Doing Academic Writing in Education

Connecting the Personal and the Professional

Doing Academic Writing in Education

Connecting the Personal and the Professional

Janet C. Richards
University of South Florida

Sharon K. Miller
University of Arizona

Routledge
Taylor & Francis Group
New York   London

Routledge is an imprint of the
Taylor & Francis Group, an informa business

Reprinted 2009 by Routledge

Cover design by Kathryn Houghtaling Lacey

Library of Congress Cataloging-in-Publication Data

Richards, Janet C.
Doing academic writing in education : connecting the personal and the professional / Janet C. Richards, Sharon K. Miller.
    p.   cm.
Includes bibliographical references and index.
ISBN 0-8058-4839-8 (cloth : alk. paper)
ISBN 0-8058-4840-1 (pbk. : alk. paper)
1. Education—Authorship. 2. Academic writing. I. Miller, Sharon K.
II. Title.
LB2369.R52 2005
808'.06607—dc22   2005040027
                                                              CIP

10   9   8   7   6   5   4   3   2   1

Dedication

*To writers everywhere—to Joshua, Noah, Madeline,
and Elizabeth, who I love dearly, and to my colleagues
and students from whom I learn every day. JCR*

*To Jim, who has always been there for me, and to my colleagues
in the National Writing Project communities from whom
I continue to learn. SKM*

Brief Contents

Contents

Foreword

Donald M. Murray

Years ago my seminar students, mostly women, and I attended a lecture by a distinguished woman scholar. The speaker opened a notebook and started reading a carefully constructed text. I wanted to be interested but found it difficult to follow the trail of her complex thinking and translate her professional diction into words and sentences I could understand.

Then, suddenly the lecturer took a quick step to the left. She freed herself from the podium and her written text. She spoke spontaneously of the topic that was obviously her passion. She was witty, clear, and personal as she invited us to explore the topic with her.

Then she made a gesture of apology and stepped quickly to her right. Back behind the podium, she started reading in an impersonal academic voice.

A few pages later she stepped left, and we heard her personal but vigorous thought. Then she returned to her written text. Again and again she stepped forth as an individual, then retreated to the academic formality she had been taught was appropriate for academic discourse.

Following the lecture, the speaker met with my students and me, but we didn't discuss her topic. Instead, the young woman scholar expressed concern that throughout their academic experience my students would have to write the "male" text she had delivered from the lectern and not be allowed to speak in the "female" voice we heard when she escaped the podium.

The issue of male and female voices was important, but her behavior was more than a matter of sexism. All of us, male and female, recognized that our profession spoke in two voices. One was the academic voice in which we spoke to the "choir," and the other was the personal voice in which we spoke to other audiences.

I find a great irony in the fact that our profession, through many of its scholarly journals of writing, encourages a professional discourse that communicates to fewer and fewer.

One of my books was reviewed a while back, and when I read the review, the language was so academic I could not tell if the reviewer approved of the work or not. I showed the review to five composition experts and received five contradictory opinions of what the reviewer had said. We need to be able to speak to each other and be understood. Our profession depends on vigorous discourse between those who explore and extend our discipline and those outside the profession who we may influence and who will instruct us. We also need to communicate to those who make academic decisions that control support for research, scholarship, and teaching.

Janet C. Richards and Sharon K. Miller have written a long-needed text that should be read by those entering the profession, those within the discipline of composition studies, and anyone interested in learning about writing. *Doing Academic Writing in Education: Connecting the Personal and the Professional* is a fine and valuable work. Its content is stimulating and significant. The authors write with both clarity and grace.

Its organization is effective, its documentation varied yet always to the point, its survey of the literature accurate and comprehensive, and the writing itself is a model of effective personal academic prose. The authors combine academic and personal voices. The writing itself teaches, demonstrating how we can combine the two languages of our profession.

After reading this book, we can stay behind the podium, yet speak with authority and wit without having to step away from the lectern to communicate what we really believe in a voice appropriate to the topic, the speaker, and a broadening new audience.

Preface

OUR REASONS FOR WRITING THIS BOOK

We didn't know it at the time, but the idea for this book originated from our work with graduate education students and teacher researchers in our research and writing classes. We (Janet and Sharon, the authors of this text) had difficulty finding just the right book for our courses. In fact, Janet's specialist degree students abandoned a text about writing because, although it appropriately focused on conventions pertinent to academic prose, it never involved real writers in the actual writing process. Janet's students became bored with the impersonal style of the book, and they refused to read their assignments.

Our conversations about the need for good books about academic writing also served as a stimulus for this text. As partner colleagues in the award-winning International Reading Association's "Reading and Writing for Critical Thinking" project, we often traveled together to work with teachers in Eastern Europe and central Asia. Waiting in airports and sitting up all night on international flights gave us ample opportunities to talk about the lack of useful books dedicated to academic writing. We also had time to share our ideas about what type of book might suit our education students' needs—a book that focused on real people as they wrote, a book that actively involved readers in the writing process, a book in which real writers told their stories and shared their reflections about their writing, and a book written for educators who wished be to enhance their writing abilities. We believe this book meets our criteria, and we think it will meet your writing needs.

Of course, this is foremost a book about academic writing. Unquestionably, our most important goals for writing this book were to help you gain confidence and acquire competence in your academic writing abilities, particularly as you write to explain concepts or present issues related to your school context, university studies, or publication interests. However, this book is also about educators who share their reflections about their past and present writing initiatives. Like many authors, some write individually, whereas others participate in supportive writing groups.

Most important, this is a book about you—you and your previous writing experiences, your current writing needs, and your reflections as you progressively enhance your writing proficiencies and develop an identity as a writer of academic prose. We are especially pleased that the activities in this book will encourage you to reflect about who you are as a writer. Perspectives of reflective inquiry conceived by Schon (1983), Dewey (1901/1933), and Zeichner and Liston (1985) postulate that it is important for educators to examine the self from multiple perspectives, think back on past experiences, critically examine one's work, and make deliberate, informed decisions. Through your reflections, you will discover how your professional, academic writing *connects to the personal—mediated by your frames of reference, and linked to your experiences* (Eisner, 1990).

WE WROTE THIS BOOK FOR EDUCATORS
WHO WANT TO WRITE WELL

We want you to know that you can improve your academic writing. In fact, you are reading this book right now because you want to achieve your potential as a writer. As an educator, you want to write well because it is important to your professional success. For example, you may be an undergraduate student in a specialized curriculum program, or a graduate student in a masters, specialist, or doctoral education program that emphasizes extensive writing as part of course requirements. You may be working toward National Board Certification, another endeavor that requires substantial evidence of your abilities to write effectively. You may be a teacher engaged in action research projects that demand explicit written documentation of your findings. In addition, you may want to publish your writing in diverse venues, such as electronic texts, practitioner and scholarly journals, newsletters, and newspaper articles.

Perhaps you are a school administrator, a school librarian, a grade chairperson, or a supervisor of instruction who is required to write to parents, fellow educators, citizens' groups, or school district personnel. Your leadership position, job success, and future promotions require that you establish yourself as a good writer—one who can use written language effectively to communicate important ideas to different types of audiences. Yet, you may be uncertain how to rhetorically frame what you write to meet various audiences' needs (Jalongo, 2002; Rankin, 2001).

Maybe you need to learn how to organize your ideas by engaging in invention (i.e., prewriting) strategies so you can begin writing a draft with assurance and authority—more informed and better prepared (see Chapter 3 on invention). On the other hand, because "every writer is different" (Fletcher, 2000, p. 4), you may want to acquire confidence in your written communication skills so that you feel free to devote less time to invention and prewriting tasks and more time to composing a first draft.

Perhaps you want to know how to determine when it is necessary to revise your writing and how to make thoughtful revisions (see Willis, 1993). Revising is a crucial part of the writing process. Maybe you seek to establish a connection between your professional and personal voice so that readers identify with you and your writing perspective. Rankin (1998) asserts that often in higher education, professors erroneously teach us to keep the personal out of our writing and therefore, we lose our power as writers and our voice—our persona. *Persona,* the root word for *person* and *personality,* in part, refers to our self-image (Sadowski & Paivio, 2001). If that is so, and if self-image is important to our writing identities, then we must consider how our academic writing represents us.

We developed this book to help you with the issues we just mentioned and to support you as you confront other writing concerns as an educator engaging in academic writing. We take a different, innovative approach than do most authors of books on writing. We have structured the activities in each chapter to help you connect your writing endeavors to who you are as a person—what we call your *personal self.* The reflective activities will help you determine what issues and concerns are important to you with respect to academic writing. You will also discover your writing strengths and confront your writing needs.

DISTINCTIVE FEATURES

We have included the following distinctive features in this book that we think will make it well suited to your academic writing needs:

- The direct involvement of educators in active writing groups, who, like you, are pursuing a variety of academic writing tasks. Their work together, their individual writing efforts, and their reflections about their writing inform some of the book's content and provide a model for your writing endeavors.
- Activities throughout the book that encourage you to reflect about your academic writing decisions and habits, and how your professional writing initiatives connect to your personal self.

- Writing samples and personal stories about writing shared by experts and educators in various contexts who also share their writing experiences and offer personal hints about what conditions, self-reflections, and habits help them write effectively.
- Educators' reflections before and after they complete a draft.
- Educators' draft excerpts that include interspersed notes to themselves about their writing decisions.
- Educators' reflections about their revisions and their decisions to return to the invention phase of writing.
- Opportunities for you to engage in invention strategies, begin a draft, revise, and edit a piece of writing that is personally and professionally important to you.
- Opportunities for you to record your reflections about your writing in a personal Think-Writing Log (see Chapter 4 for a detailed description of Think-Writing Logs).

HOW TO USE THE BOOK

We have carefully organized the seven chapters in the book to help you move progressively and confidently forward as a writer of professional prose. Therefore, we suggest that you first read the Preface, and then chapters 1 through 7 in the order in which they are presented. In each chapter, you will hear our voices, the voices of graduate students and educators who write as individuals, and the voices of educators and graduate students who collaborate in writing groups. In each chapter, we introduce a series of reflective activities, and questions designed to help you discover your writing self—your writing attitudes, behaviors, strengths, and problem areas. In chapters 3 through 7, we also include practical applications, activities designed to inform and support your own writing initiatives.

Because we cannot adequately discuss everything there is to know about academic writing in this book, we have supplied related readings that help support important information in each chapter. Refer to the related readings, as well as those in the References, when you seek additional information about aspects of academic writing that you find most challenging.

In chapter 1 you will meet us—Janet and Sharon, the authors of the text. We begin with our own personal narratives, in which we candidly talk about who we are as writers. We want you to know us as real people, who, like many of you, often struggle with professional writing. We share our beginning writing efforts and our failures, and we tell how we learned (and are still learning) how to write professional prose. Connecting to our writing selves helped us remember that although we are mindful of written language conventions and our audiences, we do our best work (as do all writers) when we blend our academic composing efforts with "who we are, what we know, and how we constitute our world" (Lunsford, 1991, p. 9).

In chapter 1, you will also meet writers who work and study in various contexts, and you will meet some of the people in our participant writing groups. When you read their narratives, you will recognize the strong connections among their writing histories, writing habits, and attitudes. You may also discover that you and they hold similar writing concerns and are confronted with the same writing dilemmas.

Chapter 2 provides information about different types and purposes of academic writing. These genres include essays, textbooks, action research projects, dissertations, syllabi, and letters, among others. This chapter also discusses concerns and dilemmas associated with expressing our individual voices within the traditional expectations of academic writing, along with educators' and noted writers' reflections about their experiences writing for an academic audience.

Chapter 3 leads you into the world of academic writing by focusing on invention strategies—techniques used by many authors before they actually begin composing. Although not all writers use specific prewriting or invention methods, such as devising lists, making concept maps, or creating outlines, many authors find invention techniques helpful for discovering what they know (and if they know enough) about a writing topic. Invention and prewriting strategies also help authors plan how they will structure and organize their writing and determine what ideas pertinent to a topic are particularly relevant to their audience and purpose for writing. In this chapter, we introduce Practical Applications. We invite you to think about and engage in prewriting that focuses on an idea in which you are particularly interested in and that you might develop further. You will have an ongoing opportunity to continue working with this piece as you progress through the book.

Chapter 4 describes how some educators, noted authors, and students sit down and actually begin writing first drafts. In this chapter, you will be invited to extend your invention and prewriting activity into a first draft. Some experts believe that prior to writing, authors should carefully research and think about a topic. Other well-known authors, like Donald Murray (2001), prefer to write "discovery drafts," gradually uncovering what they want to say as they compose. In this chapter, educators candidly share their reflections before and after writing a first draft, as well as their thinking during the composing process.

We also introduce Think-Writing Logs in this chapter. "Think-writing is talking to yourself in writing, thinking as you write" (MacLean & Mohr, 1999, p. 13). The more we think about ourselves in relation to our writing, the easier it is to write because we have an opportunity to come to know ourselves as writers, and to allow ourselves to be who we are.

Chapter 5 focuses on "big-time" revision and talks about the importance of the writing self and the reading self—the ability to compose and then step back and become a reader of your own writing. This chapter also offers a broad overview of revision. In addition, because reading and thinking about how authors write drafts are not substitutes for actively engaging in your own writing activities, we invite you to return to your draft and make appropriate revisions. You also will have opportunities to reflect about why you made these revisions and to record your revision patterns and practices.

Chapter 6 is designed to help you edit your work—usually, but not always, the last step in the composing process. Toby Fulwiler (2002), noted author and professor of writing, tells us, "To finish well, you edit" (p. 21). Although Fulwiler treats editing as the final phase of writing, he says, "It matters less when you do it than that you do it" (2002, p. 21). We think editing encompasses checking for correctness (i.e., the conventions of written language). We also believe that editing involves enhancing the clarity of a manuscript at the word and sentence level. In addition, editing includes fine-tuning the pace of your writing so that it moves along smoothly, and doesn't bore readers. Again, you will have an opportunity to edit your own work and record your editing patterns and practices.

Chapter 7, the culminating chapter, ties together all of the ideas presented in the book. In this chapter, we focus on connecting the personal and the professional through an exploration of voice and its role in academic writing. Further, we explore various avenues to finding and raising your voice in a community of writers, either within the academy or in a collegial support group. Again, the reflections of our contributing writers and some of the members of our writing groups discuss how connecting the personal with the professional helped them become more effective, confident writers. We also invite you to revisit your own reflections and writing efforts to help you discover what you might still need to learn about writing.

ACKNOWLEDGMENTS

We are indebted to Donald Murray, Professor Emeritus of English at the University of New Hampshire, who, through his extensive writing, serves as our distant teacher. Despite his heavy schedule, Don wrote the Foreword to this book, supporting major premises about connecting the personal with the professional. Because we know that Minnie Mae, his devoted wife, has always been there for him as his first audience, we are certain that we owe her a debt of gratitude, as well.

We thank the Southern Arizona Writing Project, a local affiliate of the National Writing Project (NWP),[1] which, through their Professional

---

[1]Initiated in 1974, at the University of California at Berkeley, the NWP is a successful U.S. teacher network and school–university partnership that fosters professional development in more than 175 writing/learning communities in 49 states (Lieberman & Wood, 2002a, 2002b). Contact the national office of the NWP at the University of California, Berkeley, for additional information, such as starting a local network or attending a summer institute.

Learning Communities program, provided a travel grant that allowed us (Janet and Sharon) to work together in the final stages of writing this book.

We wish to thank Priscilla Griffith, former editor of *The Reading Teacher*, current co-editor of *Action in Teacher Education*, and chair of Instructional Leadership and Academic Curriculum at the University of Oklahoma, and Elizabeth Sturtevant, Co-Editor of the *Journal of Literacy Research*, and Literacy Program Coordinator at the Graduate School of Education, George Mason University in Virginia. They offered their personal stories about writing to us when we were in the hazy brainstorming stage of this book. Their narratives helped to solidify our thinking about what direction we should take.

We are grateful to three colleagues who helped spark our consciousness about the need for writing this book: Joan Gipe, Professor Emerita, University of New Orleans; Victoria Risko, Professor at Peabody College, Vanderbilt University, Memphis, Tennessee; and Linda Labbo, Professor at the University of Georgia in Athens, Georgia.

Educators who teach and study in diverse contexts graciously contributed their writing and reflections about their writing to help make this book practical and reader-friendly. We appreciate their willingness to make their writing and their thinking about writing visible to us.

We thank participants in two writing groups, teacher researchers from the Southern Arizona Writing Project at the University of Arizona, and members of the University of South Florida Round Table Writing Group. We could not have written this book without their help. They graciously shared their personal narratives, writing models, and reflections about the writing process.

We are also indebted to Janet's students from the University of Southern Mississippi and the University of South Florida.

We thank the reviewers of the draft of this book: Susan Bratcher at Northern Arizona University, Duane Roen at Arizona State University, and Leah Fowler at the University of Westbridge, Alberta, Canada. Their insightful comments served to enhance our initial draft and improve our final product.

We are most grateful for Naomi Silverman's guidance throughout all phases of this project. As always, as we progressed with our writing, Naomi, Senior Acquisitions Editor at Lawrence Erlbaum Associates, knew when to prod, poke, push, suggest, and question to move us forward, and when to offer heartfelt support to relieve our writing concerns and soothe our psyches. Thank you, Naomi.

Contributing Writer-Educators

We are indebted to the following graduate students and educators who graciously shared their writing and their reflections on writing. Their contributions inform much of the content of this book and helped us understand their thinking as they connect the personal and professional in academic writing.

Peggy Albers, Associate Professor, Georgia State University, Atlanta, Georgia

Nancy Anderson, Associate Professor and Round Table Writing Group member, University of South Florida, Tampa, Florida

Jeannie Bailey, elementary teacher and graduate student, University of Southern Mississippi, Long Beach, Mississippi

Mary Alice Barksdale, Professor, Virginia Polytechnic Institute and State University (Virginia Tech), Blacksburg, Virginia

John Barnitz, Professor, University of New Orleans, New Orleans, Louisiana

Chuck Begnino, school administrator, Poplarville, Mississippi

Jeanette Bolte, school psychologist and Assistant Professor, University of Southern Mississippi, Long Beach, Mississippi, school psychologist and Assistant Principal

Melissa Brock, graduate student, University of Southern Mississippi, Long Beach, Mississippi

Heather Brown, high school English teacher, writing group member and teacher-consultant, Southern Arizona Writing Project, University of Arizona, Tucson, Arizona

Lindal Buchanan, Assistant Professor, Kettering University, Flint, Michigan

Katherine Chapman Carr, Professor Emerita, Central Missouri State University, Warrensburg, Missouri

Shelby Clarke, second-grade teacher and masters degree student, University of Southern Mississippi, Long Beach, Mississippi

Choyce Cochran, elementary teacher and graduate student, University of Southern Mississippi, Long Beach, Mississippi

Debbie Dimmett, middle school gifted and talented teacher, doctoral student, writing group member and teacher-consultant, Southern Arizona Writing Project, University of Arizona, Tucson, Arizona

Sandra Engoron-March, elementary bilingual specialist, writing group member and teacher-consultant, Southern Arizona Writing Project, University of Arizona, Tucson, Arizona

Jody Fernandez, recent PhD graduate, University of South Florida, Tampa, Florida

Liz Fields, second grade teacher, Mississippi.

Andrea Fishman, Professor, West Chester University, and Director of the Pennsylvania Writing and Literature Project, West Chester, Pennsylvania

Sandra Florence, Associate Writing Specialist, Composition Program, University of Arizona, Tucson, Arizona

Katie Fradley, elementary teacher and doctoral student, University of South Florida, Tampa, Florida

Shelly Gaithier, reading coach and graduate student, University of Southern Mississippi, Long Beach, Mississippi

Joan Gipe, Professor Emerita, University of New Orleans, New Orleans, Louisiana

Mary Gobert, doctoral student, University of Southern Mississippi, Long Beach, Mississippi

Gopa Goswami, elementary literacy specialist, doctoral student, teacher-consultant, Southern Arizona Writing Project, University of Arizona, Tucson, Arizona

Deborah Green, elementary reading specialist, writing group member and teacher-consultant, Southern Arizona Writing Project, University of Arizona, Tucson, Arizona

Priscilla Griffith, Professor, University of Oklahoma, Norman, Oklahoma

Karen Kelly, doctoral student and Round Table Writing Group member, University of South Florida, and Co-Director, Tampa Bay Writing Project, Tampa, Florida

Mary Virginia Knowles, doctoral student, University of South Florida.

Melinda Lundy, reading coach, doctoral student, University of South Florida, Tampa, Florida

June Markowsky, first-grade teacher and graduate student, University of Southern Mississippi, Long Beach, Mississippi

Renee Maufrey, elementary teacher and graduate student, University of Southern Mississippi, Long Beach, Mississippi

Diane McCarty, elementary music teacher, Bay St. Louis, Mississippi

Christine Miranda, Graduate Program Coordinator, University of South Florida, Tampa, Florida

Timothy Morse, Assistant Professor, University of Southern Mississippi, Long Beach, Mississippi

Sherri Nelson, Assistant Principal, and graduate student, University of Southern Mississippi, Long Beach, Mississippi

Cheryl North, doctoral student, University of Delaware, Newark, Delaware, Adjunct Instructor, Towson University, Towson, Maryland, and teacher consultant, Maryland Writing Project, Towson University, Towson, Maryland

Amy Palermo, graduate student, University of Southern Mississippi, Long Beach, Mississippi

Kathy Perez, Professor, St. Mary's College, Moraga, California

Timothy Rasinski, Professor, Kent State University, Kent, Ohio

Aldema Ridge, middle school language arts teacher, retired, teacher-consultant, Maryland Writing Project

Victoria Ridgeway, Associate Professor, Clemson University, Charleston, South Carolina

Kim Schwartz, doctoral student and Round Table Writing Group member, University of South Florida, Tampa, Florida

Greg Shafer, Assistant Professor, Mott Community College, Flint, Michigan

Kim Shea, doctoral student and member of the Round Table Writing Group, University of South Florida, Tampa, Florida

Kim Starks, graduate student, University of Southern Mississippi, Long Beach, Mississippi

Elizabeth Sturtevant, Professor, George Mason University, Virginia

Kimberly Stasny, School District Superintendent, Bay-Waveland School District, Bay St. Louis, Mississippi

Shannon Vincent, Assistant Middle School Principal and recent PhD graduate, University of Southern Mississippi, Long Beach, Mississippi

Robert Weir, Associate Professor, Bay Path College, Longmeadow, Massachusetts

Nancy Williams, Associate Professor, University of South Florida, Tampa, Florida

Rus VanWestervelt, middle school teacher, writer, teacher-consultant, Maryland Writing Project, Towson University, Baltimore, Maryland

About the Authors

Janet C. Richards, a former K–6 classroom teacher and skills strategist, is a Professor in the Department of Childhood Education at the University of South Florida (USF), Tampa, Florida, where she teaches doctoral students and supervises preservice teachers in field-based literacy and creative experiences methods courses. She initiated and mentors the Round Table, an advanced graduate and faculty writing group in the College of Education at USF. Richards's research agenda includes devising reading comprehension and writing strategies, developing methods of self-study, employing arts-based methods for qualitative inquiries, and examining changes in preservice teachers' beliefs and cognitions. Her text *Elementary Literacy Lessons: Cases and Commentaries From the Field* (coauthored with Joan Gipe) was published by Lawrence Erlbaum Associates in 2000. Her text *Integrating Multiple Literacies in K–8 Classrooms: Cases, Commentaries and Practical Applications* (coauthored with Michael McKenna) was published by Lawrence Erlbaum Associates in 2003.

Sharon K. Miller, a former high school English teacher and instructional supervisor, is a Co-Director of the Southern Arizona Writing Project at the University of Arizona, Tucson. She directs teacher research programs, which includes teaching at the Teacher Research and Inquiry Institute and consulting with local school systems for the development of on-site teacher research and inquiry communities. She conducts professional development workshops for teachers on teaching writing, supervises student teachers in the Teaching and Teacher Education program, and works with initiatives of the National Writing Project. She coauthored (with Terri Austin) a chapter overview on integrating reading and writing and responded to teaching cases in Janet Richards's and Michael McKenna's recent book, *Integrating Multiple Literacies in K–8 Classrooms: Cases, Commentaries, and Practical Applications*, published by Lawrence Erlbaum Associates in 2003. Her interest in Southwestern archaeology and history provides rich resources for future writing pursuits.

Chapter 1

Seeing Ourselves as Writers:
A Process of Personal Discovery

To reduce writing to a series of skills and prescriptions does not teach empowered creative thought. Rather, it marginalizes writers, telling them their experiences are not important. (Shafer, 1999, p. 227)

In writing, as in life, you have to ask a lot of hard questions of yourself ... never settle for easy answers ... You have to learn to trust ... the writer's voice within you ... Anything can happen; everything is possible. You just have to keep writing. (Randall, 2002, p. B2)

Good writing isn't forged by magic or hatched out of thin air. Good writing happens when human beings take particular steps to take control of their sentences, to make their words do what they want them to do. (Fletcher, 2000, p. 5)

Have you ever observed an author writing? Probably not. Much of what good writers do is concealed from public view (Fletcher, 2000). Unless they participate in an interactive writing group, authors usually work in solitude. How they plan, draft, revise, review, and edit their work are generally hidden from us. Carol Berkenkotter's case study of Donald Murray is a notable exception. Berkenkotter (1983) illuminates Murray's writing, revising, and editing strategies, and his writing habits. In addition to Berkenkotter's study, Murray's numerous books about writing offer insights and advice on the processes and the craft of writing. He frequently uses his own experiences and his own writing to illustrate a writer's struggles (see Murray, 1982, 1989, 1990, 1993, 1996a, 1996b, 1999, 2000, 2001).

In this book, we try to make academic writing less mysterious and more visible to our readers by offering an "insider's" view of the process of composing. We (Janet and Sharon, authors of this book) tell how we write. Noted authors, graduate students, and educators in various contexts also explain their academic writing habits. In addition, members of our writing groups, from the Southern Arizona Writing Project and the University of South Florida Round Table, share their drafting, revision efforts, and reflections about their writing as they work together to develop their own manuscripts for publication and university course requirements. Our combined voices portray our thoughts and reasoning about who we are and illuminate how we write as authors of academic prose. We invite you to write along with all of us—to develop a burning desire to write, and to learn how to feel at home and comfortable when you write academic prose. Georgia Heard (1995) calls this "at home" feeling *querencial* from the Spanish *querencia,* which loosely translated, means "favorite place."

GETTING TO KNOW US

Some of you may be at the beginning of your academic writing journey. Others may be somewhere along the path, facing obstacles or crossroads where decisions must be made. Still others may have enjoyed success along the way and are looking for new opportunities, challenges, and even some risks. Wherever you are now in your writing journey, we think it is important that you first get to know us (Janet and Sharon), as educators who have had some success, but who are often challenged by writing in much the same way you may be. Therefore, we introduce ourselves by including excerpts from our personal narratives. The excerpts illuminate our writing histories, experiences, and quandaries within a framework that addresses issues we believe you may also share.

Consciously reflecting about our writing pasts in the context of what academic writing is all about for us today helped us figure out who we are now as writers. We were able to comprehend how our current professional writing initiatives are mediated by long-ago writing experiences. We were also able to document who influenced us as writers, and to think about why we write the way we do (see Ellis & Bochner, 2000b, for a discussion of personal narrative). We invite you to think along with us about these same issues and reflect on how your own writing history helped to shape the writer you are today.

Connecting to our writing selves and to what we find personally important about writing jogged our memories about some of our most painful writing experiences. We remembered our teachers' names and the exact words they spoke and wrote on our papers as they critiqued our work. Thinking about our writing pasts also helped us reminisce about our mentors, and the specific ways they supported us as we worked to improve our writing. These memories underscored for us just how important response and feedback can be.

Inquiring into our personal writing selves helped us identify our writing strengths and face up to specific writing demands that continue to challenge us. When you read excerpts from our writing narratives, you will know that we, like some of you, are at times confident, at times insecure, and always anxious about submitting our work for public view. Like some of you, we are frustrated when the ideas we have don't flow out of our brains perfectly and spontaneously. Like some of you, we get annoyed and frustrated when our attempts to get words on paper are muddled and muddy.

We want you to know that we, too, are intimidated by our internal and external critics. We are proud (Janet gets exuberant) when something we have written makes it into print, or when one of our supervisors, colleagues, editors, or students compliments us on our writing. Above all, with every text we begin—whether it is a scholarly essay, a grant proposal, a less formal newsletter article, or a report about our work—we learn something new about writing and ourselves as writers.

We also want you to know that we don't know everything about writing, and we certainly won't ever learn it all. However, we plan to continue the process of connecting to our writing selves, and we invite you to join us.

Throughout this book, you will meet other educators and students who share their writing stories. Some write as individuals and others participate in writing groups. Their writing serves as a model throughout the book, and their thoughtful reflections help us understand their thinking as they progressively work through the processes of composing for academic purposes.

BECOMING A WRITER

According to Donald Graves (1983), "[c]hildren want to write. They want to write the first day they attend school. This is no accident. Before they ever went to school, they marked up walls, pavements, and newspapers with crayons, chalk, pens, or pencils ... anything that makes a mark. The child's marks say, 'I am.'" (p. 3). We can identify with this notion; we were children who wanted to write and much of who we are today, as writers, reflects our earliest experiences.

Early Writing Experiences

For both of us, writing was not associated with school, but, rather, it was something we did at home when school was out. Janet explains her experience.

I wrote often when I was young. I had an old wooden desk that sat in a tiny corner of my bedroom. The desk had a little pull-down shelf, and I would sit for hours at that desk and write poetry and stories. I never thought of it before, but I always wrote at home—never in school. In fact, I have very few remembrances about writing in grades kindergarten through twelve. I don't remember receiving any writing instruction in elementary or high school.

I won a writing prize when I was a senior in high school, but I can't remember what I wrote or who awarded the prize. I do remember that I was really surprised when I received the award because I really had no idea how to write.

Sharon's experiences were not unlike Janet's.

I was in the second grade and I wrote a book! I filled an entire composition notebook, page after page with writing. I wrote everyday. After school, I climbed into the window seat in our dining room, and I wrote my book. I remember how proud I was when I filled the final page. Looking back, I doubt that it said anything very coherent, but at the time I thought it said wonderful things. I had written a book!

Once it was done, though, it was done. The book was filled with words so it had to be a book. As a finished product it seemed less important than the actual writing. I never showed it to a teacher or to anyone, and I don't know what finally became of it. I guess it was tossed out when we moved, but I wish I still had it.

It is interesting that both of our early efforts at writing were characterized by a certain solitude and disconnect between school and writing. Neither of us showed our writing to our teachers or classmates. Janet can't even remember having any instruction in writing in elementary or high schools. Meredith Sue Willis, author of *Deep Revision: A Guide for Teachers, Students, and Other Writers* (1993), had a similar school history. She says, "At the elementary school I attended, we did not write at all. We practiced penmanship, spelling, and grammar, but we never composed anything. For me, the important reading and writing happened outside of school" (p. 23).

One of Janet's graduate students, Renee Maufrey, also has no memory of writing anything of worth during her entire school experience. Renee explains:

I cannot ever remember writing in elementary or high school. I even called my mother to ask her if my memory was distorted about the lack of writing activities in my elementary and high school curricula. She said, "No, no, you never wrote poems, little books, stories, informational pieces, or anything else."

I am convinced that I am hesitant to write today because I did not write when I was a child. I hold a belief that I cannot capture our beautiful language in my writing.

Graves (1983) maintains that, not only do children *want* to write; as many as 95% come to school believing they *can* write. When a teacher hands out paper and instructs nursery school or kindergarten children to write, they do not hesitate to begin marking on the pages. He believes, however, that some teachers fail to nurture their students' inherent desire to write, or they underestimate their writing potential. Some teachers emphasize writing correctness rather than creativity, which undermines children's confidence, and causes them to lose their enthusiasm for writing.

Mary Osborne, Writing Project Coordinator for Pinellas County Schools, Florida, agrees with Graves. By concentrating on teaching kids how to pass writing tests rather than teaching them to write creatively, she believes, "We teach the love of writing right out of kids" (in Catalanello, 2004, p. 1). George Hillocks, a retired University of Chicago English professor, researcher, and author of *The Testing Trap: How Statewide Writing Assessments Control Learning* (2002), concurs. He believes some teachers don't teach students to think critically when they write, and, "writing is thinking" (in Catalanello, 2004, p. 14A).

SOME TEACHERS MAY TAKE TOO MUCH CONTROL OF STUDENTS' WRITING

Often, teachers take control of the writing process. Unfortunately, such control can do more harm than good. Lucy Calkins (1994), noted author about teaching writing, believes that some teachers "bury students' urge to write … with boxes, kits, and manuals full of synthetic writing stimulants" (p. 4). As Graves (1983) notes, children's initial enthusiasm for writing fades away because they have to write what the teachers want them to write. William Zinsser (1988), another respected author who focuses on the writing process, says that teachers often make their students afraid of writing at an early age by assigning topics for which young writers have no aptitude or interest.

Kim Starks, an elementary teacher and graduate student at the University of Southern Mississippi, gives us an idea of just how devastating it can be when teachers take too much control of students' writing and destroy their confidence. Kim writes:

When I was in the 6th grade, a teacher made fun of my writing. She read my work out loud and made me feel stupid. I remember that one time, I worked on a story for days and my teacher read it to the class and tore it apart. It's no wonder I lack confidence as a writer.

Sadly, Kim's experience is not unique. For all of us, how our teachers approached the teaching of writing (or failed to teach it at all), and how they responded to our early efforts, established our personal beliefs about ourselves as writers. If we, like Kim, were ridiculed, we grew up hating to write and avoiding it.

Peggy Albers, Associate Professor at Georgia State University in Atlanta, remembers that she loved writing, and her teachers provided prewriting and drafting instruction. However, they undermined her self-image when they offered few compliments or no remarks at all about her writing aptitudes. She explains:

I hungered for any comments about the work that I did but when the resident priest delivered report cards, teachers made no mention about my learning. Rather, the space designated for teacher comments was always left blank, and report cards simply were records of my grades. At the end of the year we were given our report cards to keep, and in the space designated for teacher comments, I took it upon myself to write, "Peggy is a good student who likes to write."

Fortunately, Peggy recognized her own writing ability. Other young students who do not receive positive feedback from their teachers might give up because they think their writing is not good enough.

Even in college and graduate school, some professors influence students' writing initiatives when they try to take control of their writing. In fact, Gregory Shafer, an English teacher at Mott Community College in Flint, Michigan, writes about college professors who try to force students to "shed their cultural personae and learn to embrace a foreign and rather stiff language"(Shafer, 1999, p. 222). Thus, students write the way they think the teacher wants them to write, but their style does not reflect who they are (Zinsser, 1989).

Writing in a stiff, academic language results not only in loss of students' personae, but it robs them of their voice. Voice, in writing, is the personal, unique style of writing that helps readers almost hear the writer speaking (Fulwiler, 2002). Donald Murray (2001) thinks that a writer's voice is the most important ingredient in writing. He says voice is that "magical heard quality in writing [that captures readers' attention and evokes readers'] trust in the person who is saying it" (p. 65).

Debbie Dimmett, a middle school gifted and talented teacher, and a member of our Arizona writing group, believes her personal voice was disregarded and even "erased" by her college professors. Unfortunately, Debbie's teachers, in rejecting her voice, provided "no room for thought, dialogue, or growth" (Shafer, 1999, p. 224). At one of our first writing group meetings, Debbie had this to say about her experience:

> I always felt I could write until my freshman year in college. Then I realized how unremarkable my writing really was. To make the grade I adapted my style to suit those who would be evaluating me. As a result, I left out what I have come to believe is the most important dimension of professional writing—my own voice. My voice wasn't objective or professional enough for academic writing. So I borrowed the voice of others, which allowed me to write, but not to speak honestly through my writing.

> When I entered graduate school it became imperative that I have some original thoughts to write about and defend. But I learned that my voice was suppressed even more, and as my writing became more objective and more professional. I was always aware that my words never truly reflected my own thoughts. At the moment I do not even have a draft of any work in progress, which actually gives me great relief. Right now, I am a reluctant writer.

Even though she continued to struggle with finding her voice, Debbie ultimately became one of the writing group's most prolific writers. She became quite adept at code-switching; that is, adapting her own voice to her purpose and audience, which includes writing in her doctoral program, writing about her passions for Caribbean culture, and writing about her teacher research.

Jeannie Bailey, an elementary teacher and graduate student, is another writer who believed that she had to disown her own voice—her persona—and embrace a strictly academic tone. Jeannie tells a poignant story.

> I took English Comp Two in junior college. The instructor taught us how to write research papers. We just kept writing papers for grades and all I got were Cs—so I just gave up. The instructor just focused on grammar and mechanics. There was nothing about who I was as a person. But there was something terrible that he called a lethal sentence. "Do not write a lethal sentence." I can still remember him saying that.

Shelby Clarke, a second-grade teacher and masters degree student, also had an instructor who undermined her faith in her ability to hear her own thoughts and write in her own voice. Understandably, Shelby's confidence in her writing ability was seriously undermined when one of her professors actually announced in class, "The reason Shelby will probably score poorly on the GRE [Graduate Record Examination] is because she cannot not write well in an academic voice."

Because of that incident, Shelby says her fear of writing is just now beginning to go away.

I used to freeze when I wrote. Just recently, I have begun to have more confidence in me as a writer. In two of my graduate courses, Dr. Richards asked me to think about who I am as a writer. I discovered that I am the one who needs to remember that I have something to say. I need to be confident enough to write what I believe.

TEACHERS CAN MAKE A POSITIVE DIFFERENCE

Sometimes it takes years for us to get over the notion that we cannot write. If we are lucky, we encounter that one supportive teacher who will make a positive difference. Witness the experience of Sherri Nelson, an assistant principal.

I began college when I was 32 years old and I was intimidated by my poor writing skills. When I was assigned my first research paper, I was horrified! My college professor was wonderfully patient, encouraging, and kind. He helped me edit the smallest of things, over and over. I still have problems with commas and semicolons, but I am no longer afraid to ask for help with writing. I even have a new boldness and confidence when I write professionally.

Sherri's teacher made a difference by believing in her potential and taking time to help her overcome her lack of confidence. Confidence came late for Sherri, but it's a tribute to her own determination that she overcame her fears.

Greg Shafer is another instructor who makes a positive difference. He takes a stance that fosters student self-actualization and self-expression when he states, "I believe that writers should not try to please their teachers. Rather, writers need to cultivate original ideas, allow voice and passion to emerge, and reflect on their own issues and desires (personal communication, April 4, 2003).

PERSONAL REFLECTIONS

Now that you have read some excerpts from our writing stories, take time to reflect on your writing experiences. Were you a child who wanted to write? Did you feel like a writer? Did you write at home? How did your educational experiences influence your attitude about writing? Were you encouraged? Discouraged? Did teachers try to take away your personal voice or were you guided by a kind, gentle teacher? Write your reflections.

FINDING SUPPORT FOR YOUR WRITING EFFORTS

Some of us, like Sherri, were fortunate to find a writing mentor—a person who took extra time and energy to help us improve our writing abilities. Janet tells us about Bruce, her statistics professor, who took the time to respond thoughtfully to Janet's dissertation drafts:

> *When I wrote my dissertation I actually had no idea how to begin. I kept writing a first paragraph and then throwing it in the garbage. I finally learned something about academic writing from my statistics professor, Bruce Thompson. Bruce revised much of what I wrote in an initial draft. I learned from Bruce that not only must you have something important to say; you must also know how to say it.*
>
> *Bruce used a red pen and printed in capital letters to revise his doctoral students' work. Then, he placed the corrected drafts on his empty chair—which is the first place I would look when I entered his office. I hated to see all those red marks in the margins of my manuscript. Yet, for the first time in my professional and academic career, I could compare my writing with an appropriately revised version. Bruce just didn't write something like, "AWKWARD!" or "DO OVER!" Instead, he took the time to write what he thought I should have written. His efforts were very helpful, and I use his strategy with my own undergraduate and graduate students. To this day, when I write, I try to please Bruce. In fact, I am not ashamed to say that when I publish something even now, I think, "Bruce might read this."*

Mentoring generally isn't just writing notes in the margin of a composition. Sometimes, when a writer is involved in high-stakes writing, a mentor must offer multiple layers of support. For example, when Gopa Goswami, a doctoral student at the University of Arizona in Tucson, prepared a paper for her comprehensive examination, she worked with Sharon as her mentor.

> *The experience of having Sharon mentor me as I grappled with the task of editing a lengthy paper was one of the most valuable experiences I have had with writing. Sharon talked me through what I was trying to say in my paper. Revision and editing occurred at many levels. I had to rethink where best to place an analysis, where to add descriptions or examples of dialogue, and how to edit at the sentence level. I also had to learn and apply some standard rules about quotation marks and references.*
>
> *I noticed that I could explain verbally what I was trying to say and when I told Sharon my ideas, she would say, "Then why don't you write that?"*

It was as if I was seeing through a mentor's eyes how to improve my writing at all levels.

Lindal Buchanan, who recently graduated with a doctorate in English Rhetoric, and is now an Assistant Professor at Kettering University in Michigan, also had someone who worked closely with her as she completed her dissertation.

I had a mentor while working on my dissertation—a Godsend. If I'd get stuck, I could write to Carol and explain my thoughts or problems. Her knowledge in my field is so vast she could immediately suggest a book to read or see a connection that had eluded me. She mentored me in terms of seeing gaps in rhetoric scholarship and she constantly assured me that the things that interested me mattered to others. In terms of writing itself, Carol advised me about the process of turning a dissertation into a book. She made comments like, "Don't quote other people so much in this section. You say it better than they do and you need to assert your own views. This is claiming authority."

Diane McCarty, elementary music teacher, has a helpful writing mentor who lives with her. She says, "I have a mentor. I have my husband read my writing and I ask him to offer suggestions. Sometimes I take his suggestions and sometimes I don't, but having someone else read your work is very informative."

Diane makes a good point. Your writing is your property and it is a representation of your thinking. You should feel free to reject or accept suggestions from others.

Debbie Dimmett tells a story about rejecting her National Board Certification support group's advice. They kept telling her to delete certain segments from her work because "no one would want to read it." Believing that her writing was important and belonged to her, Debbie kept her writing intact, declaring that even if no one wanted to read it, she herself liked it. Debbie earned her certification and now has a group of people she is mentoring through National Board Certification.

PARTICIPATING IN A WRITING GROUP

Like Debbie, Elizabeth Rankin, author of *The Work of Writing: Insights and Strategies for Academics and Professionals* (2001) participates in a writing group. She says, "Their honest and helpful feedback has been invaluable. I owe them special thanks, not only for reading my work in progress but also, for allowing me to draw occasionally on their work and on many conversations over the years" (p. XIV).

Meredith Sue Willis (1993) also is member of a writing group. She believes:

The more experienced you are as a writer, the easier it is to become your own responder; that is by separating yourself from yourself through time, you can read almost like a sympathetic stranger. But even when you become good at having some distance on your own work, you will sometimes want a warm body, a receptive smile, an open ear. A writers' group has been an important part of my writing life for the last ten years. (p. 59)

Natalie Goldberg, whose books *Wild Mind: Living the Writer's Life* (1990), *Writing Down the Bones* (1986) and *The Essential Writer's Notebook: A Step-By-Step Guide to Better Writing* (2001), inspire us all to become writers, believes that we need contact with others for support. She advises, "Go to workshops to meet people. Don't stay isolated. Make an effort to seek out people who love writing and make friends with them. It helps to confirm your writing life" (Goldberg, 2001, p. 118).

The National Writing Project (NWP) offers educators a variety of opportunities for meeting other educators who want to write and learn more about teaching writing. For some, the invitational summer institute of a local NWP site may be their first time writing with and in a supportive community. Frequently, the atmosphere is electric in these institutes, and the writing experiences affirm our voices and confirm our writing life, as Goldberg suggests. Debbie Dimmett explains how her experience changed her.

When I participated in the Southern Arizona Writing Project's summer invitational institute, I found this to be the most nurturing experience I've ever had. I actually came to think of myself as a writer with a voice rather than a utilitarian writer who just wrote reports and professional documents. It became a little unnerving to hear my voice reflected in the pieces that I wrote. I wasn't used to hearing my voice. Finally, my erased voice was in full view.

PERSONAL REFLECTIONS

What has been your experience with a mentor or with a group? Has anyone ever supported you as you worked through the writing process? If not, how might you and some of your colleagues participate together as a community of writers? Have you discovered your writing voice—your unique style of writing that rings true to you? (See Macrorie, 1985, for discussion of writing voice.) How do you see yourself as a writer now? (Keep in mind that William Zinsser [1988] says, "It's not necessary to be a writer to write well" [p. viii]). How do readers of your work know you? Are readers able to construct a picture of you as a writer (Hillocks, 1995)? Have you ever rejected someone's writing advice? Why? Write your reflections.

BEHAVING LIKE A WRITER

"Teachers say their number one reason for not writing ... is that they don't have time" (Wilcox, 2002, p. 5). Wilcox goes on to say that most people don't have time to write, but you have to make time because just like any skill, the more you write, the better you will write. Therefore, it's important to develop a writing habit. "If you want to learn to write, you have to write" (Gardner, 2001, p. 2). How much time do you devote to writing?

Some writers write every day like the noted short story and novel writer, Flannery O'Connor, who says,

> *Every morning between 9:00 and 12:00 I go to my room and sit before a piece of paper. Many times I just sit there for three hours with no ideas coming to me. But I know one thing; If an idea does come between 9:00 and 12:00, I am there and ready for it. (cited in Murray, 2001, p. 21)*

Greg Shafer writes daily. He explains:

> *I am a very diligent and driven writer. When I latch onto an idea, I pursue it until I have it finished. It tends to haunt me and I find that when I'm working on something, it's always lurking in every activity I do. I read and reread my drafts constantly. (personal communication, April, 2003)*

Popular author and accomplished literary critic John Updike is a diligent writer. He says, "I write for three hours every morning six days a week, but never on Sunday. One thing authors learn is patience—sitting ability really" (The History Channel, March 6, 2004).

Julia Cameron, author of *The Artist's Way* (1992), thinks that all authors should write every day. She recommends that authors write what she calls, "morning pages"—three or more pages in a notebook written each morning without stopping (see free writing in chapter 3, and the section titled, "Doing What I Have To Do," in Georgia Heard's [1995] small book, *Writing Toward Home*).

Donald Graves (1994) agrees that one must write often to develop fluency. He thinks writers should write at least four days a week so that they can develop their abilities to think and express themselves through writing. We think this includes both informal and formal writing, including diaries, journals, letters, creative writing, as well as our academic writing.

Mary Renck Jalongo, author of *Writing for Publication: A Practical Guide for Educators* (2002), concurs with Graves. She believes that "anyone who writes has to commit time, to carve it out of the 24 hours allotted to every human being" (p. 42).

Natalie Goldberg (2001) agrees that writers need to give time to writing. She is emphatic about "S-T-R-U-C-T-U-R-E. Structure your time" (p. 60). She goes on to say:

> Schedule in writing time. If you have a busy week, don't beat yourself up for not being able to write every day. Look at your calendar. If next week you can fit in only half an hour for writing on Tuesday from ten to ten-thirty in the morning, good. Mark it down. Do you have another window of time? For how long? Let's push it further—where will you write? At the Blue Moon Café? OK, you've made a date, and like any other—with the dentist, the accountant, the hairdresser—you have to keep it. (p. 65)

Meredith Sue Willis (1993) also advises us to write regularly. She suggests:

> Try this, if you are having trouble, … [c]ommit yourself to a certain place and time for working … regularity is essential, whether the working time is three nights a week or every morning from 6 to 7 AM or every Saturday afternoon or one Saturday a month. Vow to sit at your work at your chosen time. (p. 157)

Donald Murray (2000) thinks acquiring the habit of writing daily is more important than talent if you want to write well. He says, "The first lesson in making writing easy is to write every day" (p. 198).

Janet writes every day.

> I am a tenacious writer. I have a need to write every day even if I write for only 30 minutes on Saturday or Sunday. In fact, I am obsessed with writing. Sometimes I sit at my computer and write for hours. When I finally stand up, my knees hurt because they've been bent so long. I often think that one reason I write so much is because I subconsciously fear that if I don't write everyday, I'll lose my ability to compose. In my work as a university professor, one of my responsibilities is to publish so I always have that "hanging over my head."

> There is another reason I write so much. I have a passion for writing, but for me, writing a draft is hard work. I love to revise. I like to think that Don Murray (2001) and Meredith Sue Willis (1993) would be pleased to know that I am happiest when I am revising and editing. I love to examine what I've written to make sure I have thought things through. I like to find just the right word, or re-work a paragraph or phrase until I think it sounds perfect.

> I don't want readers to think I've always been such a tenacious and fairly competent writer. As I shared earlier in this chapter, when I wrote my dissertation, I had no clue about how to organize the thing. I did not know how to write. I tore up hundreds of sheets of paper just trying to get a first paragraph. The garbage can was full of my writing.

I don't know where to put each and every comma in a document, and many times I insert commas in the wrong place. I also have a tendency to go over- board with exuberant descriptions. For example, I recently wrote, "The preservice teachers were obsessed with group discipline." My writing part- ner revised the sentence to read, "The preservice teachers were preoccu- pied with group management." I also write before I am ready to write. By that I mean, I just sit down and begin writing before I have thoroughly read and re- searched a topic. I discover what I need to know as I write, just like all "dis- covery drafters."

A PREFERRED TIME AND PLACE FOR WRITING

Do you have a special place and a special time for writing? Hillocks (1995) believes that a preferred context and time for writing relate to special cir- cumstances that influence a writer's productivity. Earlier in this chapter, we quoted Flannery O'Connor and Julia Cameron, who said that they like to write in the morning. Tolstoy and Rousseau preferred to compose early in the day (Goldenveizer, 1969). Janet also writes best in the morning. On the other hand, Dostoevsky always composed at night (Goldenveizer, 1969), and Janet's former doctoral student, Ramona Moore Chauvin (see excerpts from Ramona's dissertation in chapter 2) does her best writing after mid- night. Ramona even enjoys staying up all night to write if she has a deadline to meet. Although Sharon feels comfortable writing throughout the day, she prefers to accomplish most of her writing in the evening.

As writers, we not only have a preferred time of day or night to write; we also have a variety of aptitudes, concerns, interests, experiences, and pas- sions. Each of us is distinct, and we all are in different stages of our writing journeys (Fletcher, 2000). It is no wonder that we have our individual ways and styles of writing. Some of us need silence and others need background noise. Some of us make extensive notes on index cards before we can begin to write anything. Others draw sketches or make concept maps. Some writ- ers forgo invention strategies and just sit down and start writing. They ei- ther revise as they write, or they go back when they have completed a draft and make considerable, careful revisions (Golden, 1969). Ralph Fletcher, author of wonderfully informal, informative books on writing such as *How Writers Work: Finding a Process That Works for You* (2000), defines these peo- ple as the "start-writing and see what happens people" (p. 22).

Some writers struggle through a piece, slowly plodding along, revising as they write. Some of us cannot begin writing until we telephone our best friend and discuss our ideas for an academic piece. Others go for a long walk in the woods or do the dishes. Some writers can only write if they se- quester themselves for a lengthy time span. In fact, Quintilian (30–96 A.D.), the first state professor of Rhetoric under Roman Emperor Vespasian, recommended that writers detach themselves from the world so that they might "go to that place where you can hear the writing" (Bloodgood, 2002; also see Murphy, 1990).

IDENTIFYING OUR INDIVIDUAL STYLES OF COMPOSING

According to Ede (1988), writers may decide how to approach a writing task based on such factors as: (a) the nature and importance of the writing task; (b) the writer's own time schedule; and (c) the amount of experience the writer has had with a particular kind of writing. She further asserts that most successful writers have a "typical or preferred way of managing the writing process" (p. 31). Ede supplies us with four specific styles of composing, which she labels heavy planners, heavy revisers, sequential composers, and procrastinators. Donald Murray (1989, 2001) adds a fifth writing category to Ede's list: discovery drafters. One of these preferred styles, or a combination of styles, may describe your approach to writing.

Heavy Planners

Heavy planners are composers like Heather Brown, a member of our Arizona writing group, who do much of their planning prior to writing. Their first drafts are often more finished pieces of writing that require less revision and editing than manuscripts written by other authors. Heavy planners can think about and map out their writing during the course of their everyday lives. They even plan while they sleep. For some writers, this type of constant planning might be considered a self-defense mechanism. They have so little time to sit and write that their writing is done at odd times when their minds have a few moments to spare for concentration on the topic. Heather describes her writing style this way:

> For me, academic writing is a whole different can of worms than a creative or personal piece. When I'm writing an academic piece, I write lists upon lists—scribble on napkins, scribble on scraps of paper, and make bulleted lists on a computer. I copy quotes, make notes from texts, write my own ideas beside these notes. Soon, I am swimming in notes. I think my "heavy planning" style is my biggest obstacle to my writing. I plan, plan, plan. Then my task is to be less generative and more organizational.

> My biggest hurdle is synthesizing all of my ideas into a coherent piece. When I am in the midst of writing an academic piece, I think of it constantly. New ideas pop into my mind as I try to sleep. In class, my mind wanders to my writ-

ing and I may think of where to place a section, or how to organize something, and, yes, more lists come about. Somehow, miraculously, a finished piece emerges. I end up editing at the end quite a bit, but I do not revise so much because the revision component occurs while I sleep and I draft. I think I would be a better writer if I could open up more and let the personal come through. But it will take a lot of letting go.

Heavy Revisers

The difference between heavy planners and heavy revisers is a matter of sequence. The heavy planners don't seem to revise and the heavy revisers don't seem to plan, but neither is the case. It's a matter of thinking style (Ede, 1989). Janet and Sharon are heavy revisers. In fact, even while composing, Sharon continuously circles back to revise, section by section, paragraph by paragraph, and word by word. Sometimes she gets so hung up on revising that it slows down her writing and inhibits her ability to get on with it. However, that is Sharon's writing and thinking style. She had a need to manipulate words and phrases, looking for the "right" way to express her thinking, and trying to find a focus for her writing. She finds it difficult to let go of a draft and she believes that what she writes is never finished. Even when she reads one of her published pieces, she thinks, "Oh, no! I wish I had changed that last paragraph."

Sequential Composers

Sequential composers devote roughly equivalent time to planning, drafting, and revising. They are more comfortable and confident with the careful organization of the sequenced, linear stages of the writing process. They are less likely to have confidence in a loosely organized draft or a manuscript hastily planned as they ride on the subway or take a shower. Joan Gipe, Professor Emerita at the University of New Orleans, and a respected author of books and research articles on literacy, explains her sequential composing habits.

I'd say I do half and half—half planning and half revising after drafting. I do a lot of thinking and planning before I write. I make lists, like, "What I Know" and "What I Don't Know." I include all sorts of ideas. I usually know the direction I want my writing to take, but I also abandon my original thinking if I get a better idea. The computer has made me more willing to see what might develop—what might be there somewhere in my brain. I do spend a lot of time on revision. It's the fun part. I take my work to a different room and adopt a new persona. I become a red-pencil reader self.

Procrastinators

We know many colleagues who are outstanding writers, but they don't write every day like Janet. Even though every writer procrastinates from time to time, procrastinators seem to enjoy the pressure created by an imminent deadline. They appear to thrive on postponing their writing until there is nothing left for them to do except write. They delay writing until they can't put it off any longer. However, as Donald Murray (2001) explains, when the ideas in their heads get big enough and the thoughts they are listening to get loud enough, they have to write. Mary Alice Barksdale, Professor at Virginia Tech, a bona fide procrastinator, and a wonderful writer of scholarly prose, explains what she does before she can write.

> I can think of a million not very important things I have to accomplish before I begin writing. I need to take out the garbage. I have to walk the dogs again. I need to talk to a friend. I have to check my e-mail. I need to do the three little dishes in the sink. Finally, I can't put it off any longer. There's nothing else to do. I have to write.

Priscilla Griffith, who helped us find our direction for this book, is also slow in getting started. She says:

> My biggest writing difficulty is procrastination! I am not a fast writer. I tend to rewrite and revise as I go along, rather than later. I guess that makes me a sequential planner and a procrastinator. This makes me comfortable, but it sometimes drives co-authors crazy! I am a lazy writer. I will literally read a fertilizer catalog to keep from writing. The problem I have is getting started. Once I am started, I do okay, and in fact, become immersed in the process. Let me give you an illustration of what I mean by having a hard time getting started. Janet's e-mail to me requesting my writing narrative was posted just above an e-mail message from an Apple computer advertisement for the iMac. I actually started to hit the link to an Apple page, knowing full well I was not going to purchase a computer. It was just avoidance behavior.

Sharon also needs a deadline to get her writing accomplished. She recalls many late nights as an undergraduate, sitting up and completing a term paper or another writing assignment that was due the following morning at 8 a.m. That style of writing, however, is not one she recommends. She cautions, "Not much that I wrote under that pressure was usually worthy of praise—although the writing might have been adequate for an assignment. Procrastination makes it very difficult for writers to manage the writing process."

On her behalf, Sharon does not consider her procrastination style of writing to be her primary style. However, during the writing of this book,

Janet did have more than a few moments of frustration waiting for Sharon to "write her part." It sometimes is problematic when a writer who writes every day like Janet collaborates with a procrastinating writing partner. Fortunately, though, opposing styles did not interfere with Janet's and Sharon's goals, and they managed to remain good friends and colleagues.

Like Sharon, Liz Fields, a second-grade teacher, links her procrastination to a need for a deadline. She says:

> *Without a doubt, I am a procrastinator. But I don't procrastinate because I think I can't write or I am lazy. I do think a lot about what I might write, and I store ideas in my brain like the Heavy Planners that Ede (1989) describes. But I admit that I seem to write better under pressure with a deadline looming. I usually have little revision to do. Now that I reflect about my writing, I wonder if I might write better if I took more time to revise?*

Tim Rasinski, Professor at Kent State, former editor of *The Reading Teacher,* and current co-editor of *The Journal of Literacy Research,* savors deadlines just like Liz. Tim states, "Deadlines are great motivators for me—otherwise I do tend to procrastinate. But when I write, I write! I write ten to fifteen days at a time, three to five hours per day until I finish a draft."

Sometimes, writers procrastinate simply because they don't have the time they need to write. Janet's doctoral student, Shannon Vincent, explains her last-minute tactics.

> *Believe me, I didn't want to procrastinate when I wrote my dissertation. I am a first-year assistant principal in a middle school. I am also renovating a home I recently bought. I simply had too much to do between school, my doctoral classes, fixing up my new house, and writing a dissertation. Looking back, I should have recognized that good writing takes a lot of time. I barely made the deadline to defend my dissertation so that I could graduate in May rather than August. But I did it!!*

Gopa Goswami attributes her procrastination to negative feelings about her writing abilities.

> *I tend to procrastinate when it comes to writing because I don't have positive feelings about the writing process. I have fears that I must overcome. I am in a place that I call "comfortable discomfort" as a writer. That is, I am very aware that I often struggle with my writing, and, therefore, I procrastinate because I am not at ease with it. But now I'm ready to face my writing difficulties and deal with them.*

Gopa's unease with writing poses a barrier to her productivity, but, as she points out, she is ready to face her discomfort.

Discovery Drafters

Some scholars caution that the notion of writing as discovery simplifies the writing process. For example, Hillocks (1995) notes:

> *Anyone who has engaged in serious writing in the arts, humanities, social sciences, or natural sciences knows very well that writing a book or article is no simple matter of sitting down, engaging in a little brainstorming, throwing some ideas on paper, drafting and revising, and in the process discovering new ideas and concepts. On the contrary, sometimes years of research go into developing the ideas that go into a brief article, let alone a book. (p. 13)*

Hillocks (1995) emphasizes that writing is much more than simply engaging in a free write to discover what ideas might develop. Nonetheless, even as we agree with Hillocks's assertion, we also agree with Don Murray (1989), who describes the role of surprise in writing and urges us "to be patient ..., waiting for surprise to land" (p. 6). Even so, we understand we may fail to recognize such surprises, because they don't simply leap off the page as fully developed insights or life-changing ideas. It is a matter of being thoughtful about what we write in those unguarded moments when ideas are flowing and creating a writing environment, which promotes discovery and surprise.

We think discovery drafters plan, although their planning may not be evident. They simply have a strong tendency to find out what they want to say through the act of writing itself (Ede, 1989; Murray, 1989, 2001). Discovery drafters write the piece, and, as they write, they work hard at making some kind of sense out of the ideas they wish to convey. They usually find that they wrote something they did not expect to write. Then they try to unify the text around these unexpected ideas (Hillocks, 1995). These writers spend a great deal of time revising either during the drafting stage or later. Sharon explains:

> *Labeling myself a discovery drafter means that when I think I have a topic, I simply begin writing. My main prewriting strategy is summed up by the E. M. Forester quote: "How do I know what I think until I see what I say?" (cited in Rankin, 2001, p 14). I have to write to find my focus and my direction. I will write a long, long draft and then I have to struggle to find out what's important in it. Sometimes it's counterproductive, but it's what I do. After I have it down on paper, then I begin to look for the research or theories I might need to clarify my thinking. I try to keep my audience and my purpose in mind during this drafting, but I find that it is the revision stage that ultimately helps me see where I have strayed from the purpose, or I have written something that might*

inadvertently offend or confuse my audience. For me, drafting and revising
are always tied together.

Kim Schwartz, a new doctoral student at the University of South Florida
and a member of the University of South Florida Round Table writing
group, says she recently diagnosed herself as a discovery drafter.

I mull things over in my brain slightly until I have a rough concept in my head.
Then I sit down and compose, revising and editing as I go. When I've finished
composing, I generally have no concept of how what I have written works to-
gether to convey my ideas. But, after I reread my work, I do have a general
sense of whether or not I said what I wanted to say.

Noted historian Joseph Ellis, Professor of History at Mt. Holyoke College
in Massachusetts, and author of respected history books, such as *American*
Sphinx: The Character of Thomas Jefferson (1996), is another discovery drafter.
He writes, "I'm one of those people that believes you should start writing before you think you're ready. I think among my scholarly friends there's a library of unwritten books based on mounds of research that have been done,
and I think you can err in both directions" (cited in Lamb, 1997, p. 1).

OVERCOMING OBSTACLES TO WRITING: LACK OF CONFIDENCE, DOUBTS, AND FEARS

We all have been reluctant writers on many occasions. We all have experienced obstacles when we write—rocks in the road, as Georgia Heard (1995)
calls them, that kept us from writing—boulders on the highway that
blocked our confidence and delayed our journey. Sometimes these obstacles are rooted deeply, like Gopa Goswami's hesitance to confront her
struggle, or Renee Maufrey's belief that she cannot capture our beautiful
language in her writing.

Heather Brown explains that her obstacle to writing is a lack of self-
confidence.

I am much more critical of my writing now. My biggest hurdle is not only feel-
ing confident about how I express things, but also feeling confident in what I
have to say —that it is purposeful, and that others will not only want to read it
but that they will gain something from it.

Mary Alice Barksdale worries that her manuscripts will be rejected. She
confides:

I have a lot of trouble calling a piece finished and submitting it for review. I have about six papers on my computer desktop right now that I have submitted and they have either been rejected or evaluated as "revise and resubmit." I consider all of them close to being ready for a new submission or a next round of reviews. Three of them were drafted over two and a half years ago when I was at another university. I think I just need to spend a half a day or so on each one so that I can send it out—but I am having difficulty finding time for getting back to those tasks. I know that this is one of my faults. I take rejections very hard and it is very difficult for me to go back to those papers and take another chance with another journal.

June Markowsky, a first-grade teacher and graduate student in Mississippi, reveals that she worries about her writing every time she has to write an academic paper. June says, "I dislike even starting a paper for graduate school. I put it off because I doubt my abilities to write well. I need help with my writing."

"Fear of getting it right has squashed my writing" says Renee Maufrey. She continues:

I really want to write, but I doubt my writing abilities. When I write a letter to parents I make it very formal. I don't want any mistakes and so, I write with no personal voice. My school-related writing is in no way connected to my personal self because I use a formal, authoritarian style that even includes passive voice.[1] It is sad, but it is true. I just send cold memos to parents.

Georgia Heard (1995) believes that all writers have doubts and fears about their abilities to write. She advises, "Don't try to avoid the rocks. The obstacles I face—lack of time, too many projects at once—as well as the obstacles all writers face—rejection, criticism, doubts, and insecurities … are impossible to avoid and can be valuable teachers. I gather strength from them. They are an inevitable part of a writer's life" (pp. 38–39).

Tom Romano, the well-respected author of *Writing With Passion: Life Stories, Multiple Genres* (1995), maintains that as writers we all face fear and anxiety. He urges us to banish what he calls "the psychological carnivores that prey upon confidence" (p. 30). Be brave and have faith, Tom tells us—"Faith in our subject matter, faith that needed language resides in us, faith that our meaning making through writing is worthwhile" (p. 30).

---

[1]An example of active voice is, "I collected the data." In this sentence pattern, the subject is the doer of the action. An example of passive voice is, "Data were collected by me." Writers should use the passive voice specifically to emphasize the receiver of the action or when the doer of the action is unknown. Often, use of the passive voice "lends itself to a kind of muddied, heavy-footed writing" (Emery, Kierzek, & Lindblom, 1990, p. 44).

Mary Renck Jalongo (2002) agrees that "part of becoming an author ... is replacing negative self-talk with positive self-talk and silencing the critic [in you] until you generate a good, working draft" (p. 27).

Ralph Fletcher (2000) also recommends that writers exchange negative thoughts with positive ones. *"Don't be hyper-critical!"* he states emphatically. "Everybody knows writers like this. Try to identify whatever it is that gets in the way of your writing. Many of us have a little voice in our heads that says, *'That stinks!' 'This is weak!' 'Hah! A first grader could write better than this!'* It's important to silence this voice, gag it, tell it to go away" (pp. 45–46).

Edgar Schuster (2003), English teacher and author of *Breaking the Rules: Liberating Writers Through Innovative Grammar Instruction*, agrees with Fletcher. He tells us, "[t]rying to write while worrying about errors is like trying to waltz in a ballroom with loose floorboards" (p. XIV).

Bonita Wilcox, author of *Thinking and Writing for Publication: A Guide for Teachers* (2002), thinks fear of making errors and of being rejected is a common problem with teachers. Joe Check (2001), director of the Boston Writing Project, agrees with Wilcox (2002). He believes that as educators, some of our faultfinding about how we write and our fears of rejection may be connected to the education profession. Joe says we've been "trained to point out what's wrong with a piece of writing ... trained that the only writing worth reading is the professionally edited writing of books and journals. This training is of no use, is even harmful, at the onset of the writing process when what's needed is warmth, sunlight, and rich soil for our newly seeded ideas to germinate" (p. 23).

PERSONAL REFLECTIONS

Now that you have read about some of our writing habits and attitudes, and learned about personal styles of composing, take time to reflect. Part of gaining confidence in and competence with your writing abilities is to recognize what type of writer you are. Are you a procrastinator? A discovery drafter? A heavy planner? A sequential composer? A heavy reviser? A procrastinator and a discovery drafter? A procrastinator and a heavy planner? What writing behaviors work for you? Do you read and think about a topic before you begin to write? Do you make notes or create an outline? Are you a reluctant writer who initially engages in avoidance rituals, but then you turn out great work like Mary Alice Barksdale and Priscilla Griffith? Do you waste time with too much heavy planning? Perhaps you just sit down and wrestle with a whole bunch of ideas until you finally discover what you have to say like Janet and Sharon. Do you usually have difficulty figuring out what you want to write and, therefore, struggle with a first sentence and rephrase a first paragraph over and over? Do you begin writing too soon? Do you fill the garbage can with your work? Do you write every day, or do you begrudge every minute you spend writing? Do you have doubts about your writing? Do you fear rejection? Are you anxious that your writing is not good enough and, as a result, you are too self-critical? What obstacles, or "rocks in the road" as Georgia Heard (1995) calls them, keep you from writing? What self-defeating writing habits and negative attitudes do you need to change? Can you make a commitment to write every day? What type of writer do you want to be? Write your reflections.

UNDERSTANDING HOW ACADEMIC WRITING CONNECTS TO OUR PERSONAL SELVES

As you read the personal narratives and engaged in the reflective activities in this chapter, you most likely noticed a striking pattern. When we examine our writing experiences, habits, and attitudes in thoughtful, deliberate ways, we usually can begin to figure out why we write the way we do. We also can determine exactly what we need to do to become better writers.

To a great extent, our past history and current beliefs, attitudes, and writing habits influence our academic writing (Rankin, 2001). What we think about our composing abilities, how we get ready to write, and in what ways we write very much reflects who we are. We cannot separate ourselves from our writing. In fact, "our Self is always present, no matter how we try to suppress it" (Richardson, 2000, p. 923).

Peter Elbow (2000) refers to this connection between self and academic writing as the unique person and the "voice behind the text" (p. 171). Acknowledging this linkage between the personal and the professional is an important first step in improving academic writing abilities.

Janet's reflection reveals much about who she is as a writer.

What did I learn reflecting about my writing? First of all, it's a good thing I asked Bruce to be on my doctoral committee because I needed a writing mentor, and he helped me very much. To a large extent, my personality and character traits influence how I write. I don't ever give up. But I still try to write too fast and to get it over with. I discovered how I really feel about drafting and revising, that I hate one and love the other. I also learned that I start writing before I'm ready. I have to follow Hillocks's advice about thinking things through.

I'm an extrovert so it is usually nonproductive for me to sit at my computer and hope an idea will pop into my head. Writing for me is not a solitary, private act. I need to discuss and interact with others. I've learned that if I talk with a col-

league by phone, e-mail someone, or interact with a friend in a face-to-face conversation, ideas will just flow out of my subconscious. Another thing I've just recognized as I write this chapter is that I've never written within a larger community of writers like Sharon. I probably have an erroneous idea that community would slow me down. If I get ideas for writing by talking with others, then I might do well in a writing group.

Janet's recognition that working with a writing group might be a good thing led her to form a group at the University of South Florida. This group, dubbed the Round Table, is comprised of advanced graduate students, new professors, and those who wish to extend their academic writing skills; they meet once a week to share their writing efforts and offer suggestions for enhancing manuscripts.

Reflecting on her writing practices helped Sharon to see herself more clearly as a writer.

I've learned that if wishing could make it so, I'd have written the great American novel by now, but I haven't done that. Although I have the general plot outline, the characters created, and bits and pieces of chapters written, it languishes among so many other personally low priorities or competing urgent expectations. Or maybe it's a low priority as a result of my own insecurities. Did I accept the invitation to write an overview for Janet's last book and get involved in this one to avoid writing that novel? Could be. I've been known to do that before. I'm a deadline person. Give me a task and a deadline, and I'll get the job done. Leave it open-ended, and like Mary Alice Barksdale and Priscilla Griffith, I can find every excuse in the world to put it off: the bathroom needs cleaning; my teeth need flossing; my desk is disorganized. Those things I have had published came with a deadline. Someone said, "Do it by November 1st, or June 20th," and I did. Somehow I can't say that to myself; my commitment to internally imposed deadlines just evaporates. (Janet should be the one writing about commitment—she writes all the time.)

Furthermore, I don't have the experience with professional writing that Janet, Mary Alice, Tim Rasinski, and Priscilla have. Oh, I've had things published in newsletters and a few articles published in national journals, so you might be skeptical about my expertise, and I wouldn't blame you. But as a teacher of writing who has been involved with the National Writing Project (NWP) for 17 years, I am committed to the NWP principle that a good teacher of writing is a writer. To that end, I've written a great deal and have come to view myself as a writer. I've often had to write for academic reasons. I value writing communities and support groups. I certainly need someone to tell me to stop revising. I wear the "scarlet R," I've been told. I simply have to accept the fact that a piece is actually finished. So as a writer, I'm a discovery drafter, a procrastinator, and a heavy reviser.

PERSONAL REFLECTIONS

Now that you have had the opportunity to reflect on your writing past and current writing practices and habits, think further about what you have learned about yourself as a writer. What are the most important attributes and behaviors you've discovered that typify you as a writer? What specific writing attitudes and behaviors do you have that are nonproductive? Productive? What do you need to do to propel yourself in the direction you wish to follow? Do you need to find a supportive, working writing group—a community of writers? Do you need to make a renewed commitment to writing? Do you need to bolster your self-confidence? How does your academic writing connect to your personal self? How can you develop your academic writing voice? Write your reflections.

SUMMARY

Donald Murray (1994) asserts that "all writing ... is autobiographical, and that our autobiography grows from a few deep taproots that are set down in our past in childhood" (p. 208). In examining our own writing pasts we have not only exposed the "tap root" set down by our childhood experiences, but also other aspects of our growth that impact the writers we are today. Sometimes those early and later experiences were nourishing, and sometimes they threatened to stunt our growth. Those experiences, good and bad, and how we have dealt with them have shaped our attitudes about writing and influenced our belief in our writing abilities.

Some of us have persevered in the face of extremely negative experiences and have learned to overcome self-doubt. Others have blossomed in an environment of support from teachers, professors, and colleagues. Whatever our background, whatever we believe about ourselves as writers, we all face similar challenges when we are confronted with expectations of academic writing. However, whether we are in a graduate program with clearly defined writing requirements and pressures, or we are educators in school and university settings who want to contribute to conversations about teaching and learning, we have the right to be recognized and the obligation "to share our thoughts, [ideas, research findings,] and feelings with others" (Trimble, 2000, p. 161).

The right to be heard is one of our primary goals for you, our readers—which, in fact, means helping you develop an understanding of academic writing in a broader sense. We are not only talking about what we must do to earn an advanced degree, or to acquire a better position, or to earn tenured positions as university professors. We are talking about the commitment that we, as educators, have to the profession to speak up and speak out, to tell our stories and to share our individual and collective expertise. As educators, we are experts in our field, and we have a responsibility to keep "the public informed about educational issues" (Wilcox, 2002, p. 9).

Joe Check (2001) points out that when educators "begin writing they frequently enter an intense period of personal and professional examination, growth, and renewal" (p. 23). While reading this chapter, you began to examine yourself as a writer. As you read subsequent chapters, we will continue to encourage you to think deeply about your identity as a writer, understanding that your growth as a writer is nourished by both personal and professional experiences even today. The "tap roots" (Murray, 1994, p. 208) set down in our youth are only the foundation from which our writing identity grows. As we enter a new "growing season," so to speak, it is up to us to take control. Rather than allowing our writing selves to wither, languish, or fade away, we can shape and direct ourselves, but we have to know ourselves. "We can't use what someone else had—a great teacher, a terrific childhood. That is outside ourselves. And we can't avoid an inch of our own experience. Our job as writers is to wake up to everything" (Goldberg, 2001, p. 154). By knowing ourselves, we all can become better academic writers.

RELEVANT READINGS

Fletcher, R. (1999). *Live writing: Breathing life into your words*. New York: Avon Books.

Fletcher's tiny book is humorous and filled with true-life anecdotes about writing. He tells us that that his goal for writing the book is to help make writing come alive. Fletcher lists writers from whom he learns, but he says the best way to learn to write is to write on a regular basis.

Heard, G. (1995). *Writing toward home*. Portsmouth, NH: Heinemann.

When you read Georgia Heard's small book, you will want to start writing immediately. She says that writing is an act of faith that what you have to say is important. Heard equates writing with painting. She compares painters' essentials (i.e., tools) and writers' essentials (e.g., notebooks, ears always tuned in). We think you will delight in Heard's lyrical prose.

Rankin, E. (2001). *The work of writing: Insights and strategies for academics and professionals.* San Francisco: Jossey-Bass.

This book focuses on the work of writing, including the thinking, strategizing, and decision making that academic and professional writers do. It also looks at purpose, audience, genre, and voice—all of which are important considerations for writers of academic prose. Rankin includes authentic stories about writing that grew from her experiences as a leader of several writing groups. She says that all writers face similar challenges.

Zinsser, W. (2001). *On writing well: The classic guide to writing nonfiction* (25th Anniversary ed.). New York: Quill. A Harper Resource Book.

We recommend this small book for its no-nonsense, straightforward approach. Zinsser first wrote this book in 1976, and he has revised and expanded it five times to keep pace with new trends, such as technology and changes in language usage. He says that fear of writing gets implanted in American schoolchildren at an early age and that writing requires plain hard work, clear thinking, and the tools of the English language. The book, written in first-person active voice, and in an informal style, includes chapters devoted to writing style, audience, simplicity, beginnings and endings, and writing forms.

Chapter 2

Types and Purposes
of Academic Writing

*Although the range of genres is wide and varies somewhat across disciplines, a list of
the most common academic genres might include scholarly books, edited volumes,
chapters contributed to an edited collection, journal articles, book reviews, essays, textbooks, grant proposals—[action research projects, dissertations, masters degree theses,
letters, and]—even syllabi and course material. (Rankin, 2001, p. 33)*

*Certain beliefs operate as the glue to hold together the otherwise disparate community
of teachers, students, researchers, and scholars that compose the academic community
... (Fulwiler, 2002, p. 57)*

*Even when "I" isn't permitted, it's still possible to convey a sense of I-ness ... Good
writers are visible just behind their words. If you aren't allowed to use "I", at least
think "I" while you write, or write the first draft in the first person and then take the
"I"s out. It will warm up your impersonal style. (Zinsser, 2001, p. 22)*

Many educators want to write, and they are frequently expected to write as
part of their work and as students of education. It's important for you to
think how these two roles often dictate the kinds of writing you have to do,
and how you might have to reconcile the occasional conflicts that arise in
your efforts to meet diverse writing expectations for different audiences
and purposes. In this chapter, we would like to help educators become comfortable within whatever community they find themselves. As an educator,
your community is different from the one you encounter as a graduate student working toward an advanced degree, and your writing demands reflect that difference. Of course, you may occupy both communities at the

same time, which may or may not prove stressful. The degree of stress will depend on how easily you can shift writing styles to accommodate different contextual expectations.

We would also like to help you contemplate your position in the ongoing debate about three issues currently associated with traditional and innovative approaches to academic writing: drawing on personal experience; using the personal "I," as opposed to third-person singular; and employing narrative discourse. In addition, we will explore how these three issues impact writing for the academy, including dissertations, and scholarly and popular educational journals. You'll also hear again from contributing writer-educators as they reflect on their experiences with negotiating the shifting terrain of academic discourse.

RECOUNTING EARLY EXPERIENCES
WITH ACADEMIC WRITING

Most of us were initiated into the world of academic writing as undergraduates in what was called English 101, or freshman comp. Sharon recalls that when she went off to college as a wide-eyed country girl, this course was the "gatekeeper" class. If you couldn't cut it in 101, you couldn't cut it elsewhere in college. Great numbers of students simply disappeared at the end of the first semester, and it was whispered that 101 had done them in. She remembers:

In those days, many freshman comp classes were built on the "due Friday" model; at least that was the case at my college. We got the syllabus on day one, with a list of due dates for the required writing assignments—all related to short stories, novels, and poetry that we would read and discuss. We spent little time in class on actual writing—unless it was an essay test on the reading assignments. There was no writing center, no tutorial program, nowhere that we could go for additional support. We were to demonstrate our ability to write in college, not learn how to do it. It was sink or swim.

My freshman comp instructor personified this gatekeeper philosophy. He graded all papers according to criteria known only to him. When he returned a paper, we found a cryptic number inscribed at the top: for example, 91 or 87. Occasionally, we discovered numerical notations in the margins like "41c," which referred us to a section of our writing handbook where we could not only identify the error we had committed, but also read how to correct it. The only thing we knew for sure was that we must, at all costs, avoid the "seven gross illiteracies." These illiteracies included sentence fragments, fused sentences (run-ons), multiple spelling errors, and the like. If we committed these sins in a paper, we received a one-letter

grade deduction for each of the first two "illiteracies"; committing three re-
sulted in failure with no rewrites possible. And on top of all this, students
needed to get a 97 to get an A, 93 for a B, and so on. In spite of my profes-
sor's harsh expectations, I did learn a great deal about academic writing in
college, but it was more from my own determination to get an A than from his
instruction.

I was a good enough writer and proofreader that I could avoid the "seven
gross illiteracies," but how to cross that threshold from B to A remained a
mystery. I worked my way up to a string of 96s, but I never got a 97. Because
my professor's overall grading scale also required a 97 for an A in the course,
I ended both semesters with Bs. And then, inexplicably, I made it my personal
mission to eventually get an A from this man, and as a consequence of con-
sistently falling short, I ended up enrolling in every course he taught over the
rest of my college career. I even took his course for an independent study in
my final semester, and I still fell short. The experience, however, did force me
to concentrate on my writing.

Janet also remembers her confusion in Freshman Comp.

My professor's name was Mr. Bailey, and I can still remember what he looked
like. But I recall very little about the class except that most of us didn't under-
stand how Mr. Bailey wanted us to write. Like Sharon, I did not get an A in
Freshman Comp, and I never knew why. I never had another writing course in
undergraduate or graduate school, and until now, I never thought about my
lack of writing instruction. I have had to learn how to write on my own. How can
we expect our students to write well unless we provide expert instruction?

Fortunately, times have changed. With the advent of research on writing
process instruction, many freshman comp courses have been transformed
into writing workshops with a focus on writing for a variety of academic purposes. Writing centers and writing tutors are common in colleges and universities. Students have access to multiple resources for support and
assistance, and freshman comp instructors understand and use the writing
process as part of their instructional programs.

For the most part, writing instruction has remained the responsibility of
undergraduate education. Frequently, that instruction stops after the freshman year, in which students are often taught by teaching assistants rather
than highly qualified writing instructors or professors. In many teacher education programs, specific subject-matter courses may be described as writing intense, which generally means increased writing expectations, not
increased instruction in writing academic prose. Subject area classes may
have minimal or no writing requirements. For students in programs other

than English, there may be little opportunity to write beyond the sopho-more year. Not only is it important for all college students to experience more instruction in how to write successfully in the academy; they should also, as potential educators, learn how to use writing effectively in their own instructional programs. Such opportunities to learn how to use writing in instruction are inconsistently offered in teacher education programs around the country. In fact, a recommendation of the National Commis-sion on Writing in America's Schools and Colleges (2003) describes the role of higher education in teaching writing this way:

> Colleges and universities have an obligation to improve teacher prepara-tion and to make writing more central to their own programs of study. The teaching of writing at the college level should be infused across the curriculum. Formal courses in the teaching of writing (including English Composition) should be the responsibility of well-trained, qualified pro-fessional staff. (p. 27)

Regardless of their experiences with writing instruction as undergrad-uates, it is assumed that applicants for graduate programs bring with them an ability to write in response to the demands of the academy. Passing qualifying exams for admittance into a program can be difficult without writing skills. Furthermore, college graduates are expected to effectively meet the writing demands of their future careers as educators. With recent calls for the improvement of writing in public schools, educators from all areas will increasingly be expected to know and understand not only how to write, but also how to write for instructional purposes and how to use writing in their instruction.

PERSONAL REFLECTIONS

Think back to your Freshman Composition experience. What do you remember? What did you learn? What type of experience was it for you? How did instruction in your Freshman Composition class pre-pare you for the types of writing that you are now doing for your job, for school-related activities, or for graduate school? What kind of writ-ing instruction, if any, was offered in your graduate classes? In what ways have your experiences in undergraduate or graduate school sup-ported or thwarted your development as a writer of academic prose? How many writing courses have you had and how effective were they in supporting your development? Write your reflections.

IDENTIFYING THE REASONS EDUCATORS WRITE

In our opinion, there are four broad categories of writing that practicing educators must produce at one time or another. These are job-related writing tasks, high-stakes writing for a variety of important purposes and audiences, writing to tell stories, and writing for academic requirements in graduate school.

Job-Related Writing

As part of our work, we are expected to write in many ways and for many purposes, including letters to parents, letters of recommendation for students, behavior reports, syllabi, class handouts, exams, grant applications, individual educational plans (IEPs), and so on. Increasingly, we write for our instructional Internet sites, where students can get valuable information regarding the classes we teach. Work-related writing is audience-specific and creates high expectations for effective writing. The importance of accuracy and effective writing cannot be underestimated for these on-demand writing purposes.

Chuck Begnino, an administrator in the Poplarville, Mississippi, School District, describes the way he confronts such writing responsibilities:

> As part of my job, I write letters of reprimand and recommendation, I also write memos and e-mails, and I write formal reports. After I complete each piece of writing—even e-mail correspondence—I reread it carefully and check to see if the commas are in the right place. I am very aware of the people who will read what I write. I try to read my writing through the lens of the recipient. I really do consider my audience. I also make sure my writing is clear. If I write specific information that is very important, like a date, I state the date at the beginning of my correspondence and again at the end of the correspondence.

Kimberly Stasny, Superintendent of the Bay/Waveland School District in Mississippi, also emphasizes attention to audience and accuracy with her on-demand writing.

> In my job I do lots of different kinds of professional writing. I write memos, letters of reprimand, letters of recommendation, e-mail messages, and complicated reports. I pay attention to my audience and I focus on the style of writing that is appropriate for each type of message I write. I have learned to make multiple revisions when I write professionally because I represent the school district and my writing must be clear and error-free.

Sandra Engoron-March, a bilingual specialist and member of our Southern Arizona Writing Project writing group, kept a list of the kinds of writing she engaged in during the course of a single week. It was a particularly heavy writing week because, in addition to her job-related writing, she was in the midst of applying for a university program in bilingual psychology. On behalf of her teaching duties, she wrote e-mails to special education service providers, to members of special education staff and other district personnel regarding issues of current importance, and summaries of cases examined during Child Study meetings. All of these writing tasks carried high expectations of accuracy and audience awareness. Her application to the university program constitutes what we call high-stakes writing; she wrote her autobiography, updated her curriculum vitae, wrote a letter of interest, filled out official university application forms, and wrote e-mails to college staff and support persons for references.

High-Stakes Writing

This brings us to the second category of professional writing; that is, high-stakes writing for clearly defined purposes. In this type of writing task, we write specifically for promotional and career purposes, such as a curriculum vitae, a résumé, or letters of application. We may decide to pursue National Board of Teaching Standards Certification, which requires a great deal of writing and the development of an extensive professional portfolio. Sandra's application process involved this kind of writing. Katie Fradley, a doctoral student at the University of South Florida, describes her experiences going through National Board Certification.

When I decided to go through the National Board Certification process in 1999, I was one of the first local teachers to attempt certification. At the time, I had no idea what I was getting into. Although the process helped me grow professionally, I felt that in my quest to become nationally board certified, I lost my personal voice. I was so worried that what I wrote was the right answer that I was afraid to trust myself and my teaching. Ironically, at the same time, I was teaching a multiage class and preparing fourth graders for a high-stakes writing test called Florida Writes. My students did very well on this test, but at what expense? The process of going through national boards caused me to reflect on every aspect of my teaching, including the way I taught writing. One of the things I discovered during this reflection was that when I looked deeply into my teaching soul, I did not like the teacher that looked back at me. Although I was preparing my students to excel on a writing test, they were losing their personal voice just like me. It was through this reflection that I decided I could not live with the teacher I had become and it was time to leave my "A"-rated school for uncharted territory in a Title One Magnet School.

Deborah Green had a similar experience with National Board Certification, finding the process particularly stifling.

This year I decided to try to become a National Board Certified teacher. Part of the process is writing four portfolios that demonstrate my mastery of teaching. For each item I chose to include, I had to write a description, an analysis, and a reflection. It was also important to use specific vocabulary. I began by taking on the description of myself as a learner. The format is extremely restrictive in that I had to do this in only four pages, which had to be double-spaced. I had several examples of my work that I could use, but my problem was writing them up so that they fit within the format, as well as demonstrating my ongoing professional development. I began to wonder which was more important, that I see myself as a lifelong learner and continuously seek ways to improve my practice, or that I write within the restricted format? Teachers who have gone through this process tell me I will be a better teacher once I go through this process. Right now all I feel is frustrated.

We have found that writing for the National Boards is a very different experience. Because of the specific expectations and the format offered, both Katie and Deborah found their voices stifled.

University educators also experience writing demands that have extremely high standards and are related to promotion and tenure. Tim Morse, Assistant Professor of Special Education in Mississippi, explains his ongoing dilemma, which he titles "Persist and Publish."

PUBLISH OR PERISH: TIM MORSE

Throughout my doctoral studies, my professors impressed upon me the importance of publishing. The majority of my instructors conveyed—either explicitly or implicitly—that publishing was an important component of any professor's job description, and these instructors made it clear to me that I must always stay apprised about how I could get my work published. In fact, one instructor required me to read a book titled Persist and Publish (Matkin, 1991). He did this for two reasons. First, the book presented sound advice concerning how to get one's writing published. Second, the book's title provided a much more positive rallying cry for this aspect of a professor's job than the more often quoted phrase, "Publish or Perish." Given the im-

portance of publishing to obtaining tenure and promotion, I always feel pressured to write.

Unfortunately the amount of pressure I experience has increased because none of my immediate supervisors (e.g., my department chair and my dean) have given me definitive answers to two questions I repeatedly pose: (a) how many publications do I need to produce annually, and (b) what type of publications must I produce (e.g., publications in refereed or nonrefereed journals). The most straightforward response I have received to these questions has been, "Refereed publications count more than nonrefereed publications." Recently, senior administrators at my university have emphasized the importance of grant writing, but again, I receive no clear guidance concerning what I am expected to do in this area.

So, here is how I try to solve my dilemmas about the pressure of publishing. I have adopted a policy of intensive writing. Thus, I have written self-initiated and invited pieces for both refereed and nonrefereed publications. This approach has been positive in that it has enabled me to maximize my total number of publications, improve my writing skills, and generate more writing opportunities because some journal editors have liked my work, and have invited me to submit additional manuscripts.

The downside to this approach is that my plan of action has not enabled me to develop one or two areas of expertise. All university tenure-track professors MUST develop one or two areas of expertise. Since I want to end this piece on a positive note, I want you to know that my writing has helped make me a much better teacher. To prepare for each piece I have written I have read extensively about the topic, and this reading has enabled me to expand the knowledge base I call upon when I teach. And as I have engaged in the writing process (i.e., invention drafting, revising, editing), I have had to clarify any muddled thoughts and beliefs I possessed.

Overall, Tim's approach provides a positive model for educators who feel similar pressure to publish. It serves his need to continue to learn and become a better teacher while he is pursuing tenure. This illustrates the value of writing and engaging in the writing process as a vehicle of learning. We are able to focus our thinking and give expression to our theories through writing. Whenever we confront high-stakes writing expectations, as Tim does in pursuit of tenure, or in our quest for promotion or higher levels of certification or recognition, it will serve us well if we can use the experience to learn more about ourselves as writers and as educators.

Nancy Anderson, a tenured associate professor at the University of South Florida, tells a story that demonstrates how important hard work, good writing, and tenacity are when you are trying to achieve promotion and tenure.

I was at my university for about three years when I had a conference with my Associate Dean. He had reviewed all of my publications and he said, "Good Nancy! Your publications are good. Many faculty have gotten promoted with less publications than you have. You have nothing to worry about. Just write longer articles."

So I started writing longer research articles. Then we got a new university President, a new Provost, and a new Assistant Dean. I also got a new chair. They made it mandatory for all nontenured professors to have a tenure review. So you see, in one year everything had changed. In fact, I had to submit my vitae and three articles. After these new administrators reviewed my writing, they told me I couldn't possibly get tenure because my writing was inadequate and my ERIC documents didn't count. I had to submit a Professional Development Plan to my chair, and I decided I better apply elsewhere.

There is a happy ending to this story. I followed my Professional Development Plan and I went up for promotion and tenure and I was successful. Not only that, I received OUTSTANDING reviews. What happened to me shows that you have to be diligent about your academic writing. University criteria may change when administrators change. Write as much as you can and the best you can. And remember, it's never over 'til it's over. By that I mean don't count on achieving promotion and tenure until you actually achieve it.

Nancy's experiences show that writing in academe can be stressful and demanding, but perseverance pays off.

Writing to Tell Stories and Report Research About Teaching

Our experiences as educators compel us to tell our stories. Like some of the educators portrayed in this book, we may reflect about our practices and decide to engage in an action research project because we have noticed "something interesting, curious, or unexpected in the process of interacting with students" (Hillocks, 1995, p. 31). We may use a variety of qualitative research strategies, such as taking field notes, videotaping, and writing teaching cases; we may use quantitative statistical methods to examine our assumptions and hypotheses; or we may combine qualitative and quantitative methods. After we collect and examine our data and reach some conclusions, we want to share our insights and learning with colleagues. One way to inform our peers is to write about our research and publish it in professional journals.

Practicing teachers are frequent contributors to professional journals, such as those published by subject-specific professional education organizations, like the National Council of Teachers of English (NCTE), the International Reading Association (IRA), and the NWP. An important premise of the NWP is that the teacher of writing should be a writer, which is not the same as saying that all writing teachers should publish, but rather that by writing, teachers have a better understanding of their students' composing needs.

The NWP further encourages teachers to claim their voices and enter academic conversations about teaching and learning. They additionally encourage the development of supportive writing communities, like our own Southern Arizona Writing Project writing group and the Round Table at the University of South Florida. Such encouragement often motivates teachers to write for themselves, their colleagues, and for publication. Additionally, book publishers like Heinemann and Lawrence Erlbaum Associates welcome proposals from practicing teachers at all levels.

Writing in Graduate School

When we enroll in a graduate program, we encounter many writing challenges. As graduate students, we have to meet very rigorous writing demands to complete our program. We write for audiences who have authority over us (Elbow, 2000). These requirements range from writing prequalifying exams to prove that we are capable of doing graduate studies to completing comprehensive exit exams to show what we have learned. The writing we do to complete our degrees includes essays, abstracts, reaction papers, research reports, masters theses, specialist degree projects, and doctoral dissertations. Sometimes new doctoral students find that the rigors of academic writing are confusing. For example, Kim Shea at the University of South Florida says:

> *As a beginning doctoral student, I don't think I've found my writing self yet. I don't even know if there is a particular strategy I use for academic writing. When I am required to write in an academic voice, the topic is constantly on my mind as I drive, do housework, and exercise.*
>
> *I don't know if I can change this pattern of writing. It seems to be working so far for me. I just can't imagine designating a block of time for writing. Somehow, I think that would stifle my ideas. As you can see, I have a long way to go. I have to find my writing "Self." That's one reason I've joined the Round Table. There are about eight of us who meet with Janet every week at 4 P.M.*

Mary Gobert, a doctoral student in educational leadership at the University of Southern Mississippi, remembers how her experience with on-demand writing experiences failed her when she encountered academic writing in her graduate program.

When I was the grade level chairperson in my school, I was the one who wrote all of our memos and policies. All my colleagues said, "You're the best writer, Mary," and I believed them. Then I entered the doctoral program at our state university. "OUCH!" I found out in a required research/writing class that I was not the writer I thought I was. But I did become a more informed writer because of the professor's help. (It was Janet.) We all sat around and read our work to one another and Janet critiqued it. Well, critique sounds too harsh. She offered suggestions for enhancing our writing. As writers, we became more informed as the semester went on, and we began to help one another in a sort of writers' workshop format. I became acutely aware of my writing problems. What I learned about writing in that class has all stayed with me—like—DON'T WRITE IN THE PASSIVE VOICE! DON'T WRITE IN THE PASSIVE VOICE! WRITE IN THE ACTIVE VOICE WHEN POSSIBLE! DON'T USE CLICHÉS AND TRITE LANGUAGE! I can critique academic manuscripts now, and I can edit my own writing.

For Mary, a supportive professor and supportive peers helped her merge both her identity as a writer and her skills in achieving the needs of her writing expectations. However, as a doctoral student, Mary also wrestled with her dissertation topic, the methodology that might be appropriate for her research question, and how to structure this type of academic writing. Mary tells us:

This morning driving down the beach road to the university, I had an epiphany. I thought I had finally figured out how to get my three interests into one dissertation proposal. The three interests are instructional leadership, administrative staff development, and literacy. Now as I get feedback from colleagues and my committee, I am not so sure of the epiphany anymore. Two things are currently pressing. How to narrow the topic appropriately is the first thing. I thought I had zeroed in on that this morning, but alas, maybe not. The second thing is that now I have created a pure qualitative study, and I don't think I am in any way organized enough to pull one off. Not of this magnitude anyway. When I think of all that coding, I know I need some framework to plug it all into. I don't have one. And how to write this up is equally confusing. I may have to rethink all of this.

PERSONAL REFLECTIONS

Take some time now to think about the writing demands you have as an educator or as a student. Is your writing community defined by your role as an educator, as a student of education, or both? What kinds of writing do you have to do? How do you meet the expectations of the on-demand writing required of you as an educator? What high-stakes writing has been required of you? How have you handled these diverse expectations? What was challenging? What was less so? What do you need to be successful in these arenas? Write your reflections.

EXPLORING TRADITIONAL EXPECTATIONS OF ACADEMIC WRITING

Academic writing is generally held to be writing that conforms to specific expectations of language, structure, and purpose. Toby Fulwiler's (2002) undergraduate textbook, *College Writing: A Personal Approach to Academic Writing*, provides an in-depth analysis of the tradition of academic writing. He cites several beliefs that drive the writing expectations that students will encounter. Among these are belief and persuasion, objectivity, relativity, balance, and the research imperative. First, he says, writers must believe in what they write, and then, through language, they must persuade readers that what they say is true. This "truth" must be documented in the writing through the use of "observation, experimentation, statistics, interviews, or personal experience" (p. 58), along with an account of where the information was found. In other words, writers must substantiate any claims or assertions made through careful argumentation and then provide a complete list of footnotes or endnotes and a bibliography. This process ensures the integrity of the writer's claims. Fulwiler asserts that all serious writing is persuasion. After belief and persuasion, the academic writer must adhere to a strict code of objectivity. It is expected that the writer will be completely impartial and objective, and should, when doing research, be removed from the situation as completely as possible. Fulwiler further asserts, "If you want to persuade [your audience] to believe you, it's even preferable to use a deliberately objective tone (passive constructions, no first-person pronouns) and quantitative detail (statistics, graphs) in your writing" (p. 59).

Next, he cautions novice writers against making absolute statements, recommending that any assertion be accompanied by a qualifying phrase such as, "It is likely," or "in all probability" (p. 60). When writers qualify their assertions in this manner, they allow for possible error. Finally, by offering the reader an examination of alternate points of view or opposing interpretations, writers achieve a balanced argument. Fulwiler encourages the use of such balancing phrases as "On the one hand/on the other hand" (p. 60) to acknowledge opposing views. "When you use these phrases in your spoken and written language, they suggest you know the rules of the academic community" (p. 60). Again, Fulwiler emphasizes the need for academic writers to use specific phrasing to protect against challenges to their work.

The overall expectation—the research imperative—is that most academic writing will be research in some form and this is the primary purpose for writing in the academy. Academic writing, he says, is based on the "need for knowledge" (p. 60) and one comes to this "knowledge in the academic community through research" (p. 61).

THE IMPACT OF THE PERSONAL ON ACADEMIC WRITING

Students are usually introduced to the concepts of academic writing in their freshman composition classes, which is important because it is vital for them to understand that in many instances these are the standards by which their writing will be measured. Fulwiler (2002) recognizes the impact of the personal on academic writing and acknowledges that writers convey a great deal of "between-the-lines information" (p. 6) about themselves. He cautions:

- Know who you are. Be aware that your writing may reflect your gender, race, ethnic identity, political or religious affiliation, social class, educational background, and regional upbringing. Read your writing and notice where these personal biases emerge; noticing them gives you more control, and allows you to change, delete, or strengthen them—depending upon your purpose (p. 6).
- Know where you are. Be aware of the ideas and expectations that characterize your college, discipline, department, course, instructor, and grade level. If you know the context, you can better shape your writing to meet or question it.
- Negotiate. In each act of writing, attempt to figure out how much of you and your beliefs to present versus how many institutional constraints to consider. Know that every time you write you must mediate between the world you bring to the writing and the world in which the writing will be read (p. 7).

We agree that such cautionary notes to beginning academic writers are very important, and we concur with Fulwiler that (a) all serious academic writing should strive for the kind of honest presentation that persuades the reader that the writer believes the thesis, (b) absolute statements can be troublesome, and (c) providing a balanced argument is important. We contend, though, that the rule of objectivity is problematic and is at the heart of many challenges to the academic tradition. It is exactly this expectation that is the cause of so many of us finding our own voices stifled and suppressed. Too often, the focus on objectivity prohibits the use of the personal "I" or even personal experience in academic writing.

OBJECTIVITY VERSUS THE PERSONAL "I" AND PASSIVE VERSUS ACTIVE VOICE

We conducted a simple Google™ search on the Internet for "academic writing" and found 88,400 instances. Our search within those results for "objectivity" drew 1,640 results. Our brief (and decidedly unscientific) examination of some of these sites showed that a large number of them were associated with university writing centers and handbooks or resources for students. Interestingly, the sites that were most insistent regarding the rule of objectivity and the elimination of any semblance of personal language were from universities in the United Kingdom, Australia, and Asian countries. For example, the University of Wallongong, in New South Wales, Australia, provides specific online activities for students to practice the avoidance of personal language. "DO NOT refer to what you think; refer instead to what the evidence suggests." "Use the 3rd person or 'It' constructions. (It could be argued that ...)" "Use the passive voice." The site offers links to skill development exercises so that students can practice proper use of objective language in their writing (*Unilearning*, 2002).

Conversely, many of the online writing centers from universities in the United States offered a more moderate view of the use of passive constructions and personal language. Perhaps this is a sign that the trend in this country is toward more acceptance of the personal in academic writing. The Writing Center at the University of North Carolina (2002), for example, offers students an online handout called "Should I Use 'I' in My Writing? Using the First Person and Personal Experience in Academic Writing." The handout suggests that in academic writing, it is occasionally appropriate to "break some of the old rules" (p. 2), but it cautions students to check with their professors before doing so. The primary purpose of the handout is to offer students advice on how to make the decision to use the personal "I" or personal experience, and in which disciplines it might be received either favorably or unfavorably. We explore this issue in more detail later in this chapter. In the meantime, we'd like to share some experiences our colleagues have had in confronting academic writing expectations.

WHEN OBJECTIVITY SUPPRESSES TRUTH

In chapter 1, Debbie Dimmett described how her freshman composition course stripped her of her own voice. As she put it:

> *My voice wasn't objective or professional enough for academic writing, so I borrowed the voice of others, which allowed me to write, but not to speak honestly through my writing.... As my writing became more objective and*

"professional" I was always aware that my words never truly reflected my own thoughts.

It is ironic that in complying with the rule of objectivity, Debbie, like others included in this book, violated the rule of belief, which certainly suggests that, sometimes in the academic community, objectivity is more important than truth in writing.

Increasingly, academic writers have found that by strictly adhering to the academic "code" for writing, as required by many of their professors, they not only have had to suppress their own voices, but that they more often write for the assignment than for an idea that is important to them. Debbie further recounts her experience with completing her masters thesis and the committee's expectations for revisions and changes. She was not surprised that they recommended changes, as that was their purpose, but the overall impact of their guidance resulted in her loss of interest in her writing.

I didn't mind having to redraft different parts of my paper; however, I did mind the content changes that eventually gave rise to a very different piece than I first envisioned. In fact, the paper that I wrote embodied a thesis with which I didn't particularly agree. I didn't argue with my committee members because I knew all I wanted was to get the degree and get on with my life. Upon completion of the paper and my master's degree, I shoved the paper in a file and never looked at it again. That was eleven years ago. In fact, if someone asked me what it was about, I'd have to say that I don't recall. I only remember what it was supposed to be about.

Although I harbored no bitterness towards my committee members, I did lose respect for the process and for the professors who were not able to move sufficiently far enough from their own work to mentor someone whose area of interest and type of methodology are different. It took me ten years to decide to continue my education in pursuit of another degree. I anticipate that once again, I will be faced with the dissatisfaction of completing a dissertation that does not reflect the direction or methodology that I would choose.

Debbie's feelings illustrate one of Lynn Bloom's (1981) findings in her study of writing anxiety among graduate students. She suggests that for short papers, writing for a topic that you don't like or feel strongly about is something we should be able to tolerate because it is a short-term investment of time and energy. However, it is altogether different if it is a thesis or dissertation:

The selection of a thesis or dissertation topic [is] analogous to the selection of a spouse. It had better be one they love, or it will not survive the stress of intimate association…. [T]oo often the students, lukewarm at the beginning of the shotgun wedding, lose interest and eventually abandon the unappealing subject and perhaps the pursuit of the degree as well. (p. 5)

Debbie managed to get through the thesis without abandoning her degree, but her reluctance to return to graduate school and her trepidation about her forthcoming dissertation experience indicate just how painful the experience was for her.

Exactly how typical such experiences are we don't know, but they happen often enough for many graduate students to become jaded about the process of writing for the academy. Debbie found that, even now, the article she really wants to write for publication has to take a back seat to the writing needs for her degree program. As a newly enrolled doctoral student, she experienced a dilemma regarding who controls the structure and the voice of the texts she has to write.

When the Arizona writing group met in April and read the first draft of Debbie's paper, the first comment was "It reads like a class paper."

Debbie acknowledged that she had submerged much of her voice to use the topic for a paper for a class called Written Language Development. Getting the paper written had taken priority over her desire to write the article—the story she really wanted to tell, and which the group had discussed with her numerous times. Of her dilemma she said:

I have three papers to write within the next month. Each of them will have a writing style that is more suitable for the intended audience. One will require scholarly writing recognized by the field of anthropology, another by the field of education, and still another that focuses on the more practical needs of teachers. It will be enlightening for me to see how I ultimately negotiate each context and set of expectations.

CONSIDER CLASS PAPERS A PREWRITING EXERCISE

The Arizona writing group advised Debbie to look at her class paper as a prewriting exercise for the article she wanted to write. For both types of writing, the teacher research that informed her paper would still be the basis for the more personally and professionally important articles she might write later. The "final" drafts she submitted to her professors would, in actuality, be intermediate drafts along the way to what she really wanted to write. At a subsequent meeting of the group, her peers examined her "scholarly" paper and made recommendations for its revision into the article she really wanted to write.

This is, quite frankly, a productive way to approach writing for the academy when control of voice and structure is externally applied. Write about what is important to you, find its "truth," as Fulwiler calls it, cast it in the academic mold if required, and later revise it into your personal truth.

According to Donald Murray (2001), the "effective assignment writer" (p. 17) completes all of the requirements of the assignment: doing the research, reading, taking notes, and documenting sources. On the other hand, he says, the "creative assignment writer has to think: to find a meaning, a pattern, a significance in the information … collected" (p. 17). He suggests making an experiential connection to the assignment and using that connection to generate new topics and research questions. In this way, the writer can then use this personal experience "backstage" to write with the appropriate objective distance required. It only makes sense that the writer would then approach a topic that has a personal connection with more passion and interest. In this idea Murray seems to agree with Fulwiler's (2002) caution that students should know themselves and recognize how their identities can influence their work (p. 6). However, where Murray and Fulweiler's thinking diverges is in the tone. Murray encourages the exploration of personal experience as part of the writing process, even when we must write in an objective academic voice, whereas Fulwiler's ideas seem to come across as a caution.

WE CAN BECOME OUR OWN WORST ENEMY

Interestingly, sometimes we can become our own worst enemy when it comes to making decisions about what we will write. Rus VanWestervelt, an English teacher who recently earned his Master of Fine Arts from Towson University in Maryland, found himself in a quandary of his own making. In such a program, one would expect to have a great deal of latitude and freedom to make choices regarding the writing expectations for the degree. In Rus's case that was true, but perhaps because of previous experiences in the university setting, and perhaps because he believes so strongly in his own need to learn and grow, he was frustrated when he realized he was writing for the degree instead of writing for his passion. Before he received his degree, Rus wrote:

> *It was a relief to get this [manuscript] finished for several reasons. Most of all, though, was this feeling that soon I'll be graduating, and soon I'll be able to write again for publication. I know that sounds ridiculous, as the final product I've been working on for two years now is supposed to be of publishable quality. But as a stubborn, abstract/random thinker and writer, I've hated the box I've put myself in for this degree. To be extremely brief, I let my desires/needs to please my mentors hinder my writing. I did not write for me at all; rather, I wrote to fulfill a requirement and to try to be the best student in my class. What happened, as a result, was that I boxed myself into a corner with a topic that*

wasn't me at all. I chose—my choice entirely—to compose in a style of writing that I am weakest in, and my belief was that I would use this experience to be an even better, overall writer. I believe this is true. I really do. But I cannot look at this writing that I've done as anything but preparatory writing for what I do after I graduate this summer. Maybe I'll be able to salvage some sections of my manuscript. But for the most part, it was all a practical exercise that frustrated the hell out of me.

As educators we do not always have the privilege of writing for ourselves, sometimes not even as part of our job-related on-demand writing, and certainly, within the academy, we sometimes must submit work we don't believe in. Peter Elbow (1998) pointed out the irony of the situation when he said, "I'm struck at how many ways writing involves complying or giving in.... Someone other than the writer is in charge. The writing has to conform to the teacher's criteria or it's not acceptable.... When we send writing to journals, publishers, and teachers, what is the verb we use? We 'submit.'" (pp. 98–99).

PERSONAL REFLECTIONS

Have there been times when you had to submerge your voice, smother your passion, and write for the requirements rather than for the "truth?" What has been your experience with choosing your own topics for exploration or research? Think about those situations and explore how you might have salvaged them for later writing, much as Debbie Dimmett did. Write your reflections.

DEBATING OPPOSING NOTIONS OF WRITING IN THE ACADEMY

The debate over the use of the personal in academic writing probably began with Elbow's (1973, 1998) landmark publication, *Writing Without Teachers*. Elbow suggested a pedagogical approach to freshman composition that focused on becoming a writer first and an academic second. Among the writing strategies he offered were free writing, journaling, and personal writing. Such writing is generally referred to as "expressive" writing. It is probably not coincidental that Elbow's ideas emerged simultaneously with much of the research on the writing process and as composition studies increasingly validated process instruction. Elbow's and other writing scholars' influence on composition instruction in both the public schools and in universities was profound. A not-so-quiet revolution began, as evidenced by the founding, in the early 1970s, of the Bay Area Writing Project, the precursor to the NWP.

Elbow (1993) persisted in promoting a more writer-centered approach to composition. In 1993, in *Being a Writer Versus Being an Academic: A Conflict of Goals* he explored what he saw as a basic conflict between the writer and the academic. As a teacher of freshman composition, he wondered how he could teach his students "to place themselves in the universe of other writers" (p. 78). He was concerned with who controls the text that his students would produce and how to deal with the competing interests of the writer and the culture and politics of the university setting.

Not surprisingly, Elbow's approach was not enthusiastically embraced by the academy, and, over the years, much debate has occurred regarding expressive and academic writing. David Bartholomae (1995) took up the defense of the academy with the publication of *Writing With Teachers: A Conversation With Peter Elbow*. In a scathing critique of *Writing Without Teachers*, he declared that because academic writing is "the real work of the academy," there cannot be any writing "without teachers" (p. 63). He further asserted that writing courses should help university students recognize that they are writing "in a space defined by all the writing that has preceded them" (p. 64). The debate between the Elbow camp, sometimes called *expressivists*, and the Bartholomae camp, called *social constructivists*, or "not-expressivists" (Bishop, 1999. p. 10), has continued unabated, and neither side seems ready to capitulate to the other. (See Bartholomae, 1990, 1995; Bizzell, 1982; Brooke, 1988; Harris, 1983, for social constructivist discussion. See Bishop, 1999; Coles & Wall, 1987; Elbow, 1985, 1987, 1991, 1998, 2000; Fontaine, 1988; Lunsford, 1990; Sommers, 1992; Spellmeyer, 1989, for additional discussion on expressivist views.)

THE POLARIZATION OF VIEWPOINTS

The polarization of viewpoints is perhaps best illustrated by an incident in which a manuscript from Donald Murray was rejected by one reviewer in the blind review process for being "too Murrayesque" for that particular journal. The reviewer described the prose as "solid," but much more suited for "some harmless place where very few people would read it or take it seriously" (Hult, 1994, p. 26).

Clearly, for the Bartholomae camp, the traditions of academic writing far outweigh any concern with writers' control of the text or writers' belief in their topic—what Fulwiler would call its "truth." Wendy Bishop (1999) refers to an article by Stephen Fishman and Lucille McCarthy (1992), in which they summarize the antiexpressivist criticisms by Bartholomae,

Bizzell, and others regarding what they see as a pedagogy that keeps students ill-informed, untrained, and unprepared to succeed with learning the language of the academy. They charge that students, in the interest of "self-actualization" are the victims of sentimentalization (p. 11).

In that regard, personal writing in the academy is still looked on with some disdain (Spigelman, 2001). First-year writing instructors who offer students opportunities for expressive and experiential writing come under sharp criticism from the traditionalists, who charge that first-year composition students are ill served unless they are given "instruction in the academic discourse needed to prepare them to function successfully in the academic community" (p. 63). Quite often, teachers who engage in expressivist pedagogy and encourage the use of personal experience, narrative structures, and the use of the personal "I" in their classrooms are accused by traditionalists of being throwbacks to a "1960's touchy-feely pedagogy" (Bishop, 1999, p. 10).

In spite of these charges, student-centered composition courses, based, among other things, on Elbow's notions and the research into writing process have increased dramatically. The NWP has trained thousands of writing teachers, instructors, and professors in a new paradigm of writing process instruction. As a result, more and more writing instructors at the college level not only include, but also encourage the use of the personal in academic writing. For the most part, sincere efforts are made to help students make the transition to the kinds of writing they will encounter during their college careers.

Obviously, there is a middle ground between the traditional expectations for academic writing and the more flexible, innovative forms of writing that are increasingly seen in the academy. The writing center at Dartmouth offers, in its online Faculty Resources, a handout called "The 'Place' of the Personal in the Writing Classroom" that makes a reasonable case for using the personal to support students' transition to the world of academic writing. This handout advises composition staff to find a middle ground between Elbow and Bartholomae, acknowledging that the acceptance of the personal in first-year writing courses is based on students' cognitive development needs as they begin the transition to the academic community. Thus, a number of first-year writing assignments involve writing that is based on students' personal experiences and responses. The handout further acknowledges the arguments of those professors who believe that such personal writing lacks objectivity and does little to support students' development of analytical skills, and it concludes with a series of questions designed to help instructors manage the use of the personal in their assignments and then to analyze the degree to which its use in first-year writing programs supports the necessary transition into the academic community.

USE OF THE PERSONAL IN ACADEMIC WRITING

Spigelman (2001) argues that "the telling of stories can actually serve the same purposes as academic writing and that narratives of personal experience can accomplish serious scholarly work" (p. 64). She sees narrative as a "logical and legitimate mode of argument appropriate to academic writing of both composition scholars and their students" (p. 64). She points out several academic purposes achieved by personal and experiential writing and gives examples. Specifically, Montaigne's *Essais* (in Bloom, 1987) and Richard Rodriguez's *Hunger of Memory* (1983), are examples of writings in which the authors reflect on larger issues through their own stories. A scholar may frame a broader topic and speculate about it, as E. B. White does in *Sootfall and Fallout* (1995). She also cites the genre "autoethnography," which "insists that the narrative on an individual's life is both the product and process of surrounding social and educational narratives" (p. 65). Examples of autoethnography are Victor Villanueva's *Bootstraps* (1993) and Linda Brodkey's *Writing on the Bias* (1994). (See also Ellis & Bochner, 2000, 2000a, 2000b for an in-depth explanation of autoethnography.)

EXPRESSING YOUR INDIVIDUAL VOICE

Even in doctoral programs, students can find ways to express their individual voices and to control the topics of their writing. Cheryl North, an adjunct instructor and doctoral student, is a self-described "biker chick." Growing up in a working-class suburb of Baltimore, Maryland, she has sought out those professors who are willing to see her as a bright and talented young woman with considerable promise. For her, Elbow's theories and the professors who practice them provide a comfort zone in which she can grow. She states:

> Luckily, I have found some professors who are more into good writing than stuffy scholarly crap. My favorite professor always devotes one or two classes to effective writing á la Peter Elbow. I came into his class and wrote one stuffy, scholarly paper, thinking that was what he wanted. Then I got to know him and apologized for making him read that crap. We always recommend good books on writing to each other like Bird by Bird (Lamott, 1995), and On Writing Well (Zinsser, 2001). Another professor makes us write vent papers. He tells us to write what is on our mind. The first paper in that class was to write about why and how we chose our dissertation topic. He wanted the emotional reason why. So many people came into class and told him how much they learned about themselves when they were allowed to write without boundaries. ... Truthfully, I've only had one professor who has stood behind her Ivory Tower with a vengeance. Needless to say, I didn't do too well in

that class. I told her that I couldn't write or think that way because I'm not of her social class. Ha! I think that had a lot to do with my grade, too.

THE NARRATIVE VOICE MAY POSE PROBLEMS

Although a narrative voice is appropriate for a specific writing purpose, as in the stories told by teacher researchers, it may pose problems for some writers. Before she became a teacher, Deborah Green, in our Arizona writing group, worked in the field of medical research. She was skilled in writing the technical papers that were required of the field but didn't see that as "writing, since everything was right there on the workbench and in your logbook. All you had to do was write it up." Because of the qualitative nature of teacher research, which situates the researcher in the classroom experience while investigating teaching and learning, any efforts to maintain an objective distance from the question, the students, and the experience would, in fact, be somewhat dishonest. Consequently, narrative is encouraged. For Deborah, this was extremely difficult. She was comfortable with the objective voice of scientific writing and found it hard to allow herself to intrude on her text when she wrote her story. She, in fact, resisted it for some time and struggled to produce the article she wanted to write. Finally, she took a chance.

After fighting with this paper for a couple of months, I decided to try writing it in a completely different format. Although I have never used the narrative format I decided to use it to see if a different perspective would help get me past this block. I made this decision after reading several articles written in that style in NWP's Quarterly. I enjoyed those articles and the informal style in which they were written. However, since I'm not used to using this format I felt somewhat insecure and really needed the feedback from the writing group to let me know if I was on the right track.

Deborah's experience is not unusual for those who come from similar backgrounds and for those who are comfortable and successful writing in the objective, academic voice. Among the teacher researchers Sharon has worked with over the years, there have been several who, like Deborah, had difficulty using the narrative voice to tell the stories of their classroom research. At the extreme, there were those who refused to even accept qualitative inquiry as valid research. Sharon remembers one young woman who declared that such research was a "bastardization" of the research process.

Janet also occasionally fights an uphill battle with others in the academic community when she encourages her doctoral and specialist degree students to write in the active voice, use the personal "I," and include narrative. Recently, one of Janet's specialist degree students, Jennie, used the first-person active voice to present her qualitative research project. At

Jennie's oral presentation a member of the committee raised her hand and remarked in front of everyone, "I know I am of the old school, but how odd the writing is in this manuscript."

PERSONAL REFLECTIONS

Consider the voice in which you usually write. Is it active or passive? To what extent have you been encouraged to use the active voice in academic writing? Have you ever used the active voice in a manuscript only to be told to change to the passive voice? Maybe it was just the opposite—a professor might have urged you to use the active voice. How easily can you code-switch, that is, select and use a specific voice for certain types, purposes, or audiences of your writing? Have you ever used the personal "I" in your academic writing? To what extent are you comfortable using narrative structures? Write your reflections.

MEETING THE CHALLENGE OF THE DISSERTATION

For doctoral candidates, the dissertation presents a series of challenges that may be unlike any of the other challenges encountered in educational studies. According to Marilyn Vogler Urion (2002), Assistant Dean of the graduate school at Michigan Technological University, innovative academic writing is encouraged both before and after the dissertation, but not for the dissertation itself, which "must adhere to narrowly conceived notions of academic discourse and to rigid formatting requirements" (p. 1). She attributes this to the role of the dissertation as an initiation ritual. She believes that writing the dissertation changes us because it requires "us to adopt a new set of behaviors" (p. 2), and this change allows us to enter the academic community, something that echoes Bartholomae's (1995) notion of how learning the required language and style of writing earns us "admission" to the discourse community of the academy. Urion points out that "[t]he rhetorical space of dissertations remains conservative because it (1) adheres to particular hierarchies of power and privilege and (2) relies on a particular distribution of knowledge and authority, both of which maintain the dominant culture of privilege in the academy" (p. 2).

In her book, Urion records numerous stories told by women engaged in the dissertation process. Her own dissertation was an autoethnographic study of the process of writing a dissertation, which was somewhat revolutionary in its own right, as she later discovered from colleagues who told her they would never have approved such a dissertation topic. Her study participants described instances where their committee, for a variety of reasons, discouraged their topics, or the revision requirements covered both important and petty issues. One of her informants described an experience similar to the one described by Debbie Dimmett earlier in this chapter: "I was defending a dissertation that I didn't believe in, had not envisioned, and didn't like very much at all. I wondered why in the hell I had been given just enough free rein to be frustrated in ways I had never imagined" (Urion, 2002, p. 6).

Similarly, a colleague of Sharon's, Cathy Randall, found that the members of her dissertation committee were constantly at odds with one another on what she should be doing, so that every time she met with them, she was given a different direction. As an extremely busy professional development specialist for a large suburban school system, she was eventually worn down by the stress of doing her job while completing a very complex statistical study. At meeting after meeting, Cathy tried desperately to defend her own purposes and direction, to somehow convince the committee to allow her to pursue her goals in a coherent and comprehensive fashion. Finally, understanding that writing something meaningful was not an option, and recognizing that if she was to finish her dissertation with her sanity intact, she concluded that she needed to comply with conflicting expectations.

Urion (2002) asserts that "[s]uccessfully completing a dissertation that one doesn't like stifles the writerly self," but, unlike Bloom (1981), she goes on to suggest that the experience is not so bad after all. The resulting "new self" does, indeed, have an identity, which appears to be one in which the writer is defined by her existence in a "liminal space" (p. 8), between cultures. Thus, the dissertation, with all of its warts, remains an important step in joining the "continuing scholarly conversation" (pp. 8–9). Indeed, Urion concluded from her interviews, that, in general, although the writer's identity, or voice, was stifled, it was not silenced, and that most of her study participants found a new focus for their work, or ultimately found their own voices, "seven, eight, twelve years after the dissertation was completed" (p. 9). Consequently, as an initiation ritual, for Urion, the dissertation was effective in spite of the angst the dissertators experienced, because they were able to move on productively.

Do Urion's conclusions justify what for many doctoral students is a stress-filled, negative ordeal that results in a cynical attitude about the process? Is it appropriate for them to decide to simply do what they have to do to get the degree? Is it necessary for them to compromise their beliefs and smother any sense of passion about their own learning? In medieval times, "running the gauntlet" was a popular military punishment in which a prisoner had to run between two heavily armed rows of men (Taylor, 1997). The prisoner could only hope to survive the bashing. Sadly, for some, completing a dissertation may have a great deal in common with

this ancient test. You will recall that this is how Debbie Dimmett antici-
pates her experience will be.

Completing a Dissertation Can Be a Positive Experience

Fortunately, the dissertation experience can be positive even when the
topic is not the candidate's first choice. An NWP colleague of Sharon's,
Andrea Fishman, Professor at West Chester University in Pennsylvania and
Director of the Pennsylvania Writing and Literature Project, had a close
friend who was Amish. This personal connection led to a paper on Amish
literacy for one of her graduate classes at the University of Pennsylvania,
setting into motion a chain of events that resulted in a dissertation on that
very subject. Her story is best told in her own words:

> *I had no intention of doing my dissertation research on the Amish. In fact, that
> had never occurred to me. I was planning research much closer to home—in
> my own high school classroom, in fact. That was what brought me to Penn's
> doctoral program in writing: It bore direct application to my chosen life's
> work. So why would I want to do research, literally and figuratively, in some-
> one else's field?*

> *Then one evening at a wine-and-cheese reception for a guest speaker, my Lit-
> eracy: Social and Historical Perspectives professor, David Smith, put his hand
> on my shoulder and steered me toward the dean of the graduate school. "Dell
> [Hymes]," David called, "This is the woman I was telling you about."*

> *Suddenly, a different hand on my elbow pointed me to a quiet corner with
> two empty chairs. "We need to talk," Dean Hymes intoned with frightening
> seriousness. Two glasses of wine materialized. I gulped. I had never actu-
> ally met The Dean before, only seen him from a distance and heard him al-
> luded to with clearly capitalized letters. And though I was a 35-year-old
> adult, the tall, bear-like incarnation of all this respect and power who could
> snap his fingers to make wine appear and people disappear intimidated me
> more than a little.*

> *Hymes wasted no time. "David's been telling me about your Amish research,"
> he began.*

> *My "Amish research?" Did he mean the paper I was writing for David's
> course? It was just a paper, an assignment for which I'd chosen my Amish
> friends as the topic. I nodded, not knowing what to say.*

> *"No one has access to the Amish," Hymes continued, "that's why you have a
> scholarly obligation to do your dissertation on the Amish."*

"But I'm going to do classroom research ..." I responded meekly.

Hymes shook his head in what seemed a combination of disbelief and pity at my naiveté. "Anyone can do classroom research," he quietly responded. "You are the only one who can do the Amish work."

Our conversation continued not even long enough to finish my wine. Dean Hymes was adamant and I was speechless, except to agree that I'd "think about it."

The next day I sought out another professor, a woman whose course in writing theories and processes I had taken the previous semester. Linda Brodkey and I were contemporaries; we even had sons the same age. Though she was intellectually stunning and had far surpassed me in professional achievement and political acumen, Linda was someone I trusted to tell the truth I needed to hear.

I reported what transpired the previous evening. Linda's eyes never left mine as I described Dell's low-key insistence and my own meek confusion in response.

"I know you want to do classroom research, Andy," Linda replied tactfully, measuring her words. "But you're at the center of the ethnographic world here. If you really want to know what I recommend, it's this: Do what they want you to do. Get the degree. You have your whole career to do classroom research. While you're here, take advantage of what this place has to offer. Go for it."

"Will you be on my committee?" I asked, afraid to be as alone as I foresaw myself at that moment.

Linda's smile said she knew exactly what I was asking. "Of course."

And that, as they say, was that.

On its face, Linda's pragmatism seems almost like advice to sell out. Her comments could be read as suggesting I abandon some long-held personal goal in favor of political expedience. That I go-with-the-grad-school-flow. But that was not the case. In fact, Linda was pointing out a choice I had made with little awareness or forethought. She was calling me forward to claim my own stake in this "ethnographic world" I had chosen. It was time for me to move from the periphery, where I studied the newly charted literacy lands of people like the scholars whose work I had been reading, to explore my own. My boundary could be set within my classroom walls or I could take Hymes's admonition seriously, fulfilling my "scholarly obligation" and what Linda suggested was my obligation to myself at the same time. I had chosen a world where people wanted to help me grow beyond what I—and even they— knew. A world where people preferred real questions to hypothetical an-

swers. A world where people wanted me to lead, not just follow. Where it
wasn't about learning the limits of the discourse but expanding them. Where
being a member of the community meant contributing to the community, not
disappearing within it.

Because she had access to the ordinarily closed Amish community for her research, the dissertation committee gave Andrea a great deal of support and latitude in her approach to the research and to the development of the text that finally told the story. Andrea lived with her Amish friends, cotaught in their school, and completed an ethnographic study of their literacy, research that was, indeed, a "lived experience," as noted teacher researcher, Glenda Bissex, described it (Bissex, 1998, p. x). She returned to her classroom transformed by the experience, and her "story" was published under the title, *Amish Literacy: What and How It Means* (Fishman, 1988). Andrea did not choose this topic; her graduate school professors pressured her to do it. However, because it was a topic that offered her a powerful personal connection, and because her committee valued her voice, she was able to bring passion and commitment to it. Her dissertation experience was relevant both professionally and personally.

Ramona Moore Chauvin, now at Western Washington University, also had a positive experience writing her dissertation. Ramona used the personal "I" and the active voice throughout her manuscript entitled, *Constructing a Narrative of Teacher Development: Piecing Together Teacher Stories, Teacher Lives, and Teacher Education* (1995). Ramona began her dissertation by writing:

The story of my life in teaching begins back home on Bayou Lafourche with
my family, my culture, my early schooling, and the significant teachers in my
life. I grew up on Bayou Lafourche in South Louisiana before it was popular to
be Cajun. (p. 1)

In a beautifully composed paragraph that captures the significance of the personal, Ramona goes on to say:

While I cannot reclaim my Cajun accent, writing this dissertation has helped
me to reclaim pieces from my past that are continually helping me to construct
who I am as an individual and as a teacher. It has also helped me to realize that
the development of the teacher Ramona Moore [Chauvin] is inseparable from
the development of the person Ramona Moore [Chauvin]. (p. 2)

Ramona quotes Polkinghorne, a noted phenomenologist and researcher of the "Self." Polkinghorne (1988) believes, "Self then, is not a static thing, not a substance, but a configuring of personal events into a historical community which includes not only what one has been but also anticipation of what one will be" (p. 150).

Challenges to the Traditional Dissertation

In recent years, the traditions of academic writing have not only been challenged by increasing efforts to introduce innovative structures for writing, but also by the growing acceptance of alternative discourses like Ramona's use of the personal "I" in her dissertation. Because membership in the academic community is rapidly changing, it is only natural that the language used in the academy—its discourse—will be affected. Although it did not come about easily, there are now in academe more people of color, more women, more scholars from diverse cultures, and more students for whom English is not their first language. These scholars bring with them their own particular discourses and have a need and a right to blend what might have been previously described as nonacademic discourses with traditional academic discourse.

For example, Kim Shea states,

> *I am encouraged to learn that the academy is now open to diversity. I am not a White male from a privileged family. I am an intelligent African American female who attended a rural elementary school and a predominately Black undergraduate university. My voice deserves to be heard, and it will be heard through my writing even though my voice may not be the traditional voice of the academy. Bartholomae (1995) equates writing a dissertation with pledging to a sorority or fraternity. Candidates cannot be included unless they lose some of their personal self. Expressing myself in my writing doesn't make me less scholarly. What is the point of being in the academy if I cannot express myself in writing from the perspective of my African American heritage? I feel a need to control my own texts.*

This new, or diverse, academic discourse is described by Bizzell (2002) as "still academic, in that they are doing the intellectual work of the academy—rigorous, reflective scholarship" (p. 1). By blending in, rather than rejecting, with these diverse voices we are seeing more flexible use of language and dialect within the academy, and an increase in the use of personal experience and cultural allusions to support and enhance research. For example, multigenre research papers are increasingly accepted at both the undergraduate and graduate levels, even while the debate continues. A graduate course offered in the Rhetoric, Composition, and Teaching of English Program at the University of Arizona in 2002 brought together the concepts of alternative discourses and multigenre writing. Sandra Florence, an Associate Writing Specialist in the Composition Program, shares the experience of that first course offering.

> *This course drew teachers from every level—preschool, middle, high school, university, and two teachers from the Arizona Schools for the Deaf and Blind. While our purpose was to become familiar with what multigenre writing actually is, and to look at models of how to set up this form—we used Tom Romano's work for guidelines and inspiration—the course went further than this. We had Romano's (2000) practical guide to multigenre writing, Blending Genre, Altering Style, but also read, Alt Dis, edited by Christopher Schroeder, Helen Fox, and Patricia Bizzell (2002). Alt Dis focused on the place of home dialects, new literacies, and mixed forms— their emergence and whether or not these alternative discourses should be admitted into the academy. Our discussions were heated and dynamic. While the public school teachers questioned even the value of multigenre writing in their classrooms, the notion that home dialects and mother tongue be allowed raised eyebrows.*

> *First of all, I have to clarify that multigenre writing is not necessarily alternative discourse. As Romano's text illustrated ... students may be given assignments to work with many different genres in a single document, but all of these genres may remain or be considered academically appropriate ... [using] Standard Academic English (SAE). Several teachers in this class mentioned the importance of their students mastering SAE before they are allowed to write multigenre texts. However, we all know that many of our students will never master SAE. By allowing them to incorporate their alternative discourses into classroom writing, we may be giving them one of the only opportunities they will get to establish some positive connection to writing. Multigenre assignments then can be the place where students are allowed to utilize their home dialects and mixed forms. Multigenre writing can allow for an integration of forms that can help students achieve flexibility and fluency in their writing.*

It is notable that Sandra's educator-students struggled mightily with the notion of accepting alternative discourse or multigenre writing in their classrooms, even those at the elementary and secondary levels. They seemed to see such discourse and writing as incompatible with academic expectations. Perhaps there is a middle ground that will be discovered as more and more teachers and writers explore and experiment with these forms of writing.

Accordingly, it may be some time before we find multigenre dissertations approved in the academy. However, we are already seeing a variety of alternatives to the traditional approach. For example, qualitative models of research have increasingly gained acceptance. These models stretch across a wide continuum, from relatively straightforward teacher research stories and narratives, like those found in Ramona Moore Chauvin's dissertation, to more formal accounts of teacher research and formal ethnographic studies.

Electronic Dissertation Initiatives

In addition to a more widespread acceptance of qualitative models for research, alternative structures and forms are beginning to emerge. Given the widespread use of technology in university settings, it is probably only a matter of time before a more specifically technological approach to the dissertation will be widely accepted.

In 1995, Leslie Jarmon (1996), a doctoral candidate in speech communication at the University of Texas at Austin, formally requested an exemption from the "on paper requirements for Ph.D. dissertations" (University of Texas/Office of Graduate Studies [UT/OGS], 1996, p. 1). The Graduate Assembly, which approved her project, reported that the request was reasonable because her topic was nonverbal communication. They also intended to use her project as a test case to determine the feasibility of such formats. As a result of this project, the university now requires all dissertations to be submitted digitally, for archival purposes as well as to permit the use of images, sound, and video, for information that is "otherwise more difficult to capture through prose only" (UT/OGS, 1996, p. 1).

Dr. Tim Brace (1996), Senior Systems Analyst in the Office of Graduate Studies at the University of Texas at Austin, who works with students in support of their digital efforts, makes a strong case for a more technological approach to the dissertation. He points out that it is beneficial to revisit "traditions, practices, and their products" (p. 1), while at the same time, the consideration of new, technology-based structures for the dissertation is filled with possibilities. Among these are (a) the use of multimedia, which might include data that are integral to the study, including video clips, audio, art, or music, among others; (b) a nonlinear structure, which allows multiple entry points and multiple avenues of navigation through the document (in other words, hypertext); (c) the potential for interactivity, where the reader's responses may "trigger the next item"; (d) the use of internal and external links, allowing the reader to jump to another place in the document or to exit the document to examine outside sources; and finally, (e) flexibility in the display of primary data that allows the reader to more carefully examine the researcher's interpretation and analysis. Furthermore, Brace asserts that digital dissertations are easier and cheaper to duplicate, and they are more widely disseminated, either as Hypertext Markup Language (HTML) documents or as portable document files (PDF) through Internet access (pp. 2–3). For an example of a digital dissertation, which illustrates the nonlinear structure nicely, visit Jean S. Mason's (2000) dissertation, completed at McGill

University in Montréal, at http://www.masondissertation.elephanthost.com. Interestingly enough, the topic of her dissertation relates to the use of hypertext as a writing medium.

Currently, many universities require digital archiving of dissertations, but that generally means submitting the paper dissertation, along with a CD-ROM that can be conveniently archived and made more easily available for duplication and for research. For example, the University of South Florida recently announced that the days of paper submission of dissertations are coming to an end. In 1997, the university joined the networked Digital Library of Theses and Dissertations (NDLTD), a group of universities across the country creating databases of electronically formatted theses and dissertations (ETD). The program, initiated by Virginia Tech, was conceived to make the unique intellectual contributions of theses and dissertations readily available to the worldwide scholarly population. Currently, the ETD initiative at the University of South Florida is in the testing phase. Students who submit an ETD will also be required to submit a paper copy of their work. However, the Office of Graduate Studies provides a small stipend to students submitting ETDs to help defray the cost of producing a paper copy.

Collaborative Dissertations

One area that is unlikely become a reality in the near future is the collaborative dissertation. Because significant aspects of a doctoral program involve candidates individually proving their ability to succeed in the program (the qualifying exam) and proving that they have learned something (comprehensives), it is undoubtedly difficult for the university hierarchy to shift from individual expectations to an assessment model that involves a collaborative effort. How would they know whose work they were reading? How would they divide the "credit"? These are, perhaps, some of the questions they asked when Janine Rider and Esther Broughton (1994) were completing their doctoral work. During their preliminary coursework, Rider and Broughton were extremely pleased with the degree of collaboration they had been permitted. They had collaborated on a research paper and were enthusiastically encouraged by their professors, who actually suggested it would be wonderful to see a collaborative dissertation approved. They say:

> It is one thing to believe strongly in the value of collaboration, and it is invigorating to find others who share that belief. But belief only goes so far. In many practical situations, fixed attitudes and traditions implicitly and explicitly reject collaboration.... Several of our professors confirmed the need for revising the concept of the dissertation, and they went on and on in class about

how great it would be to see a collaborative one approved. More talk with them brought the reality closer; however, getting a director in our department for a collaborative dissertation was one thing, but getting it through the university approval process was another. We would have been laughed right out of graduate class. There was never a choice. (Para. 20)

In spite of Janine's and Esther's experiences, collaborative dissertations may not be outside the realm of possibility. Our Internet search for "collaborative dissertations" brought up at least one university that lists collaborative dissertations as acceptable. The University of Buffalo permits them in the EdD program in Educational Leadership. (See http://www.gse.buffalo.edu/dc/ecap/EA4.htm.)

PUBLISHING IN PROFESSIONAL JOURNALS

A large number of professional journals, including scholarly, practical, and electronic journals, provide an excellent outlet for educators who wish to write for publication. Also, many of these journals encourage the use of the personal "I" and active voice as opposed to a strict adherence to objectivity and the passive voice, even some that are scholarly journals. Gary Natriello (1998), Executive Editor of the *Teachers College Record (TCR)*, a journal published by Teachers College of Columbia University, speaks eloquently about his preference for a more relaxed approach to writing for publication. He urged writers to come from "behind the curtain," an allusion to the man in the *Wizard of Oz* who hid behind a curtain and presented his words through a "grand vision of a wizard at center stage" (p. 617). In doing so, the man created a perception of authority that both impressed onlookers and insulated him from challenges. Natriello urges writers to disclose themselves within their texts and he laments writers' common practice of distancing themselves from the text and avoiding the personal style "in an attempt to appear authoritative" (p. 617).

Furthermore, he points to the practice of using passive constructions, such as "It has long been thought that" (p. 617), rather than simply stating directly, "I agree with much of the research that suggests." He believes that such passive constructions create a perception that some data and information simply appeared magically in the "continuing progress of humankind" (p. 618) without human intervention. He suggests that it is more honest for writers to place themselves in the text and declare their practice openly.

Moreover, Natriello (1998) is critical of the practice of using complex language and convoluted sentence constructions in an effort to impress and sound important. As a result, the reader may be unable to determine if the "complexity lies in the language or in the content" (p. 619). He provides additional examples of how researchers hide behind the work of other more important agencies and emphasizes that the writer should avoid using the profound "we" to conceal personal identity. For example, "We can now see" or "We recommend" (p. 620). He believes this can be confusing, as the reader will wonder who comprised the team of researchers and why they have not been credited for their contributions.

Finally, Natriello (1998) points out that *TCR*'s reviewers often react negatively to writing styles and approaches that make it more difficult for them to understand how the researcher conducted the study and what the article is really about. And, he asserts, it is rare for *TCR*'s reviewers to react negatively to a personal style of writing. He advises authors to

> write in a straightforward style that identifies [them]. It is not easy to develop a voice that is identifiable and consistent, but authors who do so will become known for the quality of their communication, as well as the quality of their scholarship. Writing in an accessible style will also enhance the peer-review process. (p. 620)

Generally, scholarly journals maintain an expectation for compliance with the rules of academic writing. We suggest that before you submit an article to a specific journal, you become familiar with the style of writing that authors use in that journal. Read articles in various journals in your field, and jot down the preferred writing style in each publication. Contact journal editors for publication requirements.

PERSONAL REFLECTIONS

What ideas presented in this chapter did you find most provocative, innovative, or useful? Why? What challenges and encouragement have you encountered in your academic writing initiatives? How did you resolve problems that occurred? How were you encouraged in your academic writing? Can you identify with Kim Shea's desire and strong determination to allow her voice to be heard in her writing? What did you think of Ramona Moore Chauvin's use of the personal "I" in her dissertation? What do you think of Andrea Fishman's decision to do what her professors insisted she do? Write your reflections.

SUMMARY

This chapter covers a wide range of issues related to the styles and purposes of academic writing. Purposes for writing include job related requirements, such as grant proposals, letters, and supervisory memos, and writing related to graduate studies, such as essays, dissertations, masters degree theses, and specialist degree projects. Educators also write to complete National Board Certification and to share the results of action research projects. In addition, "the range of genres for educators might include scholarly books, edited volumes, chapters contributed to an edited collection, journal articles, book reviews, essays, textbooks, and even syllabi and course material" (Rankin, 2001, p. 33). All of these different types of discourse require educators to consider the boundaries of language and style that define the broad genre of academic writing.

The chapter was informed by educators' reflections about their writing. Some expressed their concerns about strict or inconsistent guidelines mandated by their dissertation committee members. Others talked about the challenges of attempting to write using first-person singular, narrative, and active voice.

Educators also shared their positive experiences doing academic writing. For example, note that Andrea Fishman's professors' insistence that she pursue the research they believed was important turned out favorably. Ramona Moore Chauvin's doctoral committee supported her goal of weaving in her Cajun identity with her study of women teachers. In addition, Ramona's committee fully supported her use of first-person singular and active voice.

It is our hope that this chapter not only helps to inform you about the wide range of writing for academic purposes, but also encourages you to consider how the demands of your work context or your professors' beliefs about what constitutes good academic writing have the capacity to influence your writing style and the content of your discourse. But also keep in mind that you can "find a way of writing that is tailored to you, your personality, … [and] strengths" (Fletcher, 2000, p. 111).

After reading this chapter and engaging in the reflective activities, we hope that you begin to think about "the kinds of knowledge writers must have or develop to function effectively as a writer in a variety of writing situations (Hillocks, 1995, p. XIX). Also, consider why you want to write and for whom, and seriously think about the forms of writing that are most appropriate for you and your particular writing tasks. Finally, as closure to this chapter, we urge you to contemplate writing possibilities—never assume that you cannot write in a style that is most comfortable for you—always explore and include your solid sense of self in your writing—never forget that your best academic writing efforts connect the personal and the professional.

RELEVANT READINGS

Elbow, P. (2000). *Everyone can write: Essays toward a hopeful theory of writing and teaching writing.* New York: Oxford University Press.

This substantial collection of essays details Elbow's thinking on a wide variety of writing topics, including voice, theory, academic discourse, and the evaluation of writing. Elbow includes an autobiographical account of personal writing problems and criticism of his writings that helped to solidify his thinking. This book will interest serious students of writing.

[Chauvin] Moore, R. (1995). *Constructing a narrative of teacher development: Piecing together teacher stories, teacher lives, and teacher education.* New Orleans, LA: University of New Orleans Library.

Ramona's dissertation provides a model for exemplary qualitative dissertations. Her writing is clear and organized, and her voice resonates throughout the manuscript. She writes in first-person active voice and connects her own life story to her research in teacher development. Teachers' narratives offer us glimpses into their lives and tell us how they decided to enter the teaching profession. We learn that a teacher's development is inseparable from his or her development as a person.

Luce-Kapler, R. (1999). As if women writing. *Journal of Literacy Research, 31,* 267–291.

This work is a feminist examination of the role of writing in women's understanding of their identity. For more information on Luce-Kapler's work, visit Luce-Kapler's home page at http://www.educ.queensu.ca/~luce-kar, where she explains that her research and teaching arise from her background in writing poetry and fiction and from her experience as an English teacher and professional editor. Her primary work centers on writing processes and technologies and the issues of gender and pedagogy that arise from these areas. Feminist and poststructural theories also inform much of her work.

Chapter 3

Invention

Prewriting—in both the amount I do and the strategies I use—depends on the kind of writing I'm doing. I begin essays by writing streams of consciousness notes. I start with obvious quotations, or a rehashing of class discussions and free-associates. I connect these with arrows, or asterisks, and continue writing about how or why these two ideas connect.... These notes aren't in full sentences, and end up looking like an annotated road map. (Evans, cited in Murray, 2001, pp. 148–149)

One piece of advice commonly given to writers is to outline a project before they begin working on it. That's not bad advice, though it oversimplifies the relation of thought to language. Because many of us do our thinking and writing simultaneously—unable to know what we think until we see what we say—outlining is not always a reasonable option. (Rankin, 2001, p. 22)

We stated in the preface that one of our most important goals for authoring this book is to help you become a better writer. Therefore, in this chapter, we move forward into invention—what writing scholars and teachers refer to as the first step in the composing process. Donald Murray (2001) says invention is anything a writer does before beginning a draft.

Although we devote this entire chapter to invention (i.e., prewriting strategies), please keep in mind that not all writers begin composing by engaging in specific invention methods, and not all writers use invention each time they write. As you know, all writers write differently. The writing process varies from one writer and one situation to another (Hillocks, 1995). Using invention strategies and determining what invention strategy to use depends on the writer's mood and inclination, persona, writing task, and the audience and purpose for writing.

Many educators are expected to write as part of their work and as students of education. In addition to their mandated jobs and university-related writing assignments, educators frequently want to write about their classroom research, teaching experiences, observations, and ideas for instruction.

As an educator, where do you find your ideas for writing? How do you determine that you have something interesting to say? In what ways do you plan, or map out what you will write? For example, you may be a school administrator, or a classroom teacher who works with students who have limited English proficiency. You may have developed some in-school programs, or devised some teaching strategies that contribute to your students' success as they acquire English language proficiency. You may want to write about your work so that other educators can learn about your students' achievements, but you don't know where to begin. Your first step might be to engage in some invention or prewriting strategies that help you discover what you really want to tell your audience.

Perhaps you are a graduate student and you are confused about how and what to write because your professor or doctoral committee has not offered you clear directions. That is exactly what happened to Sandra Engoron-March at the University of Arizona. Sandra recalls her experience:

> *When called upon to develop the literature review, I did not know where to start. I did not know how to select the most important topics from a vast array of options. This was an extremely demanding and stressful situation for me. I had to make decisions so that I could select a theoretical framework for my research. I had few guidelines other than my knowledge of what were the most widely accepted viewpoints on the subject of my research. Was I to present the theoretical perspective that at the time received the greatest support in the literature? Or was a broad overview called for? Apparently, I, and only I, would ultimately have to make this decision.*

Invention strategies might have helped Sandra make decisions about how to categorize and rank reference sources that were most relevant to her research. Engaging in prewriting activities also might have enabled her to take ownership and control of her work early in the dissertation writing process.

Janet also remembers struggling with her dissertation. As she explained earlier, the garbage can in her kitchen overflowed with abandoned first paragraphs. Using some invention schemes might have helped her figure out the direction in which she needed to go.

Of course, not all authors use specific invention strategies as a prelude to composing. Some turn to invention or prewriting schemes only occasionally. Like Janet, Sharon, Donald Murray, and many others, they prefer to discover what they want to say, what they know, and what they need to know as they compose. Other writers may get pretty far along in the writing process, and then find out they need to explore their topic further so they loop back to invention. The bottom line is this: All writers are different, and all writers write differently. There is no one best way to get ready to write, and there is no perfect prescription that can steer all of us through the writing process.

THE WRITING PROCESS

What we refer to today as the writing process developed from extensive examinations of what real writers do when they write (Berkenkotter, 1983; Fulwiler, 2002; Murray, 1990). The generally accepted stages of the writing process include prewriting (i.e., invention), drafting, revising, editing, and publishing. However, this is a simplification. Describing the stages of composing in this way implies a precise linear process; first you do this, then this, and so on. However, it doesn't work that way. The writing process is recursive; that is, it is a cyclical, overlapping process where the writer may return to earlier stages, or proceed to later stages at any time, or the writer may try several strategies at once (Flower & Hayes, 1981; Sadowski & Paivio, 2001). For example, we may be in the midst of revising a draft when we realize we are lacking information about a topic. That sends us scrambling back to the prewriting or invention stage to generate more information and details, as Choyce Cochran, a specialist degree candidate, explains later in this chapter. We may also have to return to invention because we review what we have written and decide to abandon the topic or part of the content, and start over. Our initial writing efforts have stimulated the discovery of new insights (Sadowski & Paivio, 2001).

For example, Sharon recently contributed a piece to an NWP publication, the purpose of which was to promote a network retreat scheduled to take place in Tucson, Arizona, in the heart of the southwestern desert. She, along with two other writers, was to write on behalf of those who live in and love the southwestern desert. It was to be a multivoiced writing project that would not only promote the retreat, but also invite readers to visit and experience the beauty and complexity of the desert. Sharon knew she wanted to write a simple reflection that would somehow convey the spiritual connection she feels with the desert, but she wasn't sure how she could do that in the limited space the piece was assigned. She struggled with her own relationship with the desert while trying to remain faithful to the purpose. Ultimately, she discovered she had written the wrong piece for the wrong purpose. She explains:

> I wrote a piece about riding in the desert on a quirky horse that has a split personality. He is often a part of my desert explorations and, somehow, I thought I could represent the desert best to our NWP conference attendees by includ-

ing a horse in the desert landscape. I was allotted about 300 words and, some-how, I wrote 1,000. I struggled to trim my manuscript down, and I stubbornly held on to my horse idea, while I also tried to describe the desert scenery, and my emotional response to its rugged beauty. Finally, I got the piece down to size, but I wasn't happy with it. I e-mailed it to the editor whose job it was to blend my reflection with the voices of the other writers into a unified rendering.

I awoke in the morning knowing I had to start over. I reread my work and dis-covered that the horse competed with, and distracted from, my description of the landscape. So, as much as I love that big, black gelding, I returned to invention, jotting down the specific landscape details that more clearly rep-resent the desert experience. Then I rewrote the piece and eliminated the horse. Without competition from him, my reflection focused more clearly on the desert and the powerful connection I feel for it. The final multivoiced piece as it appeared in publication had the desired effect.

Sharon discovered on her own that she needed to start over and engage in some invention strategies because she had allowed her love of a horse to get in the way of a short informational piece. Fortunately, she had time to rethink and revise her work. However, some of us may get all the way to the publishing stage when a professional editor or a group of reviewers advises us to reorganize or rewrite our manuscript. Or we may turn in what we think is a final copy to our university professor only to be told, "Rewrite this piece please, and turn it in next week. You need to clarify your thinking."

USING A VARIETY OF APPROACHES TO WRITE AN ACADEMIC PIECE

Even with what we do know about what most writers generally do, it would be a mistake to think that *all* writers do all these things *all* of the time. "True, there are interesting similarities in how various writers work, but each writer uses a process slightly different from that of other writers" (Murray, 2000, p. 3). As Ralph Fletcher (2000) tells us, there is no one-size-fits-all writing formula. Each of us has our own individual manner of writing and we move in and out of the writing stages at our own pace and in our own unique ways. There is no single way to write an academic piece. What we must remember is that while we need to recognize that there are stages of composing, we cannot reduce the writing process to linear stages, or view the writing pro-cess in a unitary way (Hillocks, 1995). Some writers may skip a stage or com-bine stages. Some authors "write in phrases and clauses with pauses between them to consider the next phrase or clause and/or review text al-ready produced" (Sadowski & Paivio, 2001, p. 140). Some people need less time to engage in invention, and more time to create a draft (Fletcher, 2000). Others need to spend more time on invention and less time composing a draft. Still other writers continually jump back and forth between writing stages. Their writing processes appear to occur at many levels simultaneously (Flower & Hayes, 1981).

BENEFITING FROM INVENTION STRATEGIES

Opinions vary about the benefits of using prewriting or invention strategies. For example, some good writers say they spend 85% of their time on invention. Penny Judson (2000), who writes about the writing process, thinks that during the prewriting stage, writers take control and ownership of their writing because this process "encourages experimentation while giving the first draft organization and purpose" (p. 1).

On the other hand, Ralph Fletcher (2000) cautions against devoting too much time and energy to prewriting because he thinks writers may become "absolutely sick of the topic" (p. 30). Quntilian, the great Roman professor of rhetoric, also encouraged his students not to waste time with invention and first drafts. He wanted his students to write "quickly and with abandon" (Golden, 1969, cited in Bloodgood, 2002, p. 35).

Greg Shafer, who encourages student self-expression, concurs with Fletcher (2000) and Quintilian (cited in Bloodgood, 2002). He believes that ideas spring from actual writing. He thinks writers should simply write, and allow words to cook and grow (personal communication, April, 10, 2003; see also Elbow, 1973).

Regardless of your own personal style of composing, there is a possibility that using invention or prewriting strategies may help you take ownership and control of your writing because these strategies help organize and structure your thinking. Invention strategies (e.g., actually putting ideas down on paper, or making a concept map) make visible all of the shadowy, obscure writing notions that float around in your head.

WRITING WITH DIFFERENT INVENTION STYLES

In general, invention may include different activities for different writers. For some, when a topic presents itself, there is a time in which they explore the topic, trying to identify a focus. Donald Murray (1989) calls this the "essential delay" (p. 29). What many of us perceive as procrastination or fear is writer's block, which Murray describes as quite natural. He encourages us to distinguish the kinds of delay that are good for our writing and lists a large number of professional writers who believe that periods of delay are good writing practice. E. B. White concurs, stating, "delay is natural" (cited in Murray, 1989, p. 30). Tom Romano (1995) calls this delay stage "percolating."

Of course, as we said earlier, some writers appear to forgo the percolating stage. They dive right in by writing a "discovery draft" (refer back to Sharon's narrative about being a discovery drafter in chapter 1). Donald Murray (1989) describes this kind of writing as "an emptying out of all we have said, read, thought, seen, felt" (p. 20). In doing this, writers write for themselves, finding the language, the message, or the point by exploring what is known and unknown. Murray (1989) aptly phrases this as, "what I find being said on my own page"(p. 20). After discovering the focus and finding what is personally known, the writer might then begin to explore what others know and have said, collecting research and various points of view about a topic.

Although we've described this invention stage as discovery followed by research, it does not preclude writers doing just the opposite; that is, research followed by discovery.

EQUATING INVENTION WITH INQUIRY

Lindal Buchanan, an Assistant Professor at Kettering University in Michigan, equates invention with inquiry. She enters notes directly into the computer as she ponders her research question. She explains:

Some issue question catches my eye in a primary or secondary source and I'll try to get what puzzles me or intrigues me on paper. This is usually quite sloppy and runs one to five pages. For example, I recently became intrigued by something the Puritan, John Winthrop said about Anne Hutchinson—basically equating her malformed children with her ill-formed opinions. The coalition of the child with the mother intrigued me and I immediately thought it was worth researching. So, I started my research. I read everything I could get my hands on and as I read, I entered notes into the computer. I wrote out basic information or background (e.g., was born in Boston in 1634). I also entered catchy or insightful quotes from sources in case I needed them later.

I continue with this process for as long as it takes until I feel pressure building and as I do this, I start to see connections or generate further questions. Sometimes I'll do some more writing to get these ideas down on paper—again very loose and sloppy. When I have enough info/ideas/pressure built up I start writing down my ideas very loosely. I do not worry about coherence, clarity, organization at this point—and I end up with a very messy hodge-podge of writing and quotes and paraphrases that is half invention, half drafting.

CHOOSING INVENTION STRATEGIES BASED ON YOUR PURPOSE FOR WRITING

It's important for you to recognize that your purpose for writing, in many instances, will dictate the type of invention that might be most appropriate. For example, if you are a graduate student writing a required paper, you might be expected to either report your own "ability to think extensively and well" or "to *communicate* good thinking" (Weinstein, 2001, p. xi), or you might be expected to report the thinking of others. If the purpose of your writing requires a synthesis of ideas and thinking from a variety of sources, as a prewriting activity you'll be gathering resources, reading, taking notes, and exploring what others have said. In all likelihood, you won't begin to draft until after the period of research seems complete. Even then, you may find yourself cycling back to researching as the draft begins to take shape and focus.

This is what happened to Janet in her early efforts with this book. She recognized that she needed a more explicit focus to guide her thinking, and she struggled with finding the focus despite a good deal of planning, drafting, and research. She had an idea but her ideas were tangled, and until she had a glimmer of a title, the focus remained unclear. Janet needed to return to invention to clarify her ideas. For Janet, the inkling of a title finally provided a beacon for this particular piece, a guide for maintaining her direction throughout the ongoing development of the text. She remembers:

I struggled for weeks with the focus of this book. I felt like I was back writing that dissertation. I knew that I had an idea—but what was the idea? I knew the text was about academic or professional writing for educators. But, what was the rest of the puzzle? I read essays about writing that were posted on the Internet. I read sections in my qualitative research texts that focused on the self because somewhere in the "back of my mind" I was trying to link academic writing with the personal, but I consciously did not recognize that that's what I was trying to do. Like Heather Brown describes in chapter 1, I began to scribble words and phrases on scraps of paper, such as memories, experiencing, sharing, writing journeys, finding voice and identity, merging, embracing the personal. Suddenly, the word personal really clicked. That's it, I thought—Academic Writing for Educators: Connecting With Our Personal Selves? Composing Our Personal Selves? Well, something like that. I finally understood the focus of the book. Would my editor Naomi, my writing partner Sharon, and the reviewers of the book proposal understand this idea, I wondered? Of course the title changed again to Academic Writing for Educators: Making Connections, and then changed again to Professional Writing for Ed-

ucators: Finding Voice and Identity. As you know, the title and the focus of this book finally evolved into Doing Academic Writing in Education: Connecting the Personal and the Professional.

There are more effective ways to think about and plan a piece of writing than to struggle for weeks like Janet did with the focus of this book. Some specific prewriting or invention strategies might have helped reduce the significant amount of time she spent trying to discover her direction. We think invention strategies may help some of you with your writing initiatives. Therefore, we offer descriptions of several invention strategies in the following sections. As you read through the descriptions, consider how each strategy might fit your specific writing task, and in what ways each technique might complement your style of composing. The strategies are intended as suggestions only. They work well as individual techniques, but they also can be combined to meet your specific academic writing needs.

CONSIDERING A VARIETY OF INVENTION STRATEGIES

Sketch Journals and Drawings

Many authors use visual representations as inspiration for their work because images "help us see more clearly connections, relationships, and patterns in our thinking" (Wilcox, 2002, p. 40). Donald Murray (1996a) believes all writers write from images, either on paper or in their minds. He says, "We write what we see ... the relationship of seeing and telling, drawing and writing is intimate, essential" (Murray, 1994, p. vii).

Karen Ernst da Silva (2001), teacher, staff developer, and noted author about writing and the arts, agrees with Murray. She explains that making a picture is a form of thinking. She believes that drawing helps writers "find ideas for writing and to make connections" (p. 7). She says, "Drawing is part of my writing process. I keep a sketch journal, and it is my text for writing and teaching." She goes on to explain:

> *Drawing slows us down and helps us notice—important skills for writers ... Using drawings in the writing process gives me time to question, note what I see, or connect to memories, ideas, and other texts that I have read. I rarely write directly about what I draw, but drawing helps me think and gives me ideas for writing. (p. 4)*

For example, Ernst da Silva once drew a picture of a rocking chair that inspired her to write about her mother's expertise in discovering valuable antiques. Donald Graves also trusts the power of drawing as a way to release ideas and memories. He thinks drawing is wonderful preparation for writing because visual art has the ability to help us "take in the world" (cited in Ernst da Silva, 2001, p. 5). Jim La March, author and illustrator of the award-winning children's book, *The Raft* (2000), agrees that drawing, thinking, and writing are closely linked processes. He believes the power of drawing helps us get closer to something and know it better.

Jeanette Bolte, a school psychologist and Assistant Professor at the University of Southern Mississippi, says she always draws before she writes. Jeanette tells us:

One invention activity that helps me plan my writing is to keep a sketch diary. I draw my ideas. When I wrote my dissertation I traveled everywhere with a very large sketchpad. I literally illustrated my thoughts. I could never outline what I might want to write. It simply doesn't work for me.

Peggy Albers says that her strong background in the visual arts helps her with her academic writing. She explains:

Writing for me now must always involve some sort of visual or some illustration to demonstrate my points. Over the past five years I have really found the impact of visual images on my writing. I am currently working on several ideas at one time on multiculturalism and diversity in Caldecott Medal winners. Each of these papers began with my study of images so, in essence, visual images initiate my ideas for writing.

Choyce Cochran finds that her visual representations serve as a high-powered spotlight—a vehicle for illuminating problems and confusions in her thinking. Choyce created the drawings in Figures 3.1 through 3.3 to help organize the methodology section in her research project. Choyce explains how drawing helped to solidify and expand her thinking.

I had too many ideas in my head about my research project. I kept thinking of global reading comprehension instead of narrowing my study to just one aspect of reading comprehension. I chose inferencing because it is such an important component of reading. So I drew stick figures of my students. I placed them in two groups, which helped me decide that after I conduct a pretest to document my students' inferencing abilities, I will teach the standard reading curriculum plus explicit inferencing strategies to one group of students, and I will offer just the standard reading curriculum to the other group of students. Then, after six weeks, I'll do a posttest with all students. After I drew my ideas, I looked carefully at my drawing and I recognized there were problems, but I couldn't figure out what they were. This made me start thinking that I had to do more research and planning (see Fig. 3.1).

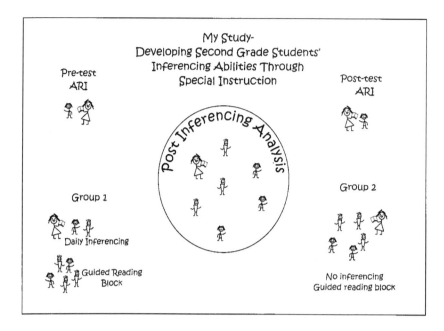

FIG. 3.1.   Choyce Cochran's first drawing.

After researching her project further, Choyce refined her ideas and created a second drawing (see Fig. 3.2).

As you can see, my second drawing is more elaborate than the first. After I spoke with Janet, who was the chair of my committee, in this second sketch I included some of the activities I will use with my experimental group (Group 1). Until then I really hadn't thought about how I might offer inferencing lessons to the experimental group. Once I created this second drawing, I thought I was ready to write a draft of my proposal, so I started writing (see Fig. 3.2).

Choyce wrote nonstop until she had completed a major part of her first draft. She began to revise her work when she ran into a few glitches.

I reread what I had written and I began to revise my proposal, but, once again, after conferencing with Janet, I realized my plan was incomplete. I had to return to the invention phase. I created a third drawing that shows what I needed to research so that I can provide crucial information to readers of my thesis—information about control and experimental groups, information about specific strategies designed to enhance students' inferencing abilities, and my third drawing illuminated a little worrisome dilemma. What am I

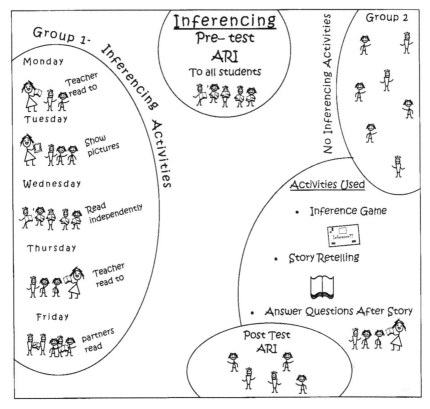

FIG. 3.2. Choyce Cochran's second drawing.

going to do with the control group (Group 2) when I am working with the experimental group? The control group will observe my instruction with the experimental group and therefore, the results of my study will be inconclusive. I still have to figure this out (see Fig. 3.3).

Not all writers think drawing and sketching are helpful invention methods. Whereas Ernst da Silva (2001) thinks drawing is useful because it slows down her thinking and allows her to visualize ideas clearly, Liz Fields, second-grade teacher in a masters degree program, dislikes drawing because she believes drawing saps her energy. She says:

Drawing saps all of my vigor. In fact, I think drawing is an obstacle to my writing because it limits my thinking. I use all of my energy trying to draw and it takes too long and I lose my ideas. For me, dumping out my ideas, free writing, and outlining work best as invention strategies.

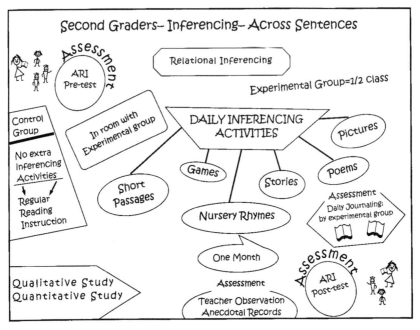

FIG. 3.3.   Choyce Cochran's third drawing.

Concept Maps and Webs

Concept maps are related to drawings. They represent an author's knowledge by visually portraying relationships and connections among ideas and major concepts. Like exemplary writing, good concept maps are usually the product of several drafts. Therefore, it is important that authors continue to refine and revise their concept maps as they extend and enhance their thinking. Another important consideration is that authors design concept maps that are clear and logical so they can follow and identify the ideas and information that they depict. There are three types of concept maps that we believe are useful for invention: spider maps, hierarchy maps, and flowcharts, (see Figs. 3.4–3.6 for examples of these types of concept maps). Each is distinguished by its format for representing information. Authors select one of the three formats as an invention strategy based on how they want to structure and present information. For example, a spider map is most appropriate for depicting the pros and cons of an issue and for brainstorming and representing everything an author knows about a topic. Authors place the central theme in the center of the map and surround the central theme with subcategories and details. A hierarchy map presents in-

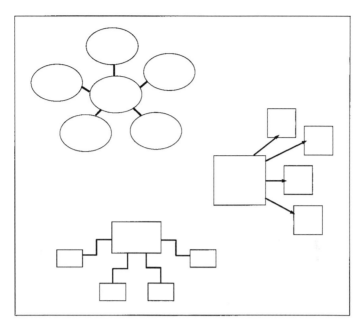

FIG. 3.4.   Examples of spider concept maps.

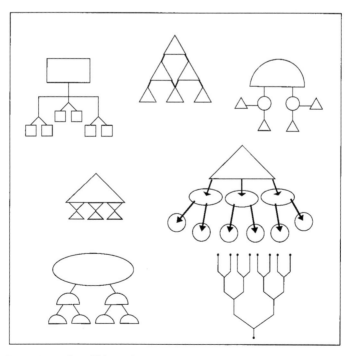

FIG. 3.5.   Examples of hierarchy concept maps.

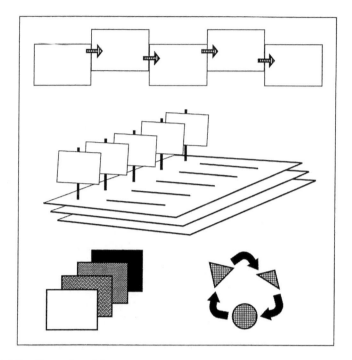

FIG. 3.6. Examples of flow concept maps.

formation in descending order of importance. A flowchart organizes information in a linear format (e.g., first, second, third).

There are many fine examples of concept maps portrayed on the Internet, and software companies offer an abundance of free concept mapping programs. Just access the Internet and search for the phrase "concept maps" to view various types of maps.

Sandra Engoron-March relies on spider concept maps to help structure her writing. She says:

> *I like to create a number of concept maps before I begin writing because this invention strategy helps me organize information about a topic. The process of creating a map helps me identify a main idea and distinguish the subcategories pertinent to the main idea. My concept maps also help me figure out what information I lack about a topic and if I have repeated information. When I number the categories that circle the main ideas in my map, I can turn the categories into sequential sections of text. I created the following map titled "Struggling Readers and Remedial Programs" for a paper I want to write and publish (see Fig. 3.7 for an example of Sandra's spider concept map).*

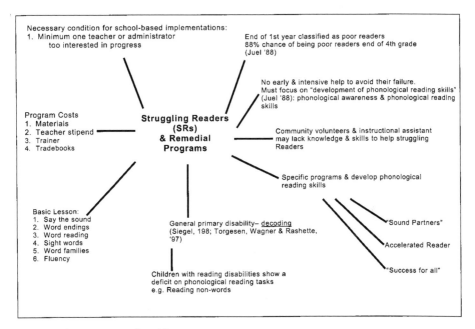

FIG. 3.7. An example spider concept map.

Katie Fradley never used a concept map as an invention strategy until recently. Katie describes her surprise at what she discovered when she switched from creating an outline to devising a concept map.

> I think I have a very sequential, goal-driven personality. Therefore, it should come as no surprise that I've always considered myself an outline type of writer. Perhaps that's why I was so surprised to find success using a concept map to help me plan my writing about a student who is having difficulty in my class. I was excited, yet frightened at the details that came from this picture. Although it was all information I knew, it was as if I was looking at a puzzle being assembled in slow motion in front of me for the first time.

When Katie switched from a linear invention strategy to a global concept map, she discovered that she could connect bits and pieces of the information into a more coherent framework.

Free Writing

Many well-known writers, including Peter Elbow (2000) and Mary Renck Jalongo (2002), find that free writing is a worthwhile invention activity. They explain that authors who engage in this practice write nonstop. They do not worry whether what they write makes sense, and they are not concerned about punctuation, spelling, or other conventions of writing. The objectives of free writing are to get your ideas down on paper, explore and generate ideas on a specific topic, improve your thinking, and alleviate writer's block.

Understandably, if you know a lot about a topic, you can easily engage in free writing. Conversely, if you have limited knowledge about a subject, free writing will not help you very much unless you use the strategy to itemize what think you might want to explore. Liz Fields used free writing as an invention strategy prior to composing a short explanation to parents about her second-grade Spelling Helper Chart. Note how Liz revised her free writing passage (see Fig. 3.8 for Liz's free write).

Brainstorming: Debbie Dimmett

Lucy Calkins (1994) says writers should ask themselves, "What do I wonder about?" (p. 210), and then they should write to explore and discover those mysteries and questions. Debbie Dimmett follows Calkins's advice. Using brainstorming as her favorite prewriting strategy, Debbie lists all of the relevant ideas she can think of that she might use in writing about a topic and

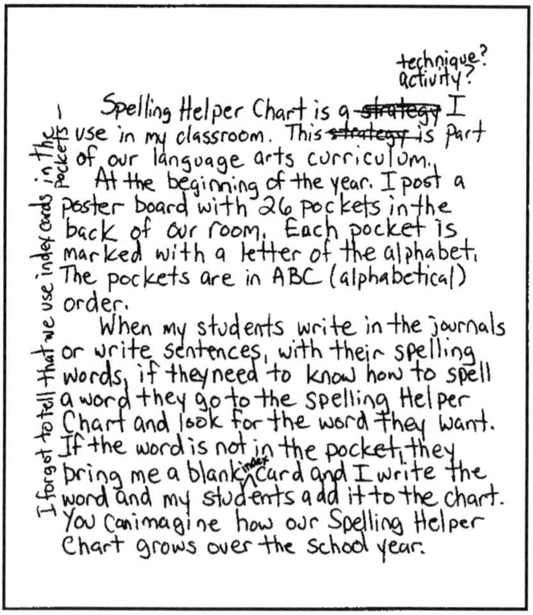

FIG. 3.8.　Example free writing passage.

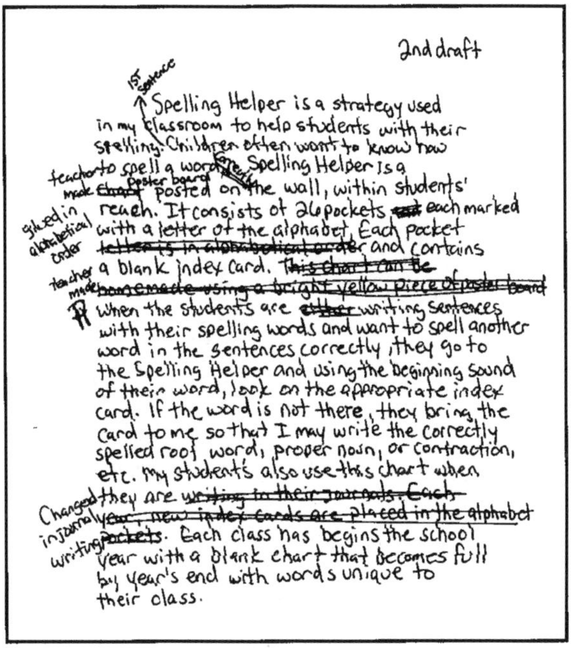

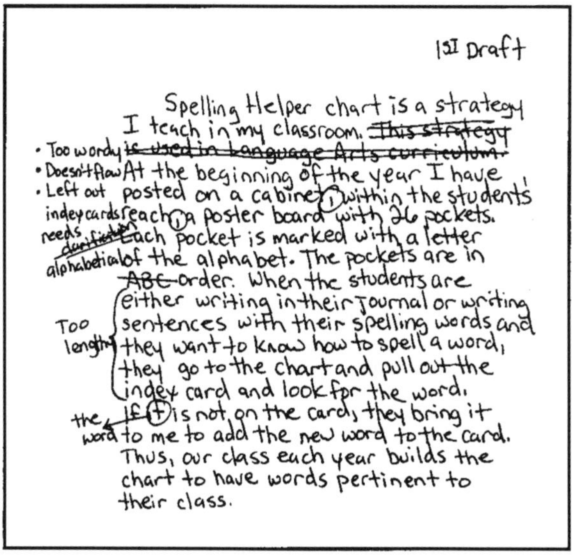

2nd draft

Spelling Helper is a strategy used in my classroom to help students with their spelling. Children often want to know how to spell a word. Spelling Helper is a ~~chart~~ posted on the wall, within students' reach. It consists of 26 pockets ~~that~~ each marked with a letter of the alphabet. Each pocket ~~letters is in alphabetical order~~ and contains a blank index card. ~~This chart can be made homemade using a bright yellow piece of poster board.~~

When the students are ~~either~~ writing sentences with their spelling words and want to spell another word in the sentences correctly, they go to the Spelling Helper and using the beginning sound of their word, look on the appropriate index card. If the word is not there, they bring the card to me so that I may write the correctly spelled root word, proper noun, or contraction, etc. My students also use this chart when they are ~~writing in their journals. Each year, new index cards are placed in the alphabet pockets.~~ Each class has begins the school year with a blank chart that becomes full by year's end with words unique to their class.

1st Draft

Spelling Helper chart is a strategy I teach in my classroom. ~~This strategy is used in Language Arts curriculum.~~ At the beginning of the year I have posted on a cabinet within the students' reach a poster board with 26 pockets. Each pocket is marked with a letter of the alphabet. The pockets are in ~~ABC~~ order. When the students are either writing in their journal or writing sentences with their spelling words and they want to know how to spell a word, they go to the chart and pull out the index card and look for the word. If it is not on the card, they bring it to me to add the new word to the card. Thus, our class each year builds the chart to have words pertinent to their class.

FIG. 3.8.   (continued)   *(continued on next page)*

final writing

technique Children often want to know
how to spell a word correctly. Spelling
Helper is ~~a teaching strategy~~ used in
2nd my classroom to help students with their
Grade spelling. Spelling Helper is a teacher-made
chart. It is constructed using a brightly
colored piece of poster-board with 26 pockets
each marked with a letter from the alphabet.
The pockets are glued to the board. At the
beginning of each school year, a blank index
card is placed in each pocket.

When the students are writing original
sentences using their spelling words and want
to spell a word in their sentence correctly,
they may go to the Spelling Helper to look
for their word. Using the beginning letter sound,
the student chooses the appropriate alphabet
~~index~~ card and looks on the card for his
desired word. If the students cannot locate the
word on the card, he brings the card to me
so that I may write the correctly spelled root
word, proper noun, or contraction, etc. The
student then takes the card to his writing
area to record the correctly spelled word in
his writing. He then returns the card to its
appropriate pocket.

The students use the Spelling Helper
for all types of writing. Not all spelling is corrected
in class, particularly during journal entries. Spelling
Helper is available to satisfy a student's curiosity
about spelling a word correctly. Each class

---

begins the school year with a blank
Spelling Helper class chart. This gives
each class ownership of their class
Spelling Helper because by the end of
the school year, it is filled with words
defined by their interests.

Dr. Richard's suggestions

Notes for final draft:
1st paragraph   change "teaching strategy"
                 to technique

                 add "second grade"
                 to "classroom"

FIG. 3.8.   (continued)

80

exploring a problem. Then, just like Lucy Calkins, she generates a list of questions that she wonders about. Debbie says:

> Before I write, I like to brainstorm and dump all of my ideas out on paper and then I can see what connections I can make. Then I discuss my ideas with my husband who is good at critiquing ideas and raising questions that I may not have considered. Then I rework my ideas until I can make further connections.

> I have always been good at thinking of interesting topics to write about, but I am not good at generating questions that would lead to further study. To facilitate this, it is sometimes beneficial if I do what I call a "brain dump." This is where I write down everything I know about the topic or what I find interesting about a topic. After that, I brainstorm questions that are raised from the lack of information that I have. Many times these questions are simply wonderings—questions that have drifted slightly off the topic.

> I find this brainstorming process particularly helpful because it allows me to make connections that I might not have made if I hadn't written them down first. The process is especially useful if I already have a lot of information about the topic, but don't know how to organize it in my head well enough to see the bigger picture in a way that will help me ask the questions that still need to be investigated. After I generate a list of questions, I usually can group certain ones together around a more specific topic. With topic and questions at hand, I begin my preliminary research, using the questions as guides for my search. The notes below are my first thoughts about a paper I will write for an anthropology class that I am taking. I have always been very interested in African languages and dialects that have continued in Cuba since the beginnings of slavery. Before I dumped all of my ideas on paper, the only question I could think to ask (i.e., to research) was why have these languages and dialects continued to exist? But after I dumped my ideas, I thought about more.

WHAT I KNOW ABOUT CEREMONIAL LANGUAGES USED IN AFRO-CUBAN RELIGIONS

- The religions include Yoruba/Santeria, Palo Mayombe, Vodou, Abakua, possibly Arara.
  - Yoruba/Santeria—the ceremonial language is primarily Yoruba (from Yoruba, Nigeria)
  - Palo Mayombe—the ceremonial language is primarily Bantu (from Congo and Angola regions). Although the language seems more fragile in its maintenance than in Yoruba traditions
  - Vodou—the ceremonial language seems to be Haitian Kreyol (a French/Fon dialect from Dahomey/Benin) and very possibly

some Spanish or a Spanish version of Haitian Kreyol. In Haiti, the ceremonial language is Kreyol.

- Abakua—the ceremonial language is that of a secret male society with its roots in Carabali (north of Nigeria). I believe it is called Anago. There is also a female equivalent which may simply be an auxiliary to the Abakua organization, called Bricamo. Bricamo seems to be located mostly in Matanzas.
- Arara—uncertain about this one; appears to use a dialect of Yoruba. Seems to have close connections to Vodou.

- Mostly priests and priestesses know the meanings attached to the words. Few practitioners know the language well enough to use it unless they have gone through the entire initiation to become priests/priestesses.
- Followers in each of the religions sing cantos but many do not know the significance of the canto, only the deity that it is being sung for, or the occasion for singing it.
- Cantos are sung in a call-and-response style where a trained singer known as the akpon guides the ceremony and leads in hailing the orishas. After his or her call, the audience responds with the same or different phrase.
- Increasingly, fewer followers know the cantos. Cantos were always taught aurally; however, fewer and fewer followers seem to be picking up on these lyrics, which frequently causes much distress in the ceremonies especially since the belief is that the orishas will not become present unless the "congregation" convincingly hail them.
- During slavery, there was a linkage of the Yoruba religion with Catholicism to the extent that African deities were given the names of Catholic saints to give the illusion that Catholicism was being practiced. The deities are still represented to some extent as Catholic saints and sometimes are even referred to as the Catholic saint (Ex. Santa Barbara is Chango). Some linkage seemed to also occur with voodoo. I don't know much about this; however, symbols of Catholic saints seem to go hand-in-hand with voodoo ceremonies and altars for the loas.
- The one Palo priest that I met knew many of the words and their significance but sometimes admitted to having to refer to a written glossary of sorts. Also admitted to shifts in the meanings of words when it was uncertain what they meant. Was he using context clues?

- Practitioners of Palo are less open about their practice and ceremonies seem to be less open. In Cuba, it is viewed as witchcraft and has historically been thought of as connected to crime.
- Yoruba religion is the most openly practiced.
- Vodou seems to be practiced mostly on the eastern part of the island (Santiago, Guantanamo) that is closest to Haiti. Vodou came to Cuba initially because of the Haitian Revolution against the slave owners. Some of the owners managed to escape with their slaves and set up new plantations.
- Arara seems to be an ethnic group located in Matanzas as well as other locales in Cuba. There doesn't seem to be a very significant group of them in Havana. Possibly in the municipality called Regla.

Questions That I Now Have:

1. What has held these languages in place for so long? (since the beginnings of slavery)
2. What is the trajectory of these languages as these religions become increasingly more accepted and mainstream?
3. How has written language interfered if at all with the aural learning of these languages?
4. What is the importance of a ceremonial language versus a common language?
5. How is language inextricably linked to the religious practice itself?

You might be surprised at Debbie's knowledge about a rather exotic and little-known topic. She has been a devotee of Afro-Cuban culture for a long time. She reads extensively about this topic, participates in an Afro-Cuban dance troupe, and has been to Cuba on multiple occasions. She recently presented a paper at the International Literacy and Educational Research Network Conference in Havana, and she does professional development work with teachers in Haiti. Debbie's brainstorming about ceremonial languages used in Afro-Cuban religions shows us that dumping all of your ideas out on paper is an effective strategy for a writer who has a good deal of information but lacks an organizational framework.

Heather Brown used brainstorming to help her discover what to write about her teacher research project that involved her Native American students. Her usual heavy planning in her head before writing didn't fit this writing task because the research was in process even as she planned her article. She had many ideas and questions that needed to be explored for her to finally tell the story of what was happening in her classroom. She sat down and brainstormed a long list of concepts, references to research, events from her teaching, concerns about instruction, references to her students, notes to herself, the curriculum, and much, much more, all of which led her to an important discovery about herself. Heather's brainstorming approach is presented next.

ARTICLE PROPOSAL: HEATHER BROWN

Real sovereignty:

Stepping away from big desk

Relinquishing control in the classroom—putting power back into the hands of the students

• my story

• influenced by Teacher Research & readings (need more on social justice—N.A.—Freire, Giroux, etc); & experience

• innovative "student-centered" techniques—still controlling problems—dialogue journals—not moving past summary—choice in books—not reading—literature circles—not discussing

even before this—at the middle school—main focus: student behavior—not really tapping into their interests/culture/background at all

What was the real problem?—not enough tools? Not enough buy-in?

two problems—too much teacher control (low student buy-in)— lack of tools ("just do it")

successes—real audience—asking to revise

• self-evaluation—honest

• pick own topics—interesting, motivated to write, better writing

literary analysis—giving too much information to them—not letting them see—still spoon-feeding

standards education—history of—adding to the problem

ask A. for suggestion of articles

research project—didn't want to publish—not whole story—still me trying to explain—my voice of authority speaking—their own story

next semester—have them create their own project—lose even the media edge if possible parameters—standards ask them what they will need (I have to help with this) real audience; motivation—see if it improves quality of work; motivation; increase in learning, etc.

what and how we teach—reinforcing the paradigm—obedience, white culture—colonization

—irony: unit on colonization—during reading assignments—you must read and respond—some responses very controlled (what is that called when you are looking for one answer?)

Mission of the school—bicultural, hands-on, authentic, real-world .... college prep and bicultural—hoping students will be leaders in their communities—am I teaching them to be leaders? AM I helping them to take control of their own education, future, etc? Am I reinforcing negative patterns despite my best intentions?

Comfort/control

My own background/other/authority

There is little organization to Heather's brainstorming, but her conflict and concerns about efforts to develop a student-centered classroom where students have some degree of autonomy are evident. The brainstorming pushed her into developing a concrete plan for the article and for modifications to her instruction that would provide her with the data she hoped would support her ideas for working with these students. She writes:

> My plan is to write an article about my shifting viewpoint as a teacher from extremely teacher-centered to relinquishing control and creating a true (or more true) student-centered classroom. I plan on having my students create their curriculum next semester. I realize that some direct instruction will be necessary, but I am hoping that by giving my students the power to create their own curriculum, they will be more invested in their education, and therefore more motivated to learn and to improve their reading, writing, and discussion abilities. In addition, I am hoping that by shifting (or at least sharing) authority, I am better preparing them to be leaders in their own communities. For the article, I will share not only my story thus far, but my experiences over the next semester.

> Originally, I had planned on attempting to publish the research I had conducted in the Teacher Research Institute, but something just kept nagging at me. I felt like I shouldn't publish it. I thought at first that I was just insecure about my writing … I got a lot of great feedback from it—from professors, my administrators, and even from a parent of one of my students.... Still, something nagged at me. I felt like I hadn't told the whole story. I felt like I didn't have the right to write this, like somehow I was putting myself in the position of being an "expert"—not only about my students, but also about their learning as Native Americans. I am not an expert. I cannot comfortably place myself in this position.

> I started thinking about these issues. I knew I wanted to write about me specifically as an Anglo woman in an all-Native charter school. There are a lot of

issues that come up—a lot of things I need to take into consideration, a lot of paradigms that I struggle to avoid reinforcing. What occurred to me was that although I am trying dynamic and theoretically sound methods in my class-room, and although I have created a bicultural, interdisciplinary, somewhat real-world curriculum for my students, I still have a degree of control that I am holding onto. As much as I have tried to create an environment of self-suffi-ciency and autonomy, I have been reinforcing the patterns that I have been attempting to have my students deconstruct.

In this instance, we can see how Heather's brainstorming activity led her to recognize that a journey into writing for professional purposes is, indeed, also a journey into herself. It is not difficult to trace her developing aware-ness of what she cared most about with regard to her teaching. Initially, she thought it was about being an Anglo woman in a Native American school, but as her article finally began to take shape, she realized it was about "let-ting go" and empowering students to take control of their own learning.

Her exploration of her teaching as a subject for writing led her to more deeply examine her identity and her role in her school and with her stu-dents. In a sense, through a brainstorming activity, Heather became aware that she is prewriting herself. It is at this intersection—of the Self and the ac-ademic—that the most authentic professional writing emerges.

Talking With Others

Some writers find it helpful to talk about their ideas before they begin to write Janet always does this type of brainstorming. As an extrovert, she gets ideas when she interacts with colleagues and students. Ralph Fletcher (2000) says that talking allows him to get comfortable with what he wants to say. He also cautions "while talking about writing can be helpful ... there is a danger that if you talk about an idea too much you can talk the mystery out of it" (p. 24).

Noted children's author Drew Lamm, who wrote *The Prog Frince* (1999) and other stories, also warns about the danger of discussing ideas for writ-ing. She states, "I definitely don't talk to anyone. If I talk, I lose that initial energy that's crucial" (cited in Fletcher, 2000, p. 24).

On the other hand, according to Ede (1989), "the romanticized image" (p. 15) of the solitary writer is not exactly reality. She points out that many writers alternate between solitary writing and social interaction with others, getting additional ideas, advice on revision, and general responses to the drafts themselves. Additionally, she asserts, many writers (like Janet) seek additional support from colleagues and friends through correspondence, telephone conversations, and e-mail.

Sometimes, getting the right "handle" on your ideas is critical to generating that initial energy Drew Lamm mentions. For some, isolation is not the key. Debbie Dimmett struggled initially to find the right topic for the article she wanted to write as part of our writing group's goal to publish. Even though the rest of the writing group had determined they would write about their work and their students, Debbie struggled with the idea of writing about an entirely different topic, pursuing her passion for Afro-Cuban and Haitian culture. However, the group interaction and support helped her make a final decision. She explains:

> *Today I realized that I couldn't use the topic that I initially decided on (Haitian schooling) because the audience was too limited, and the project would not be able to come to fruition for some time. So I decided to continue with the teacher research I had done on student self- and peer evaluation and their impact on quality of work.*

Once the discussion shifted to this topic, one that was more professionally important to her, Debbie was energized by the feedback she got from others in the group. Debbie says:

> *My writing colleague, Deborah Green raised the issue of how to get kids to want to raise the bar to something above average. This was the slant I decided to take for my paper. I hope to show how self- and peer evaluation can be effectively utilized in a classroom that follows an inquiry-based approach to learning. The evaluation instruments (rubrics, etc.) would be developed by the class or the individual student (whichever is appropriate). I will incorporate my three teacher research projects that focused on this type of evaluation. In addition, I will speak to the philosophical and pedagogical advantages. I will also need to address how this approach can be adapted to students of varying ages and abilities. Finally, I believe it will be important that I address how this type of evaluation might be accepted (or not) in a standards-based movement. I'm suddenly feeling compelled to create an outline of my paper.*

In fact, Debbie did bring an outline to the next group meeting (see her outline later in this chapter). For her, group interaction was vital to her invention and prewriting process—she came away with an overall plan for her article. She was finally able to focus and harness her energy for the writing she wanted to accomplish.

Thinking Aloud/Speaking Into a Tape Recorder

Recently, Melissa Brock, a multiage teacher in Mississippi, confided to peers in her graduate class, "I know what I want to say about my research project, but I have trouble writing it." Melissa decided to take ownership of her writing by using an invention strategy that she titled Thinking Aloud/Speaking Into a Tape Recorder. She states:

> I found that thinking aloud by speaking into a tape recorder and then transcribing my ideas was quite helpful to me. I overcame my writer's block, and my fear of typing ideas directly on the computer disappeared when I could just freely talk about my research. Of course this type of invention strategy is time-consuming. I have to verbalize and tape what I think I want to write, and then I have to transcribe my words. After that, I have to try to make sense of the transcription. I found that talking liberates me as a writer, and I can even ask and answer my own questions, such as, "Why am I writing this piece? For whom am I writing? What voice is appropriate for the piece?"
>
> Does this strategy take a lot of time? Yes. But this works for me and I'm going to continue to rely on this method.

Kim Schwartz also talks into a tape recorder to help her plan a manuscript. Kim says:

> Sometimes I walk around the house with a tape recorder in my hand just talking through my paper, trying to funnel the focus. This strategy even works for young students. I tried it with a fourth grade student of mine. She borrowed my tape recorder for three days and came in with a well-written paper.

Using Index Cards

Shelly Gaithier, second-grade teacher and graduate student from Mississippi, supplies us with another invention strategy.

> Once I have an idea in my head, I put all of the information about that idea on separate index cards. I place cards that contain related ideas next to each other. When I think of more information to add, I can easily write it on an index card and I can put the card in the appropriate place. Then when I am ready to write paragraphs, I refer to my cards. I am a kinesthetic type of person. For example, I play a lot of sports. So moving the cards around lends itself to my style of thinking and learning. A teacher taught me this technique in the eleventh grade and it still works for me.

Electronic Sticky Notes

Although Sharon doesn't use invention strategies often, she sometimes finds that a software product called *Stickies*™ by Antler Sortware (Alfke, 1994) helps keep pertinent references and writing ideas in a safe place. Electronic sticky notes work on the computer just like Post-It™ Notes work on paper. Instead of plastering the computer or a space behind or beside the computer with little paper notes, she puts them on the computer desktop. When she researches a topic, she makes brief notes on the electronic stickies to remind her where to look for detailed information. For example, one note that resided on her computer desktop for some time looked like this:

```
Voice
TasW p 84 the speaker, p.
222
Inaccessible language, pp.
123-4
EtheE. P. 35
```

Translated, this means that she can find an exploration of writing voice in the text *Teacher as Writer* (Dahl, 1992) on pages 84, 222, and 123–124. Additionally, in Donald Murray's *Expecting the Unexpected* (1989), he makes an important comment about writing voice on page 35. When Sharon gets to a point in the manuscript where she deals with writing voice issues, the note reminds her to check these sources and take advantage of expert information. If she doesn't own a book that she knows she will need, she writes more detailed information on her electronic sticky.

Making Lists as Visual Displays

Toby Fulwiler says that we make lists every day to help remind us what to buy at the grocery store or to jog our memories about what chores we need to accomplish. He finds that list making also creates a visual display of his ideas about writing. The ideas in his lists help him solve writing problems and lead him to new possibilities. His lists actually provide him with a new direction for writing.

Renee Maufrey also makes a list before she writes, but has devised a process that makes her listing more efficient for her writing task. She says,

For invention, I always make a list of ideas that are in no particular order. Then I color-code the concepts in the list according to how they are related. Next, I rewrite the list over and over, paying attention to my color-coding until all of the ideas on the list are in sequence. I make changes to my lists as I read, re-

*search, and discover new information about my topic. After I am finished with
my final list, I add notes that eventually turn into an outline. My list and my outline change as I read more about a topic and as I write my first draft.*

Making an Outline

Toby Fulwiler (2002) would approve of Renee's strategy because he believes
that "outlines are organized lists" (p. 39). We know some writers who are
wary of outlines. In fact, Georgia Heard (1995) equates outlines to recipes
that make writing flat and formulaic. Janet agrees with Georgia. An editor
once requested that Janet send in an outline for a chapter she was invited to
write. The only way Janet could supply the outline was to write the chapter
and then create the outline from the finished chapter.

Conversely, some authors can't write anything unless they first create a
well-developed outline. Tim Rasinski always writes from an outline. He
says, "I always write from a plan. I develop a series of outlines. Each outline
gets more and more detailed until I finally cast the outline into prose."

After our Arizona writing group helped Debbie Dimmett get a focus for
her writing topic (how self- and peer evaluation can be effective), she came
to our next meeting with her outline in hand. She had developed a relatively comprehensive outline for an ambitious article.

The Benefits of Peer and Self-Assessment for Improving
Student Work and Raising Student Achievement: Debbie Dimmett

I. Thesis: Peer and self-evaluation are invaluable tools for raising student
   achievement and improving the quality of student work.
   A. Both serve as measurement of evaluation as well as a tool for acquir-
      ing deeper understanding of skills and concepts.
   B. They are kid-friendly in that students understand completely and
      fully how they are being evaluated and agree with the outcome.
      a. Negative ramifications of the traditional grading system
         i. Students lack understanding about why they received the
            grade they got; many believing the grades are arbitrary.
         ii. Students don't fully understand the criteria (give 6 traits
             rubric as the example).
         iii. Students frequently are unable to frame their failures so
              that they are more successful in the future.
         iv. Students frequently don't see the connection between what
             they are told they must learn and the actual evaluation.
         v. Students frequently excel in areas for reasons even they
            don't understand

    C. Raising the question—What is the impact of a grading system that students don't understand? How might this in itself impede achievement?

    D. They have a peer support team that helps them to evaluate their own work and provides them with suggestions on how to improve it per the criteria the students have set for themselves.

    E. They develop an internal system of evaluation that becomes important as they become adults.

    F. *Cite research here.

II. Teacher Research

    A. The story of my question. Student projects were anything but good.

    B. Why self-evaluation? Assumptions.

    C. Introduction of student-developed rubrics.

        a. Difficulties of teaching rubric development (primarily getting students to be specific with language)

        b. Introduction to rubric development

    D. First sets of student-evaluated projects—hmmm, needs something more.

    E. Tweaking the evaluation procedure. The addition of:

        a. Peer evaluation

        b. Peer support teams using the tuning protocol throughout the different stages of the project

        c. Teacher evaluation using the student's scoring rubric (a three-part grade: student, peers, teacher)

        d. Student preassessment and postassessment surveys/self-reflection

        e. Had student share the project with the class, explaining the process s/he went through, time spent on the project, etc.

    F. The impact of these additions (a more focused evaluation procedure; other sets of eyes to give feedback on student work)

    G. What I would do differently

        a. Provide written feedback from teacher and peers along with the completion of the rubric.

        b. Computer-generated rubric using their own criteria

        c. Introduce other protocols that might be more appropriate for looking at student work

III. Wide Implementation

    A. Goal is to incorporate this form of evaluation as much as possible.

    B. Use with literature discussion groups and writing portfolios

    C. Planning involved

        a. Time commitment. Takes more time, but the payoff is worth it.

        b. Breakdown of time required

        c. Sample forms used

D. Alternatives (particularly for children who would have difficulty with developing an individual rubric)
   a. Class rubric or group rubric
   b. Group projects
IV. Questioning the State Standards
   A. Turn state standards into probing questions that the students will use when designing their own rubric.
   B. Return to advantages of this evaluation process for teaching and assessing the state standards without making the standards appear to be the driving force behind the evaluation.
   C. Other criteria the students develop will incorporate and tend to make more sense out of the standards.
V. Conclusion
   A. Student discussion or survey about how they are graded (traditionally). Use quotes.
   B. Return to the advantages listed in I.

Debbie tells us what she learned from sharing her outline with the writing group, and she explains how it provided clarity for the direction her first draft would take.

Although it was a rush to get something together for our Saturday writing group meeting, I found that creating an outline of my paper was really helpful in a number of ways. Not only did it help me focus and give me a renewed interest in writing about peer and self-assessment, it also helped to focus discussion about the paper. The feedback was very helpful and positive. I came away feeling that the paper was one that needed to be written. In particular, the group helped me to see how in a standards-based, test-driven environment, there is still room for peer and self-evaluation. In fact, Deborah reminded me that one of the key concerns in our district is that students don't know how they are graded. Therefore, they lack awareness of their progress. Peer and self-assessment along with student-developed rubrics will directly address this concern.

Discussing her outline with the group generated not only a clear sense of direction and a commitment to the topic, but it helped Debbie focus also on the role of her students as informants for the processes of self- and peer-evaluation in her classroom. They also emphasized the need for her to focus on her anticipated readers' needs. Debbie explains:

I plan to incorporate both suggestions in my article, because I believe that my audience will raise these questions if they are not addressed. I want to make a convincing case for these forms of assessment and, in the process, transform my own teaching so that these forms of assessments become a viable and natural component of instruction.

Using Technology

Donald Murray (1999) offers many approaches for invention. He includes technology that incorporates drawing, imaging, and word processing. The computer's flexibility with word processing offers writers many opportunities to play around with ideas and generate an initial draft. In fact, both Janet and Sharon note that using the computer has enhanced their writing abilities. Sharon explains:

> *Composing at the computer has completely replaced pen and paper for me. Perhaps it is my practice of discovery drafting as opposed to other more structured forms of prewriting and planning that makes the computer work so well. I find that I write more quickly and revise more efficiently when I can see the writing emerge on the screen. However, because there is only a limited amount of text on the screen at one time, I need a printout of my draft for a more comprehensive picture of how the various parts work together. Then I can make my revision plan and do the cutting and pasting necessary to bring it all together.*

We (Janet and Sharon) composed this book on our computers, sending e-mail snippets and longer attachments of text back and forth between us. We soon discovered that one of the significant advantages of using word processing actually presented a slight disadvantage to us. We originally wanted to capture all of our writing processes, including our invention strategies and our first and successive drafts. We thought that perhaps documenting some of our thinking about writing might be useful to this book. However, because word processing so conveniently helps writers easily revise and save their work, initial drafts are continually replaced with new versions. We didn't know how to take advantage of an option that keeps track of writing changes. Thus, we lost a great deal of process.

Now we know that Microsoft Word™ offers a Preferences option entitled Track Changes, through which writers can electronically map the revisions and edits they make in text and in formatting. We've decided that we need to take the time to learn how to use this software. Writers who are tech savvy might find the Track Changes feature very useful. (Sharon did, in fact, try using it once, and found it more than a little annoying because of her propensity to cycle back and forth and revise in process.)

ONLINE PREWRITING SOURCES

We think one of the most useful online resources for prewriting is the software titled *Inspiration*™ (n.d.) that works with both Macintosh operating systems and Windows-based computers. Because writers plan in many different ways, *Inspiration* offers diverse ways to plan and organize thinking, including developing ideas, creating diagrams, entering the main idea of a topic, and converting information to outline form. You can easily access this site by calling up the Internet and typing http://www.Inspiration.com.

One of the best all around resources for prewriting strategies and for writing strategies, in general, is the Internet. A Google™ search, for example, on "prewriting," results in an extensive list of sites, primarily posted by universities and colleges as part of their writing programs.

Some of the more helpful planning and prewriting sites include the following:

- Purdue's Online Writing Lab (OWL) at http://owl.english.Purdue. edu/handouts/general/index.html#planning
- Other college sites, such as Kansas University's Writer's Roost, offer writing support at http://www.writing.ku.edu/students/docs/prewriting.html
- The Bridgewater College (Virginia) materials posted by Alice L. Trupe (n.d.), at http://www.bridgewater.edu/~atrupe/ENG315/ pre writing.htm and http://www.bridgewater.edu/~atrupe/ENG 315/planning.htm are extremely well done
- The Writer's Complex at Empire State College (New York) at http:// www.esc.edu/esconline/across_esc/writerscomplex.nsf/home

Each of these sites, as well as numerous others, offer strategies for prewriting and planning that go far beyond the list we have presented in this chapter. We encourage you to explore the Internet for writing support and ideas. The available resources are endless.

COMBINING INVENTION STRATEGIES

In the previous section, we described several invention strategies as individual methods; however, using more than one invention strategy is also an option, depending on your writing needs and purposes. For example, earlier in this chapter, Choyce Cochran shared the drawings she created to help her figure out the design of her research project. After Choyce researched her topic and collected data, she wrote the beginning section of her manuscript. Choyce reread what she had composed, and decided that her writing was stilted and choppy. In addition, she had extensively quoted researchers and omitted her own voice. She also presented information as a series of disconnected ideas.

After conferring with Janet, Choyce made a good decision to return once again to the invention phase of composing. This time, she relied on two prewriting techniques to help organize her thinking and her writing. She devised a spider map that depicted the major categories or themes in her paper, and she created a flowchart that portrayed where she wanted to place each of the sections in her manuscript (see Figs. 3.9 and 3.10).

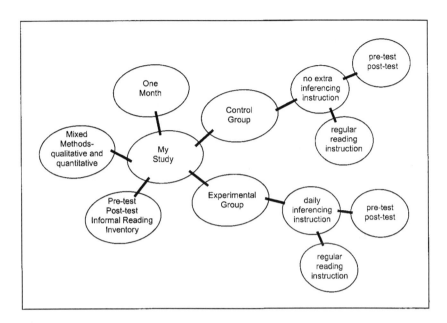

FIG. 3.9.   Example spider concept map.

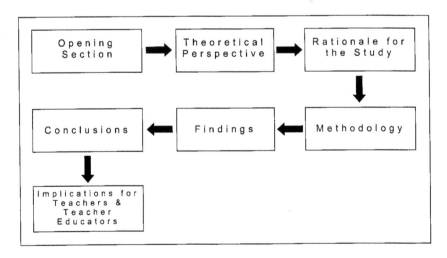

FIG. 3.10.   Example flowchart.

PERSONAL REFLECTIONS

Now that you have read about how some educators engage in invention strategies to help plan their writing initiatives, take a few minutes to reflect about how you map out your own writing. What invention strategies do you usually use? For example, do you make an outline? Do you think about a topic for a long time? Do you devote too much energy to invention and not enough time to drafting? Or is it just the opposite? Do you spend little time with invention and most of the time with drafting? Do your prewriting habits work for you? What would happen if you consciously decided to reverse your pattern of writing? In other words, if you typically don't engage in invention prior to composing, perhaps you might try one or two prewriting strategies, or if you usually spend a considerable amount of time on invention, what might occur if you just dove right in and began a discovery draft?

When you do use invention strategies, do you make drawings or sketches? Do you speak to friends about your writing ideas? Do you belong to a writing group, or have other colleagues on whom you rely for sound feedback and response? Do you read a lot about a specific topic? Do you ever plan your writing while you are sleeping? Taking a walk? Think deeply about what is important to you in this stage of the writing process and how it helps or hinders your progress. Write your reflections.

PRACTICAL APPLICATIONS: TRYING SOME INVENTION STRATEGIES

Now, think carefully about an academic writing topic that interests you (e.g., a specific teaching dilemma, a controversial situation facing educators today, an instructional practice worth sharing with others, a student who is particularly interesting or challenging, or a required class or professional writing assignment). Figure out what you already know about this topic. Try free writing, making a list, or brainstorming what you do know to get some ideas on paper.

Next, conduct an experiment that might lead you to extend your repertoire of prewriting strategies. Try using at least two invention strategies you usually do not employ. You might want to use some of the invention strategies that we discussed in this chapter (e.g., drawing, a quick write, a concept map, brainstorming, an outline, index cards, thinking aloud by speaking into a tape recorder, jotting down words and phrases, talking with colleagues or friends).

Organize your thinking about the topic you have chosen and complete your prewriting. We invite you to revisit this activity in future chapters and at subsequent stages of the writing process.

PERSONAL REFLECTIONS

What particular invention strategy felt most comfortable or uncomfortable to you? Why do you think a particular strategy was or was not most helpful for you? Did you discover any promising strategies? Were some strategies more appealing to you than others? What do you think made them appealing and promising? If you combined two or more invention strategies, which methods did you use? Why did you choose to combine these particular strategies? For what types of writing tasks and writing dilemmas might it be useful to combine invention strategies? Write your reflections.

SUMMARY

Donald Murray (1989) asserts that "the starting point of good writing [is] an emptying out of all we have said and read, thought, seen, felt. The best writing is not a parroting of what others have said—or what we have said before. It is an exploration of a problem we have not solved with language before" (p. 20). Murray goes on to describe his own practice of writing to solve problems, first and foremost for himself. He sometimes fears he has nothing to say, but he forges ahead and begins the prewriting and invention process, taking notes and waiting to see what "I find being said on my own page" (p. 20).

We began this chapter by discussing how invention strategies might help you explore and figure out (like Donald Murray), what you want to say and how you want to say it. In this chapter, Heather Brown showed how her invention activities spotlighted what she really wanted to write about—her developing awareness that her real topic really related to giving her Native American students more control over their learning. Her brainstormed list supported her discovery of what she cared most about with regard to her teaching. Through invention, Heather learned more than just the real topic of her manuscript. Heather learned about herself. She discovered that she could not separate her writing from who she is as a person and as a teacher.

We too, believe that educators cannot (and, in fact, should not) separate their personal selves from their professional selves. Therefore, when we decide that we will resolve issues with language—that is, through writing—we may find much more than words and ideas being said on our own pages. We may find that we are, indeed, like Heather, discovering ourselves.

In this chapter, we described a variety of invention strategies, such as drawing, creating concept maps, devising outlines, thinking aloud by speaking into a tape recorder, computer technology, and jotting down words and phrases. Remember that the invention strategies with which you feel most comfortable are connected to your purpose for writing, who you are as a person, and your individual style of writing.

Perhaps after reading this chapter, you discovered that invention strategies don't seem to meet your writing needs. Your choice of or your disregard of prewriting strategies is an indicator of your personal self. You will find that as you commit yourself to academic writing, you will learn more and more about yourself. Once you begin to write, you will find yourself.

RELEVANT READINGS

Gleason, B. (2001). Teaching at the crossroads: Choices and challenges in college composition. *The Writing Instructor*, a Network Journal and Digital Community for Writers and Teachers of Writing. Retrieved January 30, 2004, from http://www.writinginstructor.com/essays/gleason2.html

This invited essay delineates the origins of process writing movement. Earlier versions of the writing process offered a straightforward linear model that evolved into a recursive "two-steps-forward, one-step back" model where writers discover new ideas at any stage. Another change Gleason discusses is collaborative learning communities that arose in response to shifting multicultural perspectives because of students' cultural diversity, and learning experiences.

Hubbard, R., & da Silva, K. (Eds.). (1996). *New entries: Learning by writing and drawing*. Portsmouth, NH: Heinemann.

The 13 contributors to this edited book contend that making images is a language—a way to think, communicate, express, and explore. Teachers from elementary school through college take you into their classrooms to show how writing and drawing can be combined in different ways. The educators in this book believe that making images is as natural as speaking.

Invention Strategies. (2004). Albany, OR: LBCC Media Services (Linn-Benton Community College). Retrieved February 1, 2004, from http://cf.linnbenton.edu. depts/lrc/web.cfm?pgID=350

This short electronic paper provides tips for choosing a topic and getting started on a manuscript. The author offers tips for overcoming writer's block, and finding a focus for your paper. One innovative technique for overcoming sentence-level or

word-choice problems is to turn off your computer monitor and keep typing. Writing without frustration and concern will help you focus on ideas rather than words.

Tips on making your own concept maps. Retrieved March 22, 2003 from http://www.classes.aces.unic.edu?ACES100/mind/-c-m3.html

This electronic source offers concrete guidelines for making concept maps. The suggestions include how to gather research materials, how to select a concept map format, and how to revise and refine concept maps. The authors suggest that you keep a record of the maps you create in a visual notebook.

Chapter 4

Drafting

Every draft I write will need to be rewritten—that's what a draft is. It's a start. Then comes the next draft. And the next, and the next. Each draft is what I have so far. Rewriting is implicit in the word draft. (Cooke, 2001, pp. 27–28)

It's perfectly okay to wait before you start writing about an idea.... But once you know you're ready, it's up to you to make a start.... One paragraph is fine. Two paragraphs are terrific. A whole page of writing is heroic. (Fletcher, 2000, p. 40)

You will have to give yourself permission to write badly at first in what historian Neill Irvin Painter refers to as "zero mind drafts." (cited in Lamb, 1997, p. 142)

The good news is that you will have ample opportunity to make it better. (Jalongo, 2002, p. 55)

In the previous chapter, we focused on invention, or prewriting, often the first stage in the writing process. As we move into the drafting stage, we find that we must blur the lines between these two steps. We discovered in chapter 3 that some writers do their prewriting by drafting, as with discovery drafters. Although many writers prewrite by drafting, others use extensive prewriting strategies coupled with think time to engage in an "essential delay" (Murray, 1989). Still other writers move back and forth between invention and drafting, knowing that the discovery process involved in their writing may reveal a need to return to specific invention strategies.

In this chapter, we explore the challenges writers face when they actually sit down to get a draft on paper. We look at the various strategies our contributing writers use and what writing experts have to say about composing a draft. Drafting styles differ from individual to individual. Therefore, you will encounter conflicting notions about composing a draft that simply underscore the highly personal nature of writing. It is important to discover what works for you so that you feel comfortable with your own drafting processes.

RECOGNIZING THAT DRAFTING IS TASK SPECIFIC AND IDIOSYNCRATIC

Paul Kennedy, a Yale University professor and author, "observes that ways generating drafts are task specific and idiosyncratic" (cited in Jalongo, 2002, p. 91). Our particular styles of drafting, just as in all phases of the writing process, are usually influenced by what we write (see chapter 2, for types and purposes of academic writing), and are driven by our personal characteristics, or persona. As we explained in previous chapters, we are all different, and therefore, "everybody writes a little differently from everybody else" (Fulwiler, 2002, p. 15). So, of course, there is no perfect or ideal formula for composing a draft. What's important is that you reflect on how you usually write a draft and discover what method or style of composing is most productive for you.

Along these lines, Donald Murray (2001) recommends that writers "study the conditions when the writing has gone well and try to reproduce them" (p. 25). This is what Aldema Ridge, a friend and writing colleague of Sharon's, did when her first effort to publish was successful.

I decided to try my hand at writing an article for the National Education Association publication, Today's Education. Back in the summer of 1978, at American University, I was in a dance program and I learned some lessons I could apply to teaching. So I submitted an article. In my cover letter to accompany the manuscript, I wrote, "After eight years of being a mediocre English teacher, I changed. I am proud of the changes I made and I would like to share my growth with others."

Well, I was very lucky my first time as an author. The April/May 1979 issue contained my piece entitled, "I Became a Student Again."

I became a serious student of academic writing. I checked out books in the library on feature article writing. I attended workshops. I read articles analytically. I knew what I did in my first article and I just kept doing it.

What did I do? In that first article, I made a point about teaching and learning using personal anecdotes. I organized the anecdotes around the concrete metaphor of dance. I explained that being a student of dance was like being a struggling English student. For example, I talked about mastering the spot turn well enough one day to be asked by the dance teacher to demonstrate it the next day. But I found myself unable to do it when I needed to. In the article

*I compared my dancing experience to my students' learning experiences. Af-
ter three days of instruction, practice, and quizzes on introductory commas, I
thought my students were ready for a test. They failed miserably. Like me,
what they had done perfectly one day, they could not do the next.*

For Aldema, using a metaphor to support her thesis was a strategy she
tried to use whenever she wrote. However, the metaphors did not always
come easily. For example, when she was invited to write an article for middle school teachers, she struggled to meet the deadline because the metaphor she sought remained elusive. The article was part of a regular feature
titled, *Thirteen*, in which middle school professionals shared an experience
they recalled from their own middle school years. Aldema continues:

*I struggled to write this piece. I journaled. I made lists of ideas. I looked
through photo albums. My August deadline loomed. Then on vacation in
Labrador in July, I got it! I was on a commercial ferry and a man on the deck
pointed to the harbor porpoises. "Those little guys only live thirteen years ...
burn themselves out."*

*In a flash I had my metaphor. I thought of the pictures I'd looked at in my child-
hood photo album when I was trying to get some ideas for the article. The
photos illustrating my thirteenth year showed me stringing popcorn and
cranberries for garlands on our Christmas tree, writing, directing, and acting
in a play, and working as a volunteer at a nursing home. I had done too much
that year. I had burned myself out. I titled my piece, "Trip to Black Tickle," the
name of the harbor where I met the porpoises, and I used the porpoises to illustrate my own thirteenth year.*

You might wonder if Aldema was engaged in prewriting or drafting.
For her, the two stages of the writing process were woven together. The
drafting itself was dependent on the discovery of a metaphor. Her process
not only illustrates how a writer uses past successes to guide current efforts, but also how drafting is, indeed, idiosyncratic. Her metaphor strategy may be somewhat unconventional, but it works for her—especially
when the metaphor finally comes.

THINKING BEFORE DRAFTING

Invention involves a gathering of information, making decisions about a
topic, and thinking about organizing for a specific audience. Once we assem-
ble information, it seems logical that our next step is getting our draft written.
However, some writers find it necessary to step back to reflect on what they
have learned from their invention process and their research. They feel more

comfortable considering where they ultimately want to go. For these writers, this thinking time is akin to their personal prewriting process.

Noted authors of books on writing Herbert and Jill Myer (cited in Safire & Safire, 1992) believe it's never a waste of time to think carefully before you write. In fact, they warn against starting a draft too soon and emphatically caution:

> *The absolute first thing to do when you launch a writing project is to resist the impulse to start writing. You need to relax, to settle down, and, above all, YOU NEED TO THINK. Don't worry about wasting time; it's never a waste of time to get your thoughts in order. Who has asked you to write something? Who will read it? What purpose is the piece of writing intended to serve? To persuade? To inform? To trigger action? Ask yourself these questions—and when you feel you've got it right, then—and only then—should you move on to the first real step in the writing process. (Safire & Safire, 1992, p. 102)*

Mary Alice Barksdale, who always does the dishes before she can write, agrees that it's important to think deeply before writing. She says:

> *Most of my thinking has already happened by the time I start writing. I don't engage in any specific invention strategies—all of my planning goes on in my head. I plan by looking at the literature. I start online and end up in the library. I collect a bunch of books and articles and they sit in a pile until the due date for something draws near. Then I start pulling everything out, carrying this stuff around with everywhere and reading all the time. I stick post-it-notes in important pages that I want to refer to when I write. My prewriting is happening in my head as I read. And, I'm constantly thinking about what needs to be written and how to write it—in the car while I'm driving, during meetings, while taking a shower, while peeling an apple, while brushing my teeth, while going to sleep at night.*

> *When I have gotten through most of the reading, I am ready to write. The organization has been worked out in my head while I've been reading. Conditions have to be perfect for me to write. I have to be at home, there can be no dirty dishes in the sink, the laundry has to be done or in process, the beds have to be made. The TV has to be on, although I may not really see or hear much of anything while I write. Other than that, the house has to be quiet. I often wait to start writing until everyone has gone to bed.*

Some people might believe that this thinking time is writer's block, but for many writers, this is simply the delay Murray (1989) refers to. According to E. B. White, "Delay is natural to a writer. He is like a surfer—he bides his time. Wait for the perfect wave on which to ride" (cited in Murray, 1989, p.

30). Ernest Hemingway was of the same mind as Murray. He said, "My writing habits are simple: long periods of thinking, short periods of writing" (cited in Murray, 1989, p. 30). Above his writing desk, the famous Czech artist and existential author Franz Kafka had a sign that said, simply, "Wait" (Murray, 1989, p. 30).

Although there are no guarantees that the writing will actually come after this delay, Murray assures us that experienced writers know that it might take "days, weeks, and months" to finally get the text written. Murray further suggests that there are five considerations a writer must know or feel before writing. These are information, insight, order, need, and voice.

Information, of course, includes the facts, the specifics, and the details that come from reading and researching widely (Murray, 1989). Jon Kuckla (2003), author of a book about the Louisiana Purchase, suggests that when writers of nonfiction get mired down, they don't have writers' block, they just haven't done the research and thinking necessary to complete a successful first draft.

Insight doesn't simply boil down to your thesis statement, but rather, to your in-depth understanding of the question or problem you will explore. Planning, or mapping out the general direction of the draft, and organizing one's writing provides *order*. Murray (1989) tells us that the best writing comes from "a *need* that precedes the entire process of writing" (p. 34) and from finding the right voice for the task at hand. *Voice,* according to Murray (1989), refers to finding the appropriate style of writing for the writing task and the audience. Mary Alice Barksdale's description of her delay illustrates how she achieves Murray's writing considerations before she ever sits down to write.

It goes without saying that unless you compose a draft, you'll never get anything written. Whether we insist on finding a metaphor before writing, or we spend time thinking and planning our journey, we finally must sit down and write. Composing a draft requires writers to be sufficiently disciplined, motivated, and confident enough to deliberately stop whatever it is they are doing, sit down at a computer, or with a pen or pencil, and get their ideas on paper.

SOME WRITERS BECOME ANXIOUS AND APPREHENSIVE

Some writers become anxious and apprehensive when they get to this phase of the writing process. The hardest part for them is to take the plunge and start writing (Zinsser, 1988). It's "like facing a monster in the dark," reveals author Ben Mikaelson (cited in Fletcher, 2000, p. 39). Drew Lamm agrees. "The scary part is getting out that first draft," she says (cited in Fletcher, 2000, p. 55). John Steinbeck, one of the great writers of the 20th century, confided that when he faced the possibility of writing 500 pages, a sense of failure came over him because he thought he could never do it (Safire & Safire, 1992). Mikaelson, Lamm, and Steinbeck aren't alone. It often seems formidable when we commit ourselves to not only writing a few words, but also writing one sentence after another, and then, writing an entire manuscript. Suppose ideas don't come and we can't get started? What if we reread the two paragraphs we just composed and they seem awkward and clumsy? We need to erase those negative thoughts! Sure, writing a draft is hard work, but remember, we should never expect our drafts to be perfect. We should lower our expectations. We need to view drafts as constantly evolving and under construction. We don't need to get it perfect the first time. Murray (1989) asserts that we should write badly to write well. He tells of Calvin Trillin, columnist for the *New Yorker*, who said, "I do a kind of predraft—what I call a 'vomit out.' … It degenerates quickly, and by page four or five sometimes the sentences aren't complete.… I have an absolute terror of anybody seeing it. It's a very embarrassing document" (p. 41). Murray states that we "need to learn to write badly [as Trillin suggests] and then learn to work from there to the pieces that are published, [and] the examples of what look like effortless craft" (p. 41).

In fact, we can always fix our mistakes before anyone sees our work. If we have a deadline and we start writing early enough, we have ample opportunity to make our draft better (Lamb, 1997). We can shorten it, lengthen it, change the beginning or the ending, and, if we want to, we can even throw it away. The objective is to begin a draft—keep going—and not demand immediate perfection. "Your first version is not the only possibility" (Gardner, 2001, p. 6). You might have a bad beginning, but forget the beginning—keep going. You can always fix the beginning, or find a new beginning later (Goldberg, 2001). Remember only through the process of drafting can we organize our thoughts, figure out what we know and what we don't know about a topic, and generate new ideas (MacLean & Mohr, 1999; Zinsser, 1988). Therefore, we need to suspend judgment and banish our internal critic so we can't hear our nagging about surface issues, such as spelling, punctuation, and capitalization. Polishing comes last, after our drafting and revision efforts are complete.

DON'T FALL BACK ON WRITER'S BLOCK AS AN EXCUSE

Donald Murray (2001) tells us of Roger Simon, a columnist with the *Baltimore Sun*, now with *U.S. News and World Report* who asserted, "There is no such thing as writer's block. My father drove a truck for forty years. And never once did he wake up in the morning and say, 'I have truck driver's block today. I am not going to work'" (p. 22). Murray agrees that writer's block is a poor excuse for not writing, and he admonishes us to "[p]ut our rear end in a chair every day and keep it there until the writing is done" (p. 22). If we are writers, as we hope we are, and want to be, Murray says we must accept the responsibility that comes with being a writer. We have to do what is expected of writers in the same way we have to do what is expected of us in any job.

Rus VanWestervelt applies this to his own writing experience and elaborates on Georgia Heard's (1995) rocks in the road metaphor:

> *Sometime we meet obstacles in the road, but that doesn't mean we quit for the day. We look for the detoured routes that will get us where we need to go. Sometimes a drive on the back roads gets us there in a much better way.*

Rus's comments bring us to the idea that extensive prior thinking isn't all there is to getting started on a draft; you can take a strategic approach. Heather Brown engaged in a number of strategies that enabled her to get words on paper. First, she recorded her reflections prior to writing; next, she drafted, asking questions of herself as she wrote; and finally she reflected about her writing when she completed her draft. When you read Heather's prewriting reflections, you will see how hard she struggled over the course of a week to begin her draft. Picture Heather at her computer trying to get started.

Heather Brown's Prewriting Reflections

2/15: 2:30 P.M.

Although I haven't composed a draft yet, I have many ideas floating in my mind, scribbled on post-its and scraps of paper. I have lists and rough outlines. I have a research design. I just need to write, to put all of this down on paper. I hesitate because I'm just now beginning the classroom research. I feel like I need to plan more, read more, think more. But perhaps I'm just avoiding diving in.

2/22: 2:15 P.M.

After doing all of this research, and looking at the pile of books in front of me, I am feeling overwhelmed. Just a few moments ago, while walking through the rows of books in the library, I felt charged, excited. I wished I were a full-time Ph.D. candidate with time to read, read, read. But sitting here at the computer, the reality has hit. I am a full-time teacher and part-time student with limited time. I have a sinking feeling in my stomach. I think to myself, I'll never have time enough to do a decent job. I feel like I should just go home and do something else; maybe I'll feel just as accomplished if I do a load of laundry.

2/22: 2:30 P.M.

Ok, here it goes. I think I might just type out what I am thinking, and revise later. (There goes that little voice in my head, "No! No! That will just create more work! Don't waste time you don't have!") But I think this style is the only way I won't freeze up, dive back into the books and avoid writing. I haven't completed the research, but I do have an idea of what I am looking for, what I expect to see, and what I hope will occur in my classroom as a result. I have read some texts, so I have something to say at this point. It might change drastically, but that's okay—process not product! If anything, writing now will help my ideas to gel.

Heather's reflections prior to writing make her thinking visible to us. Some of us will recognize ourselves in that hesitancy. We see characteristics of the essential delay in her thinking, but we also see her reluctance to begin, and we can feel her internal critic's intrusion. She perseveres and begins her draft despite her concerns. Note that rather than allowing her insecurities to hinder her, she plowed right in, interspersing questions and notes to herself about what she needed to do, or what she still needed to find out. She began the draft despite her concerns.

First Draft 2/22: 2:40 P.M.

"It is a difficult balance to both assume responsibility for learning and at the same time attempt to scaffold students' abilities as they begin to assume some of their own responsibility to learn" (Oyler, 1996, p. 25). Over the past four years, I have attempted to shift my teaching practices from a teacher-centered, transmission model, to a more transformative model.

[I NEED TO EXPLAIN WHAT THIS MEANS].

When I first began teaching, I "fed" a lot of information to the kids. I used a lot of direct teaching, much of it in subjects unrelated to their lives, using assignments which had little, if any input from them (including choice). Dialogue was mainly from me to them, and sometimes (I now realize from my Chicano students, not so much my Native students) from them to me.

As I progressed, that is, as I continued to teach and reflect, and to read, and to watch other teachers, I began to use more group-oriented methods. Still, I determined the curriculum, which included assignments that were isolated, skills-based, and not very hands-on, real world, etc. The students did them reluctantly. They had no buy-in: the assignments were too irrelevant and non-contextualized. [AGAIN, I NEED TO BE MUCH CLEARER—WHAT DO I MEAN? EXAMPLES]

At Ha:sañ[1] [I NEED TO EXPLAIN HA:SAÑ], I began to build a curriculum that I believed to be more student-centered. I created units/projects that were based on my students' interests and cultural background. The curriculum was bi-cultural, interdisciplinary, and more hands-on [AGAIN I'LL NEED TO MAKE THIS CLEARER AND PROVIDE EXAMPLES HERE]. Despite all this, my classroom was still dominated by IRE discourse (teacher initiates, student responds, teacher evaluates). Much of the assignments were individual with little room for dialogue. [MAYBE I SHOULD TALK ABOUT THE DIALOGUE JOURNAL PROJECT HERE]

This year, I have attempted to keep what worked from the previous year (hands-on, bicultural, etc.) while setting up the classroom for more student-talk, more student input, etc. This has worked well. [TALK ABOUT WRITING PORTFOLIO/LIT CIRCLES]. I am pushing this further with the webpage project. My question is: What happens when students and their teacher learn together? My students are in the process of creating a webpage. I have never constructed a web page before; I know very little about the processes. I am hoping to have the technology coordinator and student experts be sources of info, while I become a guide/facilitator. By giving students a voice I hope to see positive changes:

By having them develop the project (or at least provide input) [TALK ABOUT

COMMITTEES], they will have more buy-in, and will be more motivated to learn

[SHAWN'S OBSERVATION]

By setting up an environment where students teach one another, I hope that they will see themselves as experts/sources of knowledge, which is important for leadership skills [NATURE OF SCHOOL] becoming leaders in their community; instituting change; Politics, and also for developing discussion skills for college.

By having students develop a rubric and assess themselves I hope the students will begin to see their own strengths and weaknesses (not just look to others to evaluate them) [PORTFOLIO CONFERENCE—ANECDOTE]

By having them produce a real-world product with a real audience I hope to see students caring about the quality of their writing [WHICH I HAVE ALREADY

---

[1]Located in Tucson, Arizona, Ha:sañ Preparatory and Leadership School is a bicultural, college preparatory high school designed for Native American students. Founded in 1999 by a team of parents, teachers, and community members, Ha:sañ primarily serves Tohono O'odham students. By infusing all aspects of the educational experience with elements of O'odham language and Native history, the school aims to develop students' community pride.

SEEN BY PUTTING WORK AROUND ROOM, SCHOOL, AND IN IN-SCHOOL LITERARY MAGAZINES].

Assumptions:

motivation/active participation will increase [ALREADY SEEING THIS]

students will be more invested in their learning/writing

students will feel more confident about their abilities

students will see themselves as sources of knowledge (and see the benefit of

constructing knowledge together)

by stepping back, I will allow students to go further, because my own

assumptions/control of the curriculum can restrict them [TRINA QUOTE]

After she completed her draft, Heather reflected again on her writing experience.

2/22: 3:39 P.M.

Forcing myself to write helped me solidify my ideas. I noticed that I had a lot of asides inserted in brackets. Usually, I do this after I write in order to cue my-self to do something without forgetting what I was working on. Today, I did it as I was writing so I would not forget those additions, and I would not lose my train of thought. As I was writing I would flip back to the Internet to check out Ed.D. Programs—not that I wasn't interested in the writing, but more be-cause it got me excited about future research pursuits. I really enjoy this: re-flecting on my teaching, looking to texts for guidance, ideas, etc., applying ideas to my teaching, reflecting on how they worked (or didn't). Even the re-search itself affects my teaching. By observing my students, I am forced not to intervene, which is exactly what my research is looking at. But back to the writing. Looking at it again, I realize it is less of a draft and more of an outline in prose form. I guess I really can't get away from that planning.

Heather learned a lot about herself by recording her thoughts before, during, and after writing a draft, and then reviewing her written reflections. She recognized that she was hesitant to write a draft. She preferred to con-tinue doing research and engaging in invention strategies. She also discov-ered that once she dove in and wrote the beginnings of a draft, she was able to solidify some of her ideas. In addition, Heather noted that her draft was in outline form. Her affinity for a great deal of planning influenced her style of composing even though she tried to compose her draft by typing in a free writing way (see chapter 3 for a description of free writing).

USING THE THINK-WRITING LOG

When we study Heather's notes, we can see that she recorded her thinking prior to drafting and as she engaged in drafting. Not many of us keep a record of our questions and our thinking as we prepare to write. We usually don't pause to jot down our reflections as we compose a draft. Perhaps we don't want to hesitate long enough to consciously examine and record our thoughts because we believe it would slow us down and divert our attention from the actual writing process. Similarly, when we have completed a draft, we don't want to muse about the process. In all likelihood, we're just happy our draft is complete, and we forget the sometimes brief, and often transient thought processes that have guided our writing. But what would we learn about ourselves if we did objectively step back and think about our thinking—if we conversed with ourselves about our writing behaviors (Wilcox, 2002)? What insights might we gain if we kept a drafting or a thinking log? If we recorded our thoughts before, during, and after writing? MacLean and Mohr (1999) describe this type of writing as "think-writing." "Think-writing is talking to yourself in writing—thinking as you write" (p. 13). They use this term to refer to teacher researchers' practices of keeping a journal in which they "figure things out, raise questions, and pinpoint issues of concern" (p. 13) relative to their teacher research projects. It is a place to record the type of thinking that can help teacher researchers focus on the questions they want to pursue and the types of data that might emerge. We have extended this idea to describe an approach writers can use to get started on a draft and to document information about their drafting processes. You can record your thoughts prior to and after you write a draft in a journal that we call a Think-Writing Log. However, the questions, reflections, and comments that arise as you write are best recorded directly in your draft as they occur to you.

Perhaps you already keep a journal, or a daybook, as Donald Murray (2001) calls it, in which you collect writing ideas, experiment with language, and record titles and other ideas related to writing. Perhaps this notion is new to you, and you want to begin recording your thinking. Remember, it is important to date your entries so that you can refer back to your dated reflections (Goldberg, 2001). Dating your entries will help you monitor changes and growth in your thinking and insights and your developing understanding of the writing process.

Melinda Lundy, a doctoral student in Florida, believes "think-writing" might help structure her disorganized composing style,

Think-writing really struck a chord with me. I usually write on the run—talking to myself before, during and after writing. When a word or phrase comes to me that I think I can use in my writing, I jot it down on whatever kind of paper I can find—planner, notebook, grocery list, dry cleaning tag, envelope, nap-

kin, whatever. I use whatever I can find to write with—pen, pencil, marker, crayon, permanent marker, whatever I can get my hands on—mostly in a hurried panic trying to capture my thoughts on paper before they go out of my head without the promise of returning. There is no organization to this thought dumping. It sometimes happens with no warning. After I write I re-read a lot—often smiling to myself if sentences, phrases, and paragraphs stand out, or if words in a sentence are just the right words in that hard-to-write sentence. Think-writing on the other hand is much more structured. It's talking to yourself as you write—thinking as you write, and jotting down what you think. Think-writing is intriguing to me because I think this technique can help structure my haphazard writing style.

June Markowsky, who shared her worries about her writing abilities in chapter 1, found that making entries in her Think-Writing Log helped her solidify her ideas and confront her dilemmas before she wrote a draft. June also discovered that writing in a positive way in her Think-Writing Log after she started a draft provided a boost to her ego, and it served to alter her negative thinking about her writing abilities.

Here is June's entry in her Think-Writing Log prior to writing a draft: 6/03: 2:40 P.M.

I'm getting ready to conduct research for my Graduate Seminar in Early Childhood class. We have to work with a young child and report our findings about the child's thinking and development in eight areas, such as stages of artistic development, oral language ability, and socio-dramatic play behavior. I've already started my assessments with a six-year-old boy because this class is only five weeks long, and we're already in the second week of the semester.

I am concerned about how to write up my findings. How much information should I include? If I write every single word my research partner says and describe every single action/behavior he makes, my paper will really be l-o-n-g. I have a question too—When do I cite references in the body of the paper? I have to ask my professor. I am not happy with my writing abilities either. I get anxious when I have to write. I have to begin this paper or I won't have time to do a thorough job revising and editing. Ok, I have to start my draft now—Here goes—

June's Draft with Notes to Herself: 6:03: 2:55 P.M.

On Sunday evening, June 1st, David and I sat down for the first part of the print awareness assessment. I told David that I would be showing [SHOW] him pictures of different items and I would like for him to [LIKE HIM TO] name them. He responded, "Okay, I like pictures."

We began. [WE BEGAN WHAT?] I held up one picture after another and David named the item depicted. [I NEED TO ELABORATE HERE.] I didn't know if I should coax him or not—especially when I held up the picture of Sunny Delight orange juice. He said, "I know its orange juice, but I can't read what these words say."

I said, "That's okay, just as long as you know its orange juice."

We kept going until we finished this part of the assessment [I NEED TO ELABORATE, BUT THIS IS A START].

According to Marie Clay????[WHAT DID MARIE CLAY SAY ABOUT ENVIRONMENTAL PRINT? I NEED TO REVIEW THAT.]

June's Entry in Her Think-Writing Log After Writing a Draft: 6:03: 3:10 P.M.

Well, I didn't get very far in my draft, did I? When I read it, I can see that I need to expand this section considerably. I need to consider my readers. I need to describe more of the environmental print photos and include David's responses to them. And I surely need to study Marie Clay's work. Why did I write David and I sat down? That's understood. Why didn't I write a longer draft? There I go again—doubting my writing ability. The one thing I feel good about is that I started a draft. I STARTED A DRAFT!!!

Just like Heather, June discovered a lot about herself when she took the time to make entries in her Think-Writing Log. June noted that she continued to have anxieties about starting a draft. Yet, she had the courage to begin. As she composed her draft, she was conscious of her thinking, and she inserted notes to herself, such as, "I NEED TO ELABORATE." She also inserted questions that required answers, such as, "When do I cite references in the body of the paper?"

It is interesting to note that June started off her postdraft Think-Writing Log entry with a negative stance: "Well, I didn't get very far in my draft, did I?" Yet, she ended her entry in a positive way by writing in bold, capital letters, "I STARTED A DRAFT!"

Consciously making a positive statement about drafting helped June take the first steps to control her feelings of inferiorities and her anxieties about writing. She was able to focus on her abilities to begin a draft, and for the first time since we have known June, she projected an image of herself as a writer. We think June took control of her writing when she did this. A major key to success in writing and in life is to think you will succeed. We say, "Wow! June's reflections are great." They portray her struggles, thinking, and problem-solving abilities. In addition, June's candid reflections illuminate her personal writing journey.

PERSONAL REFLECTIONS

We recognize that keeping a Think-Writing Log involves spending additional time with your writing and we know your time is valuable. At the same time, we believe your efforts to use this strategy when you feel particularly challenged will ultimately save you time in later writing endeavors. How do you see yourself using a Think-Writing Log? Would it be useful for your high-stakes writing assignments, your creative endeavors, or your work-related writing? Might inserting notes in your drafts prove useful to you? What do you think you might discover about yourself and your writing if you used the think-writing strategy? Write your reflections.

EQUATING DRAFTING WITH DISCOVERY

Heather and June's use of the think-writing strategy enabled them to discover what they wanted to write and how they might achieve their goal. Similarly, discovery drafters might find this kind of strategy useful. On the other hand, if you are a discovery drafter who wants to dive right in and just write, write, write, we urge you to do so. What works for you is best for you.

Although Murray (2001) subscribes to the importance of the essential delay, he still views drafting as discovery. He says he explores topics as he composes that reveal all sorts of things he needs to know. Toby Fulwiler (2002) also equates composing with discovery. He says, "Writing starts from ideas and ideas start from writing" (p.16). Kathy Carr, Professor Emerita at Central Missouri State University, agrees. She explains:

> *I don't do much prior planning. It's a spontaneous thing because I become inspired by something I've read and there's something I want to say so I just sit down and write.*

Janet, Sharon, and Choyce Cochran are also discoverers. They can't delay writing a draft until they are absolutely, positively ready because unless they start writing, they never will be ready. Contrary to what Herbert and Jill Myer advise, they think delaying the start of writing is a waste of time. They believe they must see what appears on the page to know what they really think.

WRITING AS FAST AS POSSIBLE

Perhaps you don't consciously think much prior to writing, and you don't want to engage in think-writing. You just sit down and write continuously until you think your first draft is finished. Natalie Goldberg (2001) thinks writers should write nonstop and say what they want to say to foster their creative thinking. Mary Renck Jalongo (2002) also thinks writing nonstop is a good idea. "Writing a first draft sometimes feels like taking a 100 item multiple-choice test in 60 minutes. You do not linger over confusing items; you simply plow through it as much as you can without pausing. Try beginning with free writing. When you free write, you jump-start your writing by getting your ideas out as quickly as possible" (p. 89).

Jalongo (2002) also recommends that authors keep moving forward on a draft even if they need to leave out certain key points. "If you need examples, but cannot think of one, just write EX [for example] and keep going. One will come to you when you least expect it. If you need facts and figures but don't have them yet, don't lose your momentum by stopping to surf the net" (p. 90).

Donald Murray (2001) is another author who writes his drafts as fast as possible without concern for spelling or punctuation. Murray states, "I write as fast as I can because velocity is as important in writing a discovery draft as it is in riding a bicycle. You have to get up to speed to get anywhere" (pp. 9–10).

Tim Rasinski also gets up to speed and stays there when he composes a draft. Once he starts writing, he works almost nonstop. He says he writes in spurts—but not necessarily every day. You may recall that he told us in chapter 1 that when he writes, it may be for "ten to fifteen days at a time, three to five hours per day." He simply writes nonstop until he is finished.

Like Tim Rasinski, Choyce Cochran composes drafts without interruption.

I just sit down and start typing on the computer. I type, type, type until I can't think of another idea. Then I reread what I have written. Sometimes, I discover that I need to go back to the invention stage because as I read my draft, I think of information that should be included but it is not. That's what I had to do with my research proposal. I planned to do a study about my second graders' inferencing abilities. I did a lot of research and I thought carefully about what I wanted to write. As I explained in chapter 3, after I wrote a first draft, I recognized that I had to return to invention. I had not planned my proposal as carefully as I thought. Then, after I completed a second draft, I discovered I needed to return to invention once again. Finally, I sat down and wrote the beginning section of my research project.

Choyce brings up a good point. Just because we are in the drafting stage of our work, it doesn't mean we cannot or should not return to an earlier stage of the writing process, if necessary. As Jalongo (2002), Hillocks (1995), and writing experts explain, the composing process is never orderly and sequential. Writing is recursive and writers often loop backward and forward, organizing, composing, and revising at the same time (Miles,

1990). The important thing is to recognize if we need to return to invention, whether we need to let our ideas "percolate" for a few days, or if we need to conduct additional research before we can move on. Experienced writers know when to make these types of interactive writing decisions.

DRAFTING AND REVISING SIMULTANEOUSLY

Frequently, discovery drafting is a messy process involving simultaneous writing and revising. Sometimes writers write a sentence or a paragraph and then, rather than moving on to the next paragraph, they stop to rewrite and revise that sentence or paragraph until it is perfect. That's what Janet did with the beginning sentence of her dissertation. However, she ultimately concluded that it was non-productive, and time consuming. Somehow, she finally moved forward.

Although for some writers, such behavior is rooted in procrastination, that's not always the case. Revising while you write doesn't always mean focusing on single words or sentences to the exclusion of moving forward. In-process revision is frequently purposeful. Amy Palermo does that "just to make sure that things are going OK."

Janet and Sharon understand what Amy means. They have always revised when drafting. In the days before computers cleaned up the look of Sharon's drafts, her first attempts were always messy with lines scribbled out, margin notes, words and lines inserted between lines, sentences circled, and directions to other locations indicated by large arrows. She says:

> As I write, I stop periodically and go back to read what I've written. I read purposefully to check how what I've added fits with what I've already written, how it fits with my purpose, how it will sound to my audience, how it represents my voice. Along the way, I also correct spelling and punctuation and I recast sentences if needed. All of these editing tasks are not just because I want to correct spelling, punctuation, and the like. When I draft, I circle back and forth between old and new text. I monitor the progress of my draft to see if I have maintained my focus.

Elizabeth Sturtevant explains her in-process revision tactic:

> I always revise as I write a draft, but I don't think this is the best way. It is just how I seem to write best. I think of new things when I write. Sometimes I do too much revising as I write and I get hung up on making the draft perfect. My colleagues do better by plowing through a draft and revising later. I also revise when I have completed a draft—multiple times. Generally, if I put a draft away and come back to it a day or so later, I can make a lot of improvements. But I cannot wait too long or I forget what I have written. If I hit a snag while

*writing a draft—if I feel like I have hit a block, I do some additional research
and reading just like Jon Kuckla suggests. I always stop at the end of sections and read back to make sure they fit with other sections.*

It is interesting that Elizabeth says, on the one hand, that in-process revision is probably not the best way to write, but on the other hand, it is how she
writes best. We might contend that if it works best for her, then it is the best
way. She has a clear perspective on when it works and when it doesn't, and
she recognizes other roles for revision as well. Each of us has our own best
way to write and we need to acknowledge our personal writing preferences
and use them to full advantage.

PERSONAL REFLECTIONS

Think for a moment about your usual method of composing a first
draft. Are you like Mary Alice Barksdale and Tim Rasinski, thinking
things through carefully before you write, or are you more like Donald
Murray, Kathy Carr, and Choyce Cochran, discovering as you compose? Do you write a page or two and then go back and reread it before
you progress ahead like Amy Palermo and Elizabeth Sturtevant? Do
you engage in nonproductive drafting behaviors like writing a beginning sentence and then revising it over and over until you consider it
perfect like Janet did with her dissertation? Do you linger over a paragraph and re-evaluate it 45 times because you are stuck and can't move
forward? Do you write a page or two and then go back and reread it before you can allow yourself to progress ahead? Examine your own
drafting behaviors and determine how they work for you. Identify any
nonproductive drafting behaviors you have as well as those that help
you move forward. Write your reflections.

EXPLORING OTHER DRAFTING CONSIDERATIONS
AND HABITS

Perhaps you have learned that you need to calm yourself when you sit down
to write a draft. Katie Fradley discovered that she needed to get rid of her
anxieties before she was able to write a good draft. Katie shares her relax-
ation technique here.

*When I write a draft I find that if I tell myself, "It's just a draft," it takes the pres-
sure off and my writing is much better than when I sit down with an outline and
formally try to write. My most productive drafting occurs after everyone has*

gone to bed and I write as I drink a glass of wine. It loosens me up a little bit. The next day I go back to revise without the wine and I'm often surprised at the ideas I was able to produce when the pressure was off.

We don't necessarily recommend drinking wine as an aid to writing, but Katie makes a point about shedding anxieties and just getting down to writing.

Kim Shea found that she too, needed to relieve her stress about drafting. Kim examined her writing self as she tried to draft a statement of intent for graduate school (see chapter 2 for types of academic writing). Because this type of writing has high-stakes expectations, it created considerable anxiety for her. She exhibited some typical stress-related behaviors as she tried to compose her statement of intent, but ultimately she understood that she wasn't writing well enough because she didn't have sufficient information. However, after overcoming this particular writing challenge, and being admitted to the doctoral program, she faced entirely new expectations. She discovered that drafting on a computer didn't work for her. Kim explains:

Jalongo (2002) says we must allow ourselves to write badly. That's what a draft is all about. When I read Jalongo's ideas, it made me feel better. I should have read Jalongo's book prior to writing a statement of intent to get into graduate school. When I began writing my letters of intent/statement of purpose for graduate school admissions, I procrastinated because I didn't know what to write. As time moved along, I decided I'd better write something, but what I wrote was awful. I'd always taken great pride in my writing abilities, but this time my ideas just didn't flow. When I looked at what I had written and I showed it to my husband, we both asked, "Is this it?"

I couldn't believe it. I had written in such simplistic terms that my statement really didn't make a statement. I realized that I wasn't sure what graduate schools were really looking for in statements of purpose so I doubled back and did some research. After perusing many books and articles, I got the information I needed and I sat down to write again. This second draft reflected me—who I am as a person. It was great if I say so myself! Two colleagues, a professor from Xavier University in Louisiana, and my husband, reviewed my draft. I made a few minor changes and I had a statement I was proud of. And I got accepted into seven Ph. D. programs.

Right now I am having a difficult time. I am new to advanced graduate studies and my confidence in my writing abilities is waning. I'd planned to complete a draft of a writing assignment for my Monday night's class and I just couldn't do it. I was at a loss for words. I couldn't sit down at my computer. Finally, I decided to do things the old fashioned way. I sat down with a pen and a notebook. Words began to flow. I drew arrows all over the pages wherever I needed to insert an idea that came to me later on. Through this style of draft-

*ing, I realized that I am a writer who needs to be doing and feeling as I com-
pose—a kinesthetic type of writer. As my pen met my paper, I could feel my
thoughts come together more clearly. Yes, this seems like additional work
because, after handwriting, then I had to type my paper. But what I found out
was that if I can't draft, changing my mode of writing might help.*

Kim Schwartz is another doctoral student who doesn't compose a first
draft on a computer even though she's a computer expert.

*I draft in pencil and I don't erase. I cross out. I use a big legal pad and I dou-
ble-space. I do not write a first draft on a computer, which is interesting because I am a computer type person. I carry a laptop with me everywhere. I do
write second and subsequent drafts on the computer. I am a chunk type of
drafter. I write in chunks of thoughts and then group my ideas.*

Deborah Green also drafts in chunks and then works to bring the chunks
together to make sense.

*When I write something I don't write straight through. I may start out with a gen-
eral outline or an idea about how I want to organize a piece, but then I might
work on a single section. If I get stuck on one section, I leave a note that says,
"Write more," and then I move on to a different section. This sometimes causes
problems weaving all the sections together. It also is difficult if one section
starts to take over and takes me away from the focus of the piece I am trying to
write. If I get to a section that is not coming together I will make a list of ideas
that might work in that section. I will also stop in midsection if an idea occurs
that doesn't quite fit and I type that idea in bold so that I can come back to it and
I won't forget it. As might be expected, all of this jumping around often makes
me produce a paper that lacks continuity and flow of ideas.*

Deborah believes that having a writing buddy helps her overcome her
tendency to jump from one section to another. She emphasizes how important it is to have someone you trust provide feedback on your draft. In her
role as a member of the Teacher Research Collaborative of the NWP,
Deborah writes with a group of teachers who worked together to develop a
set of resources for other teacher researchers. When they meet, they write
and respond to one another's work. Writing in a group setting makes the
writing easier because there are trusted colleagues and friends willing to
discuss one another's work.

Debbie Dimmett, also in our writing group, explains how her drafting
process is carefully organized with a specific focus, purpose, and audience.

To initiate a draft, I first look at my research question and my notes to formu-late a thesis statement. My thesis statement is what I intend to prove—the main point. Normally, I put this in the first paragraph and proceed with writing the introduction that will lead to my thesis statement. Sometimes I need one or two introductory paragraphs before I introduce the thesis. I use an outline to inform the paragraphs that follow the introductory paragraph. The margins of my notes include the section of the paper those notes belong in. By the way, my notes are always typed verbatim unless I am translating from Span-ish into English or vice versa. I do this because it's much easier to keep track of the type of citation that I need to give. I put my own ideas in brackets.

The introduction is always the most difficult to write for me because I have to hook my audience and set the tone of the article. However, I usually give it my best and return to it later when I'm revising. I find it very difficult to write per-sonal narrative that I know others will read because I feel completely naked putting my persona "out there."

What if no one agrees with me? What if they think I'm a nut? Or that I have a weird agenda? So, before I write, I think about the main idea I want to share with my audience. I begin the first paragraph by thinking how I might begin a conversation about the topic and I keep my audience in mind at all times.

TURNING TO THE ARTS

Many educators aspire to creative writing, or they may try to find creative approaches to their academic writing. In either case, the creative process can inform us in very different ways when it comes to getting our ideas down on paper. Rus VanWestervelt describes his approach to drafting more cre-ative pieces.

Most of the time (all of the time with the pieces that I feel best about) I spend the most amount of time prewriting so that when I am ready to start writing, I have a story to tell. It is in me, and it is crying to come out. When I don't do this, I find that what I write is often nothing more than "pushed purple prose," where I am relying on the language rather than the specifics to tell the story.

This illustrates what Donald Murray (1989) means when he talks about the writer's "need" to tell the story. As he says, "the writer has an itch that must be scratched" (p. 34). Rus describes his own unique strategy for getting one of his creative pieces down—for scratching that itch.

Often, when the story is ready to be written, I'll imagine that I am "on location" to wherever the place is that I am writing about (fiction or nonfiction), and see the story unfold in front of me as I dictate it into a tape recorder just as I see it. In actuality, I am getting as close as I can to "filming" the scene. For fiction, I bring life to my characters and see what they will do with the story I've set up. Every time I've done this, I have been shocked with where they have taken the story, and I cannot imagine the slower process of physically writing ever leading them through such remarkable scenes that required the instant and spontaneous creativity to be captured as it was happening. In a short story I wrote, titled "Alice Flows," about a dying woman's request to have her ashes released in a running brook, I was able to place Alice in the middle of the running stream surrounded by rocks that redirected the current around her. In the still of the pool of water where she stood, I saw her cup her hands in the water and bring her own reflection to her lips. It was in this image—where Alice's spirit was already in the water—that I knew how I was going to end the piece. I went home that night, typed up the scenes that I dictated into the tape recorder, and my draft emerged. Only a light edit was needed, for I merely captured the story as, in my mind, it had actually happened.

For nonfiction, or even for academic writing, I do the same procedure, but I have to be saturated with the facts—all of them—before the scene can take place. I did this recently with a manuscript I was working on concerning the death of Baltimore's mayor in 1904, just months after a fire wiped out over 140 acres of downtown Baltimore, including its entire financial district. I had read dozens of accounts on the mayor's reported suicide, but there was just something about the wife's role in the mayor's last few minutes that bothered me. I took advantage of a rare opportunity to reenact the mayor's death in a townhouse just a few doors down from where he actually died. The layout of the house had not changed since 1904, so we played out the final minutes, dictated it all on tape, and realized that it was improbable that he killed himself; rather, the evidence, combined with the actual setting, strongly suggests that the mayor was murdered. Again, just like I do with fiction, I typed up the "scene" as I drafted it on tape, and very little revision was necessary.

For both fiction and nonfiction, bringing the characters alive in the established setting allowed my draft to unfold naturally. I, as the writer, merely got out of the way to let them do their thing. And every time I do this, I am surprised by what they teach me.

Ralph Fletcher (2000) and Donald Murray (2001) talk about writing "discovery drafts" to get the stories that are in our heads onto paper. In essence, that is what I am doing when I am drafting on tape. However, writers need to remember that there are different purposes for drafting. Sometimes, the purpose for drafting is to simply let the real story emerge. You might write several pages before you get to what the story is really going to be about (and, even though this is "drafting," it is still an extension of prewriting). Or, if you are sat-

urated with the specifics (fiction) or the facts (nonfiction) that are necessary to write your story, all you need to do is get out of the way and begin writing. It's hard for many writers to remember that the characters are using them as a transmitter to help bring the story to life.

It's interesting to imagine how Rus's process can support our academic writing endeavors. We may not always think about the dramatic elements of fiction and creative nonfiction in our efforts to meet the requirements of our academic expectations. However, we invite you to think about the degree to which you can infuse your writing with a lively energy by using personal experiences as illustrations and examples of the points you are trying to make. Can you, also, "get out of the way" of the story and let it "unfold naturally"? Moreover, the idea of drafting on tape seems an interesting challenge—one worth trying.

PERSONAL REFLECTIONS

Now that you have learned how some writers create drafts, revisit your earlier reflections on your drafting process. We asked you to think about your own drafting process, what you do, and how you feel when you begin a draft. Do you feel like Ben Mikaelson—"facing a monster in the dark" (cited in Fletcher, 2000, p. 39) and therefore, you don't want to begin? Are you too tough on yourself and when ideas don't come you get depressed and stop writing (Fletcher, 2000)? In the process of drafting do you get distracted because your mind wanders? Do you keep your mind and hand moving when you sit down to write and don't stop? Natalie Goldberg (2001) thinks that writing nonstop fosters creative thinking. Do you revise as you write, or do you plow through to the end of a piece, and then revise your work? Write your reflections.

COMPOSING A DRAFT: SOME HELPFUL HINTS

Because we all write differently, there are no foolproof formulae for composing a draft. Whatever works for us is the way we should write. However, certain drafting habits and strategies are more helpful than others (Fulwiler, 2002). We offer some of these drafting strategies here. They come from a variety of sources—noted authors, our colleagues, our students, the members of our writing groups, and us. We hope you will find these ideas useful when you prepare to write a draft and when you actually engage in writing.

One helpful suggestion about drafting is to keep your main idea in mind (Fulwiler, 2002). You might even display this main idea above your computer, or as a continuous header in your computer document (Rankin, 2001). If you are unsure of your main idea, you might follow the advice of MacLean and Mohr (1999), who suggest that we write notes to ourselves that summarize what we are trying to say. Debbie Dimmett suggests that teacher researchers who are trying to report their findings should write their research question and then develop a short summary that answers the question. Debbie cautions that if you insist on writing your first paragraph before you continue, ask yourself what inspired you to write about this topic. You can use this as the basis for your introductory paragraph. Later, after your draft is written, you can revisit your main idea to see if it still works.

Earlier we spoke about not having to write a perfect draft immediately. You can skip over parts that elude you, particularly the introduction (Crème & Lea, 2000). Deborah Green does just that. She reminds us that writing in chunks is an easy way to write a longer piece.

Some of our students suggest that you might want to write a draft in longhand if the idea of writing on a computer makes you anxious or distracts you from generating ideas. They also say that soft music has a calming and creative effect.

Donald Murray (2001) recommends establishing clear, realistic, and achievable deadlines, to which Rus VanWestervelt adds "that you can and will meet." To meet deadlines, Murray (2001) explains that he works "backward, breaking the project down into a series of small daily tasks" (p. 23). Because he knows what task is to be accomplished each day, he always knows exactly what he should be doing the next day when he returns to his writing desk. Planning ahead is critical to keeping up with our self-imposed expectations as well as those imposed by our work or academic requirements.

MacLean and Mohr (1999) tell us to write as if we were talking to someone about our work. Because we are often passionate about our work and about the topics that drive us to write, Tom Romano (1995) reminds us to "[w]rite with passion. Moderation didn't get Guernica painted or Normandy invaded and moderation doesn't get writing accomplished" (p. 26). He insists that we should trust ourselves and our experiences. If we write without passion, where are we in the writing we produce?

Elizabeth Rankin (2001) also wants us to be passionately and personally involved with our writing. She says, "If you find yourself consciously avoiding any mention of the personal in your academic writing, ask your self why"(p. 69). Exploring your views on use of the personal with colleagues and your professors may open up more opportunities for you to write from your personal viewpoint. Crème and Lea (2000) urge writers to call on the personal by writing in the first person. They believe if your professor doesn't tell you otherwise, write in the first person singular. "Don't pretend you don't exist," they say (p. 194). Write with authority and don't be afraid to put yourself into what you write. Claim your right to have a voice.

It is important to make a "writer's place" as Murray (2001) suggests, be it a room, a desk, a dining room table, or whatever space you carve out for yourself. "Study the conditions when the writing has gone well and try to reproduce them" (p. 25). Once you have a place to write and you recognize under what conditions you write effectively, you can no longer put it off. MacLean and Mohr (1999) urge you to make a pact with yourself to write for a set amount of time without stopping (perhaps 20–30 minutes). Then, stop and read what you have written.

We (Janet and Sharon) would also like to offer some thoughts about writing a draft. As we noted in chapter 1, some people like to write in the morning—others enjoy writing at night. Compose your draft during your optimal writing time, and guard your writing time. University committee meetings, shopping trips, too much time spent on e-mail, talking on the phone to friends, or visiting in the hallway with colleagues all erode your writing time.

PRACTICAL APPLICATIONS: WRITING YOUR OWN DRAFT

In chapter 3, we asked you to engage in some specific invention strategies that focused on a particular academic topic of interest to you (e.g., a specific teaching dilemma, a controversial situation facing educators today, an instructional practice that you think is worth sharing with others, a student who is particularly interesting or challenging, or a required class or professional writing assignment). Return to your invention now, and carefully review your work with the intent of writing a draft. Then write a Think-Writing Log entry that candidly portrays your thoughts about beginning your draft. If you prefer to think and plan extensively before you compose, like Myers and Myers suggest earlier in this chapter, you might want to write more than one entry. Remember, Heather Brown wrote two Think-Writing Log entries before she began her draft.

Review your reflections, and then sit down at the computer, or with paper and pencil, and take the plunge. Compose a draft. Compose in your usual style. You can revise as you write like Elizabeth Sturtevant, or you can write nonstop like Choyce Cochran and Tim Rasinski. You might try inserting notes to yourself in your draft like Heather Brown and June Markowsky did. After you complete your draft, review it. In the reflection that follows, we invite you to return to your Think-Writing Log and reflect on the experience of writing this draft.

PERSONAL REFLECTIONS

Read the Think-Writing Log entries you wrote prior to drafting. Were you anxious or confident? Were you reluctant to begin or were you eager to write? What does your Think-Writing Log reveal about your prewriting frame of mind?

Reflect on your drafting process. Did you pause often to review what you had written? Did you write nonstop in a free writing style? Were you aware of your thinking as you composed? Did you insert notes to yourself in your draft? How do you think your draft turned out? Now that you have created a rough draft, how might you refine it and make it better?

What have you discovered about your writing process and your beliefs about yourself as a writer? Were there similarities between your prewriting thoughts and your later reflections? Remember how June Markowsky's Think-Writing Log entries illustrated her lack of confidence before she wrote, but then her later entries reflected her surprise and delight at what she had accomplished? How do you feel as you look forward to continuing to work with this particular writing? Do you think you might continue using the Think-Writing Log approach? Why or why not? Write your reflections.

SUMMARY

We all approach drafting differently. Some of us do considerable planning before we begin. Others just sit down and type on a computer, or scribble with a pencil on a scrap of paper to see what happens. Sometimes, how we typically begin a draft just doesn't seem to fit our current writing task, and we have to alter our usual approach. You will remember that Janet had to think of some possible titles for this book before she could move forward with the proposal. For some unknown reason, she had to rely on a potential title as a beacon for her ideas. Yet, she never had to do that with her previous manuscripts, and we don't advocate concentrating on or worrying about a manuscript title until you have completed a piece. You will also remember that drafting is highly idiosyncratic. Aldema Ridge's need for a metaphor provides a unique example of the idiosyncrasies of writing. The important thing is to figure out what works for you as you compose a draft. Remember, words and ideas rarely flow out of our brains the first time we sit down to write. As Ralph Fletcher (1999) notes, "Most of us have to work at our writing" (p.

4). Joe Hardawanes (2003), a career strategy advisor, agrees, but he believes we must fashion our opportunities. He writes, "The artist doesn't find a beautiful statue; he sculpts it from shapeless marble. The musician doesn't find an intricate melody; she composes it" (p. 2). We think what Joe says can be applied to writers. A writer doesn't find a finished piece. A writer makes a conscious effort to compose a draft. The important thing is to write. "Once you've written something (anything!), you have material you can work with" (Gardner, 2001, p. 5).

We introduced Thinking-Writing Logs in this chapter. "Think-writing is talking to yourself in writing, thinking as you write" (MacLean & Mohr, 1999, p. 13). The more we think about ourselves in relation to our writing, the easier it is to write because when we consciously put our thoughts on paper, we come to know ourselves. When we use our Think-Writing Log, we can document what hang-ups, confusions, anxieties, or joys we have about starting a piece.

We can also consciously monitor our thoughts as we write. For example, as you discovered in this chapter, Heather Brown and June Markowsky utilized their Think-Writing Logs in different ways as they composed. Yet, by consciously thinking before they composed and also during the drafting process, they both became aware of what additional ideas and information they needed to include in their drafts and how they approached drafting.

Think-writing is also useful for promoting reflection after writing a draft. Heather rediscovered that she continued to rely on her main composing style because she felt most comfortable doing considerable planning prior to writing. June recognized that although she continued to doubt her writing ability, she did settle down and start a draft. June's wonderfully exuberant closing thoughts in her Think-Writing Log, " I STARTED A DRAFT!!!" may help propel her hypercritical attitude about her writing abilities toward positive thinking.

In this chapter we provided some helpful hints from writing experts, our students, us (Janet and Sharon), and members of our writing groups. Only you can determine how and if these suggestions might help you. In fact, we have a strong hunch that after reading chapters 1 through 4, and participating in the chapters' reflective and composing activities, you have some good advice about drafting that you can add to these suggestions.

In summary, only you can decide what works best for you as a writer of academic prose. The more you write, the more you'll get to a place where you are in charge of your writing. Then the lines between your personal and professional writing self will begin to converge. You will learn to connect in meaningful ways all the bits and pieces of your experiences with your academic writing requirements (Hillocks, 1995). As we said in chapter 2, that's when your best academic writing occurs.

RELEVANT READINGS

Crème, P. & Lea, M. (2000). *Writing at university: A guide for students.* Philadelphia: Open University Press.

This small book helps university writers develop an awareness of the complexities of the writing process, and offers activities designed to help authors take control of their academic writing. We especially recommend chapter 7, in which the authors provide an extensive discussion of originality and personal perspective in academic writing and use of first-person, "I."

Fulwiler, T. (2002). *College writing: A personal approach to academic Writing.* Portsmouth, NH: Heinemann.

We wholeheartedly recommend this book to our readers. Fulwiler starts off his informal, informative book by stating that all writers, regardless of the writing task, teacher-assigned or self-assigned, involves making choices about all sorts of things—topics, approaches, stances, claims, evidence, order, words, sentences, paragraphs, tone, voice, style, titles, beginnings, middles, endings, what to include, and what to omit. He says authors can simplify this choice-making process by asking themselves three questions: Why am I writing? Under what conditions and constraints am I writing? To whom am I writing? "In other words, your purpose, situation, and audience determine the tone, style, and form of your writing" (p. 3).

Hillocks, G. (1995). *Teaching writing as reflective practice.* New York: Teachers College Press.

This is not an easy book to read, but it is worth the effort. Hillocks writes in a scholarly manner that, at first, might intimidate readers. We found that the more chapters we read, the more we became fond of Hillocks's style of writing. He operates from the basic assumption that writing is at the heart of education, presenting theories that drive writing instruction. By reading and learning about these theories, as writers, we can determine how many of these theories may apply to our academic and professional writing efforts.

Jalongo, M. (2002). *Writing for publication: A practical guide for educators.* Norwood, MA: Christopher-Gordon.

This book is written for professional audiences who write nonfiction. Jalongo describes nonfiction as "those works that are true rather than fabricated, grounded in theory and research, and rooted in the lives of practitioners" (p. XIX). She believes that writing is a craft and a set of skills. Therefore, writers can improve their work through practice. Appendices offer readers numerous resources to support their writing development. Jalongo also supplies a helpful listing of references at the end of each chapter.

Chapter 5

Revision: The Heart of Writing

If you want to improve your writing, from now on, plan for revision. (Fulwiler, 2002, p. 168)

Writing is revision … Through revising we learn what we know, what we know that we didn't know we knew, what we didn't know. (Murray, 2001, p. vii)

You only write as well as you make yourself write. (Zinsser, 2001, p. 203)

The purpose of revision is not to cure a seriously ailing manuscript, but to enhance writing that has promise. In this chapter, we explore a variety of revision issues that relate to your academic writing initiatives, and we situate your revision decisions and initiatives within a personal framework.

As you might expect, we do not offer a lock-step prescription for this stage of the writing process. We all engage in invention strategies differently, and we all compose drafts differently. Therefore, it is no surprise that we all revise differently depending on our mood, inclination, and specific writing task (see chapter 2 for types and purposes of academic writing). As you learned in chapters 1 and 4, "there are all kinds of writers and all kinds of methods, and any method that helps you to say what you want to say is the right method for you" (Zinsser, 2001, p. 5).

As you read through the chapters of this book, you met writers who compose an entire draft before they reread and revise their work. Tim Rasinski, for example, explains: "I enjoy the revision process. I let my work sit for a while and then I go back to it. That's when I find a lot of problems. I like to do an entire draft before getting into the revision and editing of the piece."

You've met others who prefer to revise as they compose a draft. They write a few sentences, perhaps a paragraph or two, or possibly 5 or 10 pages.

127

Then, they stop and read what they have written to fine-tune their ideas. They feel most comfortable when they adjust and test their unfinished manuscript as they write. They might even stop to edit along the way, inserting a comma, correcting a typo, or mending a run-on sentence (see chapter 6 for editing). Toby Fulwiler (2002) says, "There are certain times when I can't develop an idea further until I get a certain sentence or paragraph right" (p. 168). When they have completed a draft, they might revise once more. As we mentioned in previous chapters, writing is recursive, and writers often loop backward and forward, organizing, composing, and revising at the same time (Miles, 1990).

THINKING LIKE VISUAL ARTISTS

Regardless of their personal revision style, all good revisionists adopt the persona of visual artists. Like painters and sculptors, they step back from what they have created. They separate themselves from their text (their reading self), and they critically look at their work with a "new" eye (their writing self). They scrutinize their work to review what they have previously accomplished, and they determine how they might make their writing better (Fletcher, 2000; Fulwiler, 2002; Jalongo, 2002; Willis, 1993).

CONFUSING REVISION AND EDITING

Often, writers don't distinguish between revising and editing, and they label any changes they make in their writing as editing. Perhaps this confusion is related to the role of professional editors. Professional editors guide writers through the publishing process and they frequently offer suggestions for making changes in the content and organization of a manuscript. Many writers thus assume that such substantive changes are editing changes. In addition, some revision and editing tasks are similar. Bratcher and Ryan (2004) offer a model that shows how revising may flow into editing, and includes a few comparable activities, such as attending to word choice and sentence fluency (see Fig. 5.1).

Kim Shea used to think revising and editing were the same processes. She explains:

> *I've always thought of revising and editing as being the same thing. I never considered the differences between them until we discussed this difference in the USF Round Table Writing Group. Now I'm thinking how much better and more polished my writing could be if I really did take the time to revise carefully.*

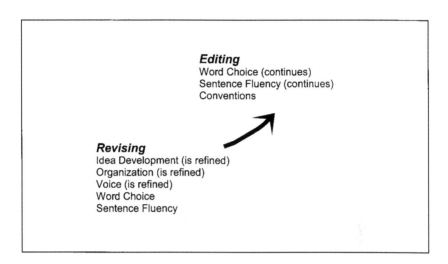

FIG. 5.1. Similarities and differences between revising and editing.

I'm beginning to understand that I have neglected revision because I concentrated on the mechanics of writing—comma, typos, that sort of thing.

Writer and professional editor Dana Andrew Jennings (2001) points out that beginning writers often think that revision means mending "a few fixed-up typos and [doing] some comma math" (p. 249). In actuality, it is important to make the proper distinction between revision and editing so that we can engage purposefully in both processes. In general, revision "is re-seeing, re-thinking, re-saying, [while] editing … is making sure the facts are accurate, the words are spelled correctly, the rules of grammar and punctuation are followed" (Murray, 2001, p. 2).

ATTEMPTING BIG-TIME REVISION

When Ralph Fletcher (2000) and Meredith Sue Willis (1993) speak about revision, they, like Murray (2001), are not talking about fine-tuning words and sentences, fixing typos, or adjusting paragraphs during the composing process. They introduce us to the world of big-time revision when they tell us the only way we can revise is to become experts of our own writing—to separate ourselves from ourselves, to reread our completed drafts over and over again, and to focus on our audience and not on ourselves. Lucy Calkins calls this ability to step back from what you have written, "passion hot, critic cold" (cited in Fletcher, 2000, p. 59). Hillocks (1995) refers to it as the ability "to divide yourself from the text" (p. 7).

WHY AUTHORS REVISE

Authors revise because they want to improve their work and write the best they can. Most published authors don't hesitate to abandon a piece of writing if they think it is not worthy of revision. They revise because they want to make a good piece better. As Ben Mikaelson explains, they polish their "manuscript as smooth as they can, like a rock" (cited in Fletcher, 2000, p. 81). They scrutinize their writing to determine if they need to expand their ideas, make their writing more precise and interesting, explain their thoughts in a better way, make sure they haven't left anything out, confirm they haven't included unnecessary information, and verify that the ideas they put down on paper accurately match the ideas they have in their heads. Good writers know that revising is crucial. They concur with Donald Murray (2001), who says, "All writers write badly—at first … then they revise" (p. 1). Good writers know that first drafts are rarely as good as they can be, but they often know when a badly written first draft is worthy of the required investment time and energy (and sometimes anguish) of serious revision.

REVISION: THE BEGINNING OF THE WRITING PROCESS

Donald Murray (2001) tells us that revision is not the end of the writing process, but the beginning. He urges us to celebrate as we revisit and refine our work because in the process, we discover ourselves. We clarify our views, expose our beliefs, and illuminate our convictions. We learn what is important to us, and we discern how our past experiences and current relationships shape our thinking. Unless someone at the university, or in our work context, insists that we write in a formal, academic tone, as we revise our drafts, we come to understand that, to a great extent, who we are defines not only what we write, but how we organize what we write. In a sense, when we revise, we revise ourselves. We rework our writing so that it represents and re-presents us.

Jerzy Kozinski, Pulitzer Prize-winning author of *Steps* (1968) and *Blind Date* (1977), metaphorically equates revising to playing an accordion. "You open it up and then you bring it back, hoping that additional sound—a new clarity—may come out. It's all about clarity" (cited in Safire & Safire, 1992, p. 210).

Rachel, one of Toby Fulwiler's college writing students, aptly describes the purpose of the revision process. She says, "Rewriting isn't just about correcting and proofreading, but about expanding my ideas, trying experiments, and taking risks" (Fulwiler, 2002, p. 167). Rachel understands the personal nature of revision that encompasses her ideas, her decisions, and her willingness to attempt new ways of articulating her ideas.

Melinda Lundy also appreciates the personal power of revision. She says:

I love what Donald Murray says about revision being the great adventure of the mind. It reminds me of writing for National Board Certification—trying to communicate what I had inside my head about the teaching process and my analysis of my students. I remember vividly, the revision process of cutting, reshaping paragraphs, moving sentences around. That was the most writing I had done up to that point and it required so much of ME. I now recognize the need to revise—to stretch as a writer—to go on an adventure!

SOME WRITERS RESIST REVISION

Zinsser (2001) believes that the idea of rewriting is often hard for some writers to accept. That's probably true. It's easier for us to believe that we did it right the first time. We want to assume that our initial version is perfect, and our writing task is accomplished. But that isn't usually the case, is it? We don't often get it right the first time. All drafts can be improved, tightened, and refined (Zinsser, 2001). That's a lesson every writer has to learn (Gardner, 2001).

Even if we recognize that our writing isn't perfect, we might still resist revision because we believe it is difficult. We don't want to mess up what we have already written by moving paragraphs around and adding or subtracting ideas and information. We think we might make our writing worse instead of making it better. We lack the discipline to roll up our sleeves, sit down, and take the time to think like a reader, and not like a writer. Elizabeth Cooke (cited in Murray, 2001), writing teacher and novelist, prefers the term *patience* rather than *discipline*. She says:

Patience is what allows me to linger over a paragraph, to reconsider a line twenty-five times, to search for a word or the meaning I am trying to find. Patience is returning to the first line over and over again until I am ready to go on. In writing one novel, I spent nearly three months revising the first twelve pages; then I went on to write the rest of the story—over four hundred pages—in six months. That's patience. (Murray, 2001, p. 29)

For some writers, the simple fact is they have not been taught how to revise or why this process is important. As a result, they may be apprehensive or uncomfortable about revising. They develop what we term *revision aversion,* and, according to Mary Renck Jalongo (2002), approach it like a root canal procedure.

Dorie Garziano, a graduate student studying elementary education, has a revision aversion, but she acknowledges the benefits of refining her work. She says:

My professors in college always wrote on my papers, "Off topic" and "Stay focused!" So, now I read and rework my writing until it drives me crazy and it makes writing torture. But guess what? All of my rereading and revising pays off. I just got an 'A' on my research paper.

Katie Fradley candidly sums up her revision aversion:

Until now I had honestly never thought about my personal revision plan. Actually, most of the time I just pretended editing was revision and moved on. To put it bluntly, my views on revision can be summarized in this brief statement: I hate to revise and will avoid it at all costs. I especially detest revising on paper and rely heavily on the computer using cut and paste simultaneously. There are many reasons why I hate revising so much. First, it forces me to analyze my writing and to accept the fact that in any piece there is room for improvement. Next, revising is hard work that forces you to think on your own, not relying on someone else's views. Finally, because I am a perfectionist, who thrives on closure, writing in general frustrates me. The following questions keep swirling around my mind as I reflect on revision. When writing, are we ever truly done, or is each piece forever in revision? Do we just come to a place where we say, "All right it's good enough"? Isn't there always room for improvement? As I reflect on this I think about how this affects my teaching in my classroom working with struggling second graders. When writing, my students constantly ask me, "Am I done yet?" Actually, I should be asking my students, "I don't know. Are you done?"

PERSONAL REFLECTIONS

What is your typical revision behavior? Do you tackle revision with patience and courage, or do you have a revision aversion? Do you revise as you write, or do you wait until you have completed a draft? How do you generally distinguish between revising and editing? How did you learn to revise your writing? Are there specific books or writing experts to which you can turn for ideas? Who were the teachers or professors who helped you and taught you how to revise? Do you generally follow a revision plan when you have finished a first draft? Describe your "revising self." Write your reflections. (You might want to begin using your Think-Writing Log for these reflections.)

REFLECTING ON REVISION

Often, when we are composing, revising, and editing along the way to a finished product, we focus our attention straight ahead. We look for the end of the process—getting that manuscript finished. We don't give much conscious thought to what we did along the way. We push those early drafts aside, sometimes tossing them into the trash without a second thought. Or, in using our word processing software, we just save and save and save until the draft is finished. Unless we make a hard copy along the way, early drafts are frequently lost. Sometimes, we need someone to ask us to stop and reflect on the changes we made in the draft. That's what happened to Deborah Green. Each time our Southern Arizona Writing Project group met, writers brought a current draft, which meant they had a draft-by-draft record of their writing. It was a valuable archive.

Both the April and May versions of Deborah's article are shown here with the changes marked. By using the Compare Documents feature of Microsoft Word, we show changes, with deletions lined out and additions underlined.

There I was standing in front of a groupmy class of second graders feeling as if the writing lesson had gone very well. But, as I walked around the room I had that sinking feeling that despite the planning, the discussion, and the modeling that I had done, I had yet again failed to motivate my young writers.

As a follow up to a story we had read we had had a pretty goodThat morning we had read Where's My Bear?. We then had a discussion about stuffed animals. We made a list of our favorite stuffed animals and we discussed how we would feel if we lost our favorite stuffed animals. We had come up with an interesting graphic organizer that listed types of stuffed toy animals, how we had gotten them, where we might lose them, and how losing one would make us feel. Now it was time to start writing. I modeled what I called free writing. I explained that when we do free writing we don't worry about spelling or getting the story just right. The important thing was to write the story as it came into our head. On the overhead I wrote about a teddy bear I have that is as old as I am. After I had talked and written my way through about half the story I announced that for the next 10 minutes everyone was going to do their own free writing about their stuffed animal. I assumed from their enthusiasm during our discussion that everyone would get right to work. OnlyAs I walked around the room, only a few students seemed to be doing any writing. What had gone wrong?

Description of class? [a note inserted in the revision]

For most of my teaching career I have been trying to find ways to unlock student's creativity and to show them how to write freely about the things that interest them. I have read articles in professional journals and resource books. I have gone to numerous conferences and workshops. After each of these experiences, I would return to my classroom ready to use the latest method or process. I have had some success having children write through "authentic" experiences, such as our pets or the field trip we had just gone on, using mini-lessons and small group conferences. At the same time I have been faced with the need to prepare students for high-stakes testing, students who are English language learners, and increasing time constraints.

Three years ago I got involved inhad the opportunity to be part of a teacher research project.pilot program in our district. As part of the project we took the Teacher Research Institute through the Southern Arizona Writing Project. I wanted to find a new way of looking at my teaching and I was looking forward to using my students' work to find out what was going on in my classroom and to see if I could find something that really worked.classroom. I wanted to find ways to motivate reluctant writers, help students think and write in an organized manner, and help each other edit and revise their writing. I started by asking, "Would short conferences between the teacher and a small group of students not only improve student's writing, but also improve peer conferences?" ThroughI thought that through modeling the questions to ask and how to give feedback theythe students would start using the same techniques with each other. After When I looked at my student's work I could see anseveral weeks, my students' work showed improvement in some areas, butareas such as use of details and staying with a single idea. But, their stories still lacked organization.

When Deborah reflected on the two versions of her article, she described different reasons for making specific changes.

In the May version, I left a question for myself about the description of the class. As I was reading the Montano-Harmon information [the background research], I realized I had never said these kids were second language learners. I think I had put that into an earlier version, but in going from the more academic writing to the narrative, I had left out that part where I had described the population of children I work with. Because I tend to write and then revise one section at a time, I have to go back every so often and make sure all the pieces still hold together.

The changes I made in paragraphs one and two came about in response to the writing group's feedback and to reading it myself after letting it sit for a while. Both paragraphs were vague. Any time I asked myself a question, I added more information. For example, in paragraph two, I thought it would be helpful to have the name of the book we read. I also thought the first sentence was too long.

I have never liked the 4th paragraph. The first sentence never sounded right—"got involved with" sounds involuntary and somewhat ominous. I also did not say what I was looking for or how I wanted to change my instruction. I think when I first wrote this paragraph I was just trying to get my general thoughts down on paper with the idea that I would go back and fill in the missing pieces and smooth off the rough edges later. If I spend too much time trying to get each sentence perfect, I lose my train of thought and I obsess over each word and don't get anything written. I'm not one of those people who can revise as they go. I need to get something down and then go back and work with it.

I have this vague feeling that if the reader can make a better connection to who I am as a teacher, they will be better able to understand what I am writing about. Right or wrong, a lot of the changes we make in our instruction are based on what we think or feel is the right thing for students. This is something I never even thought of when writing papers for biology or anthropology. In those papers, the writing was about the research and the data and the less said about the researcher the better.

Several common revision practices are made public in Deborah's reflection. She talks about the reader's need for information, about stepping back and waiting before revising, about using feedback from others, about her struggle with academic versus narrative structure, and about revealing herself through her text.

REVISING: A PURPOSE-DRIVEN ACTIVITY

When we have completed a draft, or when we are making revision decisions during the composing phase, our approach is probably not unlike Deborah's. We identify a need for change, and we address it.

As Lindal Buchanan told us in chapter 4, she connects invention and drafting. Then she revises her "messy hodge-podge" and thinks about organization and focus as she revises. She says:

I revise to bring some order into the chaos. This process takes a couple of drafts. As I draft and revise, I hear critics in my mind and I try to respond to them. They say things like, "Where's your proof for this assertion?" "So what?" "Why did you put this idea here?" "Who cares?" "Why should I believe you?" I strengthen and move sections in response to these voices. When I think my manuscript's "skeleton" (that's how I think of the argument/organization) is solid and fleshed out, then I read closely for style and editing issues, although I start thinking about style and expression earlier to be honest.

Lindal's focus on bringing organization to a draft demonstrates how writers make purpose-driven, personally relevant revision decisions. Debbie Dimmett, too, is purposeful when she revises. For example, after meeting with the writing group, and getting response to a draft, she made a detailed plan for her next steps:

My plans for revising my article include the following:

1. Clarify areas that were unclear per the recommendations of the group.

2. Reorganize my outline so that it will include some of the new information, such as the case study with Tracey.

3. Rework the paper to align with the outline.

4. Add examples of successes and failures from other teacher research projects.

5. Weave Tracey and these other examples throughout the piece.

6. Do a better job of showing my own frustrations and successes with self-evaluation.

7. Include the model for self-evaluation that I developed, which includes a competency-based component but still gives students the responsibility for evaluation. Write how I arrived at this final piece in the puzzle.

8. Add a component on teacher–student conferencing since this will be among the most important roles the teacher will play in evaluating student work.

Furthermore, Debbie decided she would try using a Think-Writing Log to gather insights into her revision processes.

In the future, I plan to reflect upon, and record the changes I make as I write. I think recording my revision decisions will help me become a better writer because I'll be able to illuminate specific patterns in my writing that always give me trouble.

PRACTICAL APPLICATIONS:
KEEPING A RECORD OF YOUR REVISIONS

Toby Fulwiler (2002) believes that writing informally about your revision agenda will help you advance your writing; consequently, we urge you, like Debbie, to use your Think-Writing Log to record your revision decisions (see chapter 4 for a description of a Think-Writing Log). We think it's important for you to engage in your own revision activities so that you can determine your revision strengths and problem areas. Try this. Look over the draft you wrote as part of the activities suggested in chapter 4. Revise your draft once and keep a record of your revisions. After you make a number of Think-Writing Log revision entries you might consider making a file labeled: "All I Know About Organizing a

Piece of Writing" (Murray, 2001). Murray believes that if you keep a revision file, "you will discover how much you know and realize you have a method of discovering how much you know that can help you to face a 'new' writing problem that isn't new after all" (p. 153).

CATEGORIZING YOUR REVISIONS

Once you have an ongoing record of the revisions you made, you will find that if you categorize your revisions, over time, you will discern emerging patterns. For example, you might find out that you often write a first draft in the passive voice, and then you go back and transform passive sentences to active ones. You might learn that you have a tendency to construct consecutive paragraphs or larger sections of text that confuse readers because they do not relate to one another. Therefore, your revisions usually focus on making your manuscript orderly so your readers don't get lost in that vine-tangled, unmarked forest. You might discover that your manuscripts usually contain too much information and you actually have two or three papers combined into one. You might find out that your literature review reads like it is taken directly from the original sources and that you string ideas and descriptions of research studies together one after the other, as Choyce Cochran did in her first draft (see chapter 2). Therefore, your revisions center on paraphrasing and making your own voice heard.

Choyce Cochran decided to extend her Think-Writing Log entries to include her most common revision patterns. She explains why she made this decision:

> I decided to take the time to add a revision section to my Think-Writing Log because when I worked through my research project, I was not satisfied with my writing abilities. As I explained in chapter 3, I had some difficulty with discovering a focus. I also paraphrased too many researchers' ideas. Then Janet pointed out that my paper continued to suffer from lack of organization in subsequent drafts. After many revisions, and many conferences with Janet, I am happy to say that my manuscript is finally finished and I successfully presented my work to my Specialist Degree committee. But I have this nagging voice in my head. The voice keeps saying, "So you completed this paper—OK. But how about any other writing you want to do? Janet and your committee aren't always going to be available. Suppose you want to keep writing? Who will help you? How can you help yourself become a better writer? How can you be your own teacher of your own writing?"

So I came up with the idea of extending my Think-Writing Log to include a list-
ing of the revisions I made in my action research project, and I have decided
to continue making entries in my Think-Writing Log for every manuscript, let-
ter to parents, or whatever I write.

Choyce shares her Think-Writing Log revision patterns here.

My Revision Patterns: 6/03: 11:40 a.m.

I looked over the revisions I made in my research project and I discovered the
following patterns.

1. I had to rework/revise entire sections of my manuscript because I wrote a
bunch of non-related ideas—including sentences, paragraphs, and larger
sections of text.

2. I discovered that I omitted important subheadings. When Janet pointed
this out, a light bulb went off in my head. Subheadings are really important be-
cause they tell the writer if ideas and concepts are ordered/placed correctly.
Subheadings also alert readers to information that will be presented.

3. As I revised my manuscript, I learned something new. It was almost like an
epiphany. I realized I had editing problems. So I discovered that careful revi-
sion can alert writers to editing requirements that need to be accomplished
in the next stage of the traditional writing process. For example, I used awk-
ward sentence constructions and excessive wordiness such as, "I am pre-
pared to share my insights of what I feel these students need in inferencing.
This hindered my revision work. I couldn't revise any further until I edited this
sentence to read: "I am prepared to share my insights about my students'
inferencing needs."

REVISING WITH THE SUPPORT OF OTHERS

Obviously we revise to communicate our ideas to readers in better ways. It is
at this point in the writing process that we might benefit from supportive
colleagues, such as the writers in the Southern Arizona Writing Project, or
the University of South Florida's Round Table Writing Group. Deborah
Green's experience with the Teacher Research Collaborative in California
provided her with a group of colleagues who supported her writing. She
tells us how important their feedback was:

Revision is always difficult for me. However, this summer I had the opportunity
to have three intensive days of writing, reflection, and revision at a National
Writing Project meeting. My group consisted of four, Hilda, Frank, Tom, and

me. Hilda is from Cuba and Spanish is her first language. I mention this because she was very good at pointing out when something did not make sense. She often asked for clarification, and when I explained what I was trying to say, I gained a better understanding and clarification of what I was trying to write. Frank is a former high school English teacher who was great at helping me see how I could rewrite to make the piece flow. Tom was our leader and did a very good job of leading us through reflection and clarification sessions.

On the surface the process was simple. After writing for three hours often at a huge conference table, we would read our paper aloud, ask for specific help, and then the group would read the paper silently and make notes that might help the author. We then used a discussion protocol that allowed readers to discuss the paper while the writer took notes. The readers would go page-by-page discussing everything they had read and making suggestions that pertained to the original request of the writer. Everything was done in a positive, helpful manner.

I leaned a great deal about writing in those three days. The combination of having to explain my thinking and working with people who understood good writing helped me write more clearly.

We may be fortunate to work with a professor who views our various drafts and gives valuable advice. Even so, we may feel uncomfortable sharing our writing at this stage. Katie Fradley explains:

As part of my doctoral coursework, I recently completed an independent study that I am hoping to turn into a journal article. My professor offered to help me with the revision process. Although I feel very appreciative that she is helping me, I also feel very uncomfortable each time I turn in a draft to her. My deepest fear is that she won't think it's good and will think less of me as a doc student. I have a vision of her sitting at her desk sighing in frustration as she reads my work. When I think about meeting with her, I keep catching myself thinking, "I wonder if she'll think my paper is done?" When in reality it's up to me.

I definitely have issues when asking others to read my work. Based on what

I have learned about myself as a writer, this does not surprise me. Because I lack confidence as a writer, I am extremely sensitive and it makes me extremely uncomfortable to give my work to others to read. I hope that this feeling will go away the more I have others read my work

Hubbard and Power (1999) urge us to get responses to our drafts before we send them off for publication. They recommend asking specific guiding questions to encourage effective, useful feedback. For example, a question like "What's the story here?" will help you determine if you have successfully conveyed your main ideas. However, they also caution you to "[s]tifle the urge to accept or reject the advice of your reviewers immediately" (p. 183). Think carefully about the advice, both negative and positive, and try to decide what you can use from them that will help you improve your writing.

REVISING WITH AN AUDIENCE IN MIND

When you involve others in your revision process, you gain an advantage. Collegial revision strategies are often easier than revision strategies you might use when you are acting as your own personal revision coach. When you are part of a writing group or if you have a writing partner, you have the benefit of "new" ears and eyes to give you a different perspective on what you have written. For example, you might read your draft aloud to your "writing buddy," as Deborah Green calls it, while both of you listen for gaps in content or for "ambiguities of language … and problems of transition from one thought to the next" (Emmerich, cited in Murray, 2001, p. 180).

You can expect your partner to hear problems in the text, but you'll be surprised at how easily you hear them yourself just because your partner makes you more audience aware, and "competence as a writer is linked to audience awareness" (Wollman-Bonilla, 2001, p. 187), Another strategy that promotes audience awareness is to tell your text to your buddy, rather than reading it. Just talk about what you have written (or what you intended to write). Then have your partner check the actual draft to see if you have included what you intended. Or your partner might ask clarifying questions (e.g., "I'm not clear on your data collection strategies. What is your plan?" "Do you have any research to support your theory that these scaffolding strategies will result in increased spelling competence?") The questions your buddy asks will make clear to you the information that your later readers will need. You will have a clear view of an audience perspective by involving readers in the revision process.

Whether you use a "buddy," a formal group, or an informal group for feedback on your writing, you are likely to get conflicting responses from time to time. Remember, different readers bring different perspectives to a text, so you should be prepared to examine and weigh the feedback before you commit to making the revisions.

Peter Elbow (1997) advises, "When you get conflicting reactions, block your impulse to figure out which reactions are right. Eat like an owl: take in everything and trust your innards to digest what's useful and discard what's not. Try for readers with different tastes and temperaments" (p. 118). At the end of the day, we have to make our own choices and decisions about revising our texts, but we also have to remember that we are writing for readers, and we must be audience aware.

If you don't have a writing buddy or a group, that doesn't mean you can't use audience awareness strategies to do your revision. To do this, you have to imagine yourself as the reader, the audience for the text you have written.

A GOOD READER OF YOUR OWN WRITING

As your own audience, then, you must become a good reader of your own writing. We cannot revise anything unless we recognize there is a need for improvement. Hillocks (1995) calls on deconstructive theory to explain the ability to identify problem areas and strengths in our writing. He says, "to write well, you have to become a good reader, to divide yourself from the text (from self), to generate a second, third, or fourth self to see what is written from the outside" (p. 7). His advice reminds us of Calkins's idea of being "passion hot, critic cold" (cited in Fletcher, 2000, p. 59) when reading your own writing. As a writer, you might bring the heat of passion to your writing, but you need to divide yourself from yourself, so to speak, and become the cold, hard-hearted critic to revise effectively. Falling in love with your words won't get your paper revised. Ask the hard questions: Have you left your readers in a maze of tangled forest trails with no signposts to guide them? Is your passion, or your commitment, evident in the text?

Deborah Green points out that her experience with the two writing groups she has worked with, the Teacher Research Collaborative of NWP and our Southern Arizona Writing Project writing group, has brought about a shift in her thinking and enabled her to look more objectively at her own writing.

I think my attitude about writing has changed. I know I can do it, but it takes me a very long time. I do a lot of staring at the computer. But I also do a lot more free writing by hand and going back and picking out the bits and pieces that might work. I can let things go now. When I look back at my original piece, I am surprised at how much is still the same. My writing style hasn't changed; I still write in piecemeal form. But I used to never want to cut anything out because it had taken me so long to get anything down on paper. Now I can see the advantages of either putting some parts aside to use at another time or just sending them off to word heaven. And I can cut out whole sections that don't work without having an emotional breakdown.

PERSONAL REFLECTIONS

Good writers know that revision is the heart of the writing process. They also consider their audience. How easily can you put yourself in the place of your readers? How effectively can you think objectively about your writing in the same way your readers will? Do you put your writing away for a few days so you can reread at it like an artist—with "new eyes"? Do you read your work aloud? Do you serve as your best critic? Can you divide your passionate writer self from your critical reader self? In what ways do you distance yourself from your writing? Do you ask others to read and comment on your work? Have you ever thought about what revision plans you follow or need to follow? Write your reflections.

REVIEWING OUR STUDENTS' DRAFT EXCERPTS AND REVISIONS

In the following section, we invite you to explore the revision process further by reviewing some of our students' initial drafts and their subsequent revisions. Our students also explain why they made specific changes to their writing. We think that studying others' efforts will help you recognize that revision takes perseverance, concentration, and a strong focus on a specific audience rather than self.

As you compare our students' original and revised drafts, consider how they transformed their writing, in what ways their revisions contributed to the improvement of their work, and how they rhetorically considered their audience. Keep in mind that their revisions are not the only ones that might be made. There are many possibilities for sharpening and clarifying sentences, paragraphs, and longer sections of text.

Mary Gobert, the doctoral student who described her concerns about writing a dissertation in chapter 2, wrote the first passage as a requirement in an advanced graduate writing course. Her professor stipulated that each student should write only one paragraph that explained a personally relevant educational process or activity. Mary's audience was her professor and her peers.

The National Board Certification Process: Mary Gobert

Three years ago, I successfully completed the grueling, difficult, year long National Board for Professional Teaching Standards certification process. This certification process includes a ten-part portfolio reflecting my educational theory and current practice. I also completed the required daylong computer based assessment designed to cover any aspects of my practice not examined in the portfolio.

Before I took this test, I wondered if I was going to pass it, but it all worked out okay.

I revised my passage in the following way.

Three years ago, I successfully completed the rigorous year long National Board for Professional Teaching Standards certification process. As required, I submitted a ten-part portfolio that portrayed my beliefs about teaching and learning and my reflections about my teaching practices. In addition, I completed an extensive computer-based assessment that highlighted dimensions of my teaching that were not portrayed in my portfolio.

Mary Explains Her Revisions in Her Think-Writing Log

I think I revised and edited at the same time, but that's what I do. I knew that I used the passive voice in my original paragraph so I went back and made sure I used the word "I" followed by a strong verb. Using this structure always helps me write in the active voice. Ross-Larson (1996) says it is better to use the active voice whenever possible because it is more direct, and I got rid of the descriptive words, grueling and difficult. These two words have similar meanings. In addition, these two words appear negative to me and might cause teachers considering National Board certification to drop out of the process. I decided to use the word rigorous to describe the process. The next to last sentence of my original paragraph was another problem. The sentence was wordy, which would confuse readers, and the vocabulary was trite (e.g., the word cover). Therefore, I edited the vocabulary by using my computer thesaurus to generate professional, powerful words, such as highlighted and evident. I also deleted the last redundant sentence.

In chapter 4, Amy Palermo explained that when she drafts, she writes a page or two and then goes back and rereads it "just to make sure that things are going ok." She wrote the following short passage for a masters degree class assignment in which students were asked to describe a teaching scenario or a schoolwide program. Just like Mary, Amy's audience was her university professor and her classmates.

The Accelerated Reader™

In my classroom we use the Accelerated Reader™ (AR). All of the second grade teachers I work with decided to go more in depth with the way we actually use the program this year to get more out of it than we have in the past.

Each student takes a test at the beginning of the year. This test uses vocabulary skills and reading comprehension to determine the student's reading level. A second grade student in their first month of the school year should be reading at least on a 2.0 reading level. So the students will read books on the level they score, we decided to require the students to read and pass 5 books on their level before they can move up to the next level. After they pass 5 books they may read a free book before they move up a level. This gives them the opportunity to read a book they might have been interested in but is not on their level.

Amy used her Think-Writing Log to record her ideas about her revision plans. She wrote:

I need to add information so my readers will understand what I am trying to convey about the AR program. My goal in this first revision is to add information and details. I need to change some verbs to past tense. I think I wander around too much. I need to consider my readers.

Amy's First Revision

In my classroom we use the Accelerated Reader™ Program—AR. All of the second grade teachers I work with decided we needed to utilize more of the program this year than in the past. We wanted to track our students' progress throughout the year.

Each student takes a test at the beginning of the year. This test uses vocabulary skills and reading comprehension skills to determine the student's reading level. (A second grade student in their first month of the school year should be reading at least on a 2.0 reading level. In the fifth month of second grade they should be reading at a 2.5 reading level or better.) The students will start reading books on the level they scored on the STAR test. We decided to require the students to read and pass five books on their level before they can move up to the next level. After they pass 5 books with 70% or better, they may also read a free book before they move up a level. This gives them the opportunity to read a book they might be interested in reading but is not on their level at the time.

Amy reread her revised passage and determined that her writing was still confusing. She wrote in her Think-Writing Log:

I still did not write what I really want to say about the AR program and I have to delete extraneous information or I'll lose my readers just like Donald Murray (2001) says. My explanation about second grade students' reading level is still confusing.

Amy's Second Revision

In my second grade classroom we use the Accelerated Reader™ (AR). All of the second grade teachers in my school decided that we needed to restructure our AR programs so we could track our students' reading progress throughout the year. Therefore, during the first week of school all of the second grade teachers gave our students a test to assess their vocabulary knowledge and reading comprehension level.

We require our students to read five books on their specific reading level with a 70 percent pass rate before they can move to the next reading level. Once students pass to the next level, they have an opportunity to select and read a book on any reading level.

Amy read her second revision and wrote this in her Think-Writing Log:

I still am not happy with my description of the Accelerated Reading Program. In the first and second sentences I use the same three words: second grade teachers. I know I could handle this when I edit my work but, it is glaring at me and I have to fix it now. My second draft does sound better though. I used strong verbs and my description of the program is clearer. But I still think I can do better. Questions readers might have are: 1) Who publishes this program? Who determined that our school would use AR? 3) What are the tests like? 4) How are the tests scored? 5) How do students choose their books? 6) What level books do students read when they have an opportunity to choose a book? I need to insert all of this information. It seems that in Revision #1, I took redundant information away. Now, in revision #3, I'll need to add information. I find that when I write out my revision thoughts in my Think-Writing Log, it helps me consider my readers.

Amy makes a good point. Any revision technique is a good practice if it helps writers seriously consider their readers as they restructure their manuscripts.

Amy's Third Revision

I am a second grade teacher and all of the second grade teachers in my school use a school district mandated reading program entitled Accelerated Reader™ (AR), published by? [I NEED To Find Out the Publisher.] Recently, we decided we needed to restructure our AR program so we could keep better track of our students' progress. Therefore, during the first week of school, we gave our students an AR test to determine their vocabulary knowledge and current reading comprehension level. (A second grade student in their first month of the school year should be reading at least on a 2.0 reading level. In the fifth month of second grade they should be reading at a 2.5 reading level or better.)

We require our students to read five books on their tested level, and then take a test and achieve a 70 percent passing rate before they move to the next reading level. The AR tests are short and easy for teachers to score, however recording these tests requires a lot of book keeping.

When our students pass a graded AR test, they have an opportunity to read a book of their choice on any reading level. Students usually choose a book that interests them regardless of specified grade level.

Amy gradually transformed her drafts into a coherent piece, even though succinctly describing the complicated AR program is not an easy task. Note how Amy considered her AR-uninformed readers and took the opportunity to carefully explain the program so that she could meet her readers' needs.

When Choyce Cochran drafted her research proposal for a class assignment, it looked like this:

Research Proposal

Various factors will be investigated to note the importance of incorporating inferencing instruction in my classroom. Different strategies and approaches will be addressed. The amount of time spent incorporating the various essential elements of literacy development will also be noted.

Many different programs are implemented to teach reading in the school district. Stories are read and studied while all subject areas are integrated into the subject areas. Mini lessons are included to teach phonics, decoding, writing mechanics, spelling, and study skills. Students' inferencing abilities are poor.

Choyce Explains Her Revisions in Her Think-Writing Log

I reread my draft and realized that it contained a number of problems that I needed to fix. I wrote in the passive voice. I rambled on about various factors and my rambling made no sense. I supplied my readers with little information about why I wanted to conduct this research project. My draft contained two unrelated paragraphs.

Choyce's Revision

My second grade student's inferencing abilities are underdeveloped. My school district's required reading/language arts curriculum includes differ-

ent reading/language arts published programs, but none of these programs concentrates on developing students' inferencing expertise.

I have decided to conduct a research project to determine if explicit instruction in inferencing will improve my students' abilities to make inferences from text and from text book illustrations.

In my study, I will have a control group (15 students) and an experimental group (15 students). I will teach both groups of students using the school's required reading curriculum. In addition, I will offer 12 inferencing instructional strategies to the experimental group. I will work with these students (the experimental group) for 30 minutes per day, five days a week for six weeks.

Do you notice that Choyce's revised draft is much clearer than her original draft? She followed her notes in her Think-Writing Log to rework her piece. She wrote in the active voice. She explained why she decided to conduct an action research project, and she provided her readers with a succinct description of her teaching/research plan.

Mary-Virginia Knowles's Action Research Project

Mary-Virginia Knowles, a doctoral student at the University of South Florida, decided to submit the first draft of her manuscript to the Round Table Writing Group. First, she first made some notes in her Think-Writing Log about the purpose of her research project. She also included her thoughts about what she perceived might be possible problems with the manuscript:

Sept. 12: 9 A.M.

I have too many ideas in my head. I want to write about my English as Second Language Students' reading of quality children's literature. I conducted an action research project on this topic and that's what I should include in my piece—just that. But right now I have many other ideas I want to write about and I have to get my thoughts in order.

Following one of the guidelines of the writing group, when Mary-Virginia submitted her work to the writing group, she included a cover sheet that alerted group members to the purpose of the piece and to the concerns she had about her first draft. (This is, by the way, an important practice for writing groups. It helps the group give a focused, useful response.) Here's what Mary-Virginia wrote to the group:

The purpose of this piece is to report on an action research project that I conducted to determine if introducing multicultural literature into my ESOL class would reduce my students' disengagement with reading. It also focused on the strategies I used to make literature study effective. The intended audience is other ESOL or secondary teachers. I think that I might need to tighten the focus of the paper and that I'm trying to do too much. I've thought about taking out the critical literacy aspect. But I'm not sure about that because the students produced a binder containing letters to the principal addressing their interests in having more books to read. Despite the letters, the principal has resisted purchasing books and so I purchased books for my students. This unfortunate situation may not be something I wish to include in my manuscript, however frustrating it is. My literature is also lacking. Also, I want to write about the book celebration the class had at the end of the semester upon completion of the book. I think all of my ideas are too many ideas and I may have three articles in mind rather than one.

The following is an excerpt of Mary-Virginia's first draft. Notice that before she revised her piece, she reread it and inserted questions to herself within the body of the draft to help guide her revisions. In a similar way, Heather Brown and June Markowsky wrote interspersed notes to themselves as they wrote first drafts (see chapter 4).

Turning Over A New Leaf:

Engaging ESL Students in Reading Multicultural Literature

[I need to change the title. "TURNING OVER A NEW LEAF" sounds trite. Maybe I should title this piece, "I Want To Read": Motivating ESL Readers with Multicultural Literature. This new title will have less than 13 words, which is always a good idea, and it tells my readers what the piece is really about.]

"I want to read!" were the words my student used to greet me one morning during the last month of school. {Why didn't I use this student's name? Maybe I should begin this way: "I want to read!" Jose said loudly as I walked into our classroom. I couldn't believe my ears! [Should I keep this sentence, or not? Does it sound professional enough?] After I had recovered from my surprise at his [JOSE'S] request, I realized that what I had formulated as one of my goals at the beginning of the year was occurring [had occurred]. My students were becoming [had become] interested in reading. What had caused this change? As I analyzed the steps [not steps I might use the word, actions.] I had [Get rid of had?] taken over the previous ten months, I concluded that because of the decision to include multicultural literature, my students' engagement in reading had increased. [I have to get rid of the weak 'ing' verb, occurring. Perhaps I might simplify this entire part and write: After I recovered from my surprise at Jose's request, I thought about what might have motivated him to want to learn to

*read.] Before I decided to incorporate multicultural literature, I used pop-
ular texts [books] of [published by] well-known ESL publishers. The se-
lections in these books did little to engage the [my] students' interests.
With the arrival of accountability and standardized testing, my focus
quickly became these tests. [Explain more here.] However, my students'
interest in reading flagged. Although bright and eager to learn, the students' behavior was resistant, characterized by using Spanish almost ex-
clusively for responses, or ridiculing peers for giving correct answers. [I
need to check on this sentence. Who said this? I need to remember to
write in my voice—to connect the personal with the professional.] My use
of non-fiction passages was well-meaning because I wanted my students
to achieve passing test scores, but I ignored literature [place elsewhere].
My students' resistance and disengagement with reading spurred me to
question the texts I was using [we used]. I decided it was time to turn over
a new leaf [I need to revise here also. I need to get rid of the phrase "turn
over a new leaf." My sentence constructions are not strong. I use too many
weak 'ing' verbs. I need to tell my readers right here or in the beginning of
the piece that for the past nine months I infused quality multicultural to our
reading curriculum and the literature seemed to motivate all of my students to read.]*

Mary-Virginia used her interspersed notes and comments and suggestions from the Round Table Writing Group to help guide her revisions. An
excerpt from her second draft follows next. As you compare her first and
second draft, think about these questions: (a) What are the specific differences between Mary-Virginia's first and second draft? (b) Which draft is easier for you to read and why? (c) In the second draft, Mary-Virginia deleted a
large amount of text that she included in her first version. Do you think her
deletions weaken or strengthen her paper? Did her deletions help to make
her second draft more reader friendly?

"I Want to Read": Motivating ESL Readers With Multicultural Literature

*"I want to read," Jose said decisively as he greeted me one morning in April. I
was stunned by his words. And then I realized that my goal for the year [I decided that one of my goals for the year had been met.] Jose, and some of my
other reluctant readers had become interested in reading. What had caused
this transformation, I wondered?*

*As I reflected on my teaching over the year, I decided that Jose, and the other
young adult readers in my class became [had become?] excited about reading when I integrated quality multicultural literature into our curriculum.*

My Teaching Context

Spanish is the first language of the majority of my 9th and 10th grade students who come from diverse countries such as, Cuba, Puerto Rico, Venezuela, Colombia, Honduras, Argentina, Ecuador, Peru, and Mexico. [I don't need to name all of these countries.] Parents often work late hours, and because of family economic circumstances, many of my students are employed after school. Based on the realities of their lives, my students' engagement in reading was problematic. Reading did not play an important role in their lives. That's when I began to wonder if culturally specific literature might motivate my students to want to read.

Previously, I taught my classes using English as Second Language (ESL) texts that focused on oral production of English. These books proved useful for the newest of my English language learners. However, once my students acquired a good command of English, the books did little to engage their interests. I tried to focus on comprehension strategies with the passages in the series. But despite my efforts, my students' resistance to reading grew. It was my responsibility as an ESL teacher to stimulate their interest in reading. Therefore, I began to question the texts I used. I concluded that my students needed to read about young adults like themselves—young adults whose first language was Spanish, and who came from diverse Hispanic/[Latino?] countries like they do. Only then could my students connect what they read to their own experiences, and only then, would they want to read.

What do you think of Mary-Virginia's last draft? Can you see how she worked through each draft, gradually refining her ideas? Did you notice that Mary-Virginia's voice is apparent in all of her drafts? She had no problem writing in her own voice. Her writing difficulties were in organization.

THINKING STRATEGICALLY ABOUT REVISION

By applying specific revision strategies to your text, you might find it easier to resolve some of your specific writing problems. For example, you might return to some of the invention strategies you used. You might create a concept web that portrays the ideas presented in each section of your manuscript. Check the concept webs for accuracy. Is information repeated? Are concepts presented in a logical order? Another invention strategy you might use is to create a flowchart. Chart your ideas and then look for gaps or repetitions in your writing (Willis, 1993). (See chapter 3 for an example of a flow chart.)

Sometimes you might use an outline as an invention strategy—that's often true of our careful planners—but making an outline after you've written the draft can be quite useful in recognizing problems in organization and content. Study your outline carefully, crossing out irrelevant or repetitious information and adding what is missing. Then you can follow your new outline when you revise your manuscript (Murray, 2001; Willis, 1993).

Determining how well you have developed your thesis is an important consideration in preparing to revise. Read through your draft and, for each paragraph, write one sentence that represents the central idea. Reread the sentences to determine whether or not they make sense and then decide what you need to do. Or as Murray (2001) suggests, "Quickly read … your draft and put a check in the left-hand margin whenever you give the reader specific, accurate information. Then go through it again and put a small arrow where you might [need to add] specific information that would help readers, think, feel, and experience the draft" (p. 34).

You might also consider some artistic approaches to revision. This is especially effective if you are writing a narrative. Create a storyboard, that is, a series of numbered boxes with sketches, like a comic strip, that shows the progression of the story. You can decide how to rearrange parts of the text, where ideas can be deleted, or where they need to be added.

Finally, distance yourself from the text. Wait a day or so, and then go back to reread. Read like a reader, trusting yourself and your ideas. Reread what you have written and pay attention to what your piece tells you, or what it fails to tell you. You might find that if you relax, you can discover ideas that would benefit from a deeper exploration. Add these new ideas to your manuscript (Heard, 1995).

PRACTICAL APPLICATIONS: ENGAGING IN YOUR OWN REVISION ACTIVITIES

Good writers know that most of their writing requires multiple revisions before they can be satisfied. For that reason, we invite you to go back to your writing and revise it again, and perhaps yet again. This time, try using some of the strategies we suggested, try getting feedback from colleagues or a "writing buddy." Work with it until you think it is as good as it can get. Continue to keep a record of your revisions in your Think-Writing Log. Again, list and categorize your common revision patterns.

PERSONAL REFLECTIONS

Think carefully about the work you accomplished in this chapter. We have focused extensively on revision and we've asked you to engage deeply in revision. We also focused on the importance of stepping outside of yourself and reading your writing like a reader. Now, we invite you to reflect on your revision activities in this chapter. Revisit your

Think-Writing Log. Did the patterns you identified on the first revision still apply? Did you find new patterns? What strategies were particularly effective? How did your revisions contribute to the improvement of your writing?

How easy or difficult was it to engage in the "passion hot/critic cold" behaviors? Could you be a tough critic of your own writing? If you got feedback from others, could you accept negative criticism without feeling personally assaulted?

Throughout this book we have asked you to put yourself into your writing, and in this chapter we have asked you to step out of it. How easy or difficult was it to write or compose in close connection with the self, and then revise apart from the self? Write your reflections.

SUMMARY

Regardless of our preferred style of writing (see chapters 1 and 4 for writing style preferences) we have to recognize that an important key to good writing is revision. Consequently, we need to engage in significant revision activities.

Rigorous revisions take considerable time and intense concentration. To revise effectively, we have to learn to distance ourselves from our writing—to move from one dimension of ourself—our writing self—into another dimension of the self—our reading self. Ralph Fletcher (2000) aptly describes this process as wearing two hats—a writing hat and a reading hat. He says, "skilled writers alternate the hats they wear—first writing, then rereading, often switching back and forth many times while writing a single piece" (p. 59).

We cannot emphasize enough the importance of wearing two hats—again Calkin's "passion hot and critic cold" idea (in Fletcher, 2000, p. 59)—to divide ourselves from the text (i.e., from one part of the self) when we revise (Hillocks, 1995). Neophyte writers often have trouble placing themselves in this role—imagining themselves in the role of audience. However, accomplished writers may actually possess the ability to play dual reader and writer roles simultaneously rather than engage in distinct pauses to shift persona.

Have you come to the conclusion that revision is not only crucial to good writing—it is difficult and time consuming? It also requires patience. If writers are to make their writing their own, "they must struggle with the details, wrestle with the facts, and rework raw information and dimly understood concepts into language they can communicate to someone else" (National Commission on Writing, 2003, p. 9). They have to discover and uncover major flaws in the organization of their work and correct minute imperfections in their choice of words. Like Choyce

Cochran, they must determine if they have left out important information or descriptions that might help their readers. Like Mary-Virginia Knowles, they have to figure out if they have two or three articles embedded within one manuscript. Like Deborah Green, they have to be willing to send some parts off to "word heaven" or cut out sections "without having an emotional breakdown."

We close this chapter by restating an important fact: We can only make deep, meaningful revisions when we consider our readers and we step outside of our writing self. That does not mean that we forgo our personae. It means that we recognize what self, the writer self, or the reader self, is most appropriate at any given time in the writing process.

RELEVANT READINGS

Willis, M. (1993). *Deep revision: A guide for teachers, students, and other writers.* New York: Teachers and Writers Collaborative.

This book is filled with practical ways to revise both fiction and academic prose Willis is joyful and enthusiastic about revising. She provides revision exercises and examples of her students' work. She states that writers can learn to revise by revising others' work and she believes revision is a natural process.

Murray, D. (2001). *The craft of revision.* New York: Harcourt College.

Murray states that writing is revision. He organizes this book around revision principles: (a) Revise to consider the information communicated in a draft. (b) Revise to illuminate your own voice. (c) Revise to delete superfluous information. (d) Revise to provide form—whether the form is provided by our professor, editor, or boss. (e) Revise to provide order.

Chapter 6

Editing

I think editing is the easiest part ... you just have to check for the obvious stuff: spelling, grammar, all that. And if it's not obvious to you, this is the part where someone else is welcome to jump in and help. (Drew Lamm, cited in Fletcher, 2000, p. 84)

Yesterday I had to get a letter out to a publisher, and I reread it about three times, each round making subtle changes in wording so that the message was more precise. (Priscilla Griffith, former editor of *The Reading Teacher*, Co-Editor of *Action in Teacher Education*, and Chair of Instructional Leadership and Academic Curriculum at the University of Oklahoma, personal communication, July 3, 2002)

Editing is finishing. Editing is making a text convey precisely what you intend to say in the clearest way possible. Editing is sentence-level work, attended to after a text's ideas are in order. (Fulwiler, 2002, p. 178)

If you can say it in plain English—DO SO! (Robert Weir, Associate Professor of History and Liberal Studies, Bay Path College, MA, personal communication, March 9, 2004)

As a prelude to this chapter, we want to share some truths with you about our previous conceptions of editing. Until we authored this book, we never gave much thought to the editing process. In past years, we think we did a fairly good job of editing our own writing, and we helped our students edit their own work, but we never examined the editing process in any detailed way. We just edited on automatic pilot. We didn't think there was very much to editing—just attend to errors and oversights related to the mechanics of writing. In fact, we dreaded writing this chapter because we believed that

154

editing was a dull and boring topic. We worried that we wouldn't have much to say to our readers. After all, there are a multitude of stylebooks that offer advice about using appropriate conventions of written language.

However, as we reviewed our colleagues' narratives about editing, many of which are included in this chapter, and conducted research on editing, we discovered that editing can be just as exciting as other stages of the writing process. We also learned that thoughtful editing involves much more than correcting grammatical errors. Thoughtful editing includes enhancing the clarity and pace of a manuscript. Most important, we concluded that just as in all stages of the writing process, a large part of editing involves making personal choices. The editing choices you make determine if you will write as clearly as possible in an active, vigorous way that moves and directs readers along so that they will want to continue to read what you have to say (Barzun, 2001; Marek, 1993). In this chapter, we situate the editing process within the writer's personal domain, and explain three basic editing premises.

EDITING WITH VARIOUS STYLES

As we pointed out in earlier chapters, authors choose different invention techniques, and they draft and revise differently. Therefore, it is no surprise that their editing styles also vary. Some adhere strictly to the traditional composing process because that approach feels most comfortable to them. Like Timothy Rasinski and Choyce Cochran, they write their drafts nonstop. Then they revise their work. They scrutinize their texts to determine if they need to expand their ideas. They reread their manuscripts to discover how to make their writing more accurate and interesting. They put their work away for a few days and then look at it with "new eyes" to see if they can explain anything in a better way. They look carefully at what they've written to make sure they haven't omitted anything or included unnecessary information, and they verify that the ideas they put down on paper accurately match the ideas they have in their heads. When they are satisfied with their revisions, they carefully edit their manuscripts, checking grammar, spelling, punctuation, capitalization, word choice, and sentence and paragraph-level considerations.

Other writers prefer to draft, revise, and edit recursively. As they write, they stop along the way to repair run-on sentences, mend misspelled words, and insert or delete commas. Like Amy Palermo, they feel most comfortable when they periodically check what they have written to determine that "things are going OK." As Nancy Anderson advises, "If you notice a writing problem, no matter how small, fix it immediately. Why wait?"

Mary Alice Barksdale adheres to a similar "fix it immediately" editing approach. She says:

I don't even think very much about editing after I finish a piece. I just do it as I write—sometimes even before I get a complete sentence on paper. Editing as a final process is very weird for me. I edit constantly from the moment I write the first sentence. Every time I complete a paragraph, I go back and read it to make editing corrections. And then, every time I finish several paragraphs, I go back and edit what needs to be fixed. For me, writing, revision, and editing are ongoing recursive processes.

WHAT STYLE OF EDITING IS BEST?

Well, what style of editing is best—saving editing tasks until your first draft is completed, editing as you draft, or a combination of both? You already know the answer to this question. There is, of course, no one best editing technique. "Logically speaking, polishing and editing come last" (Willis, 1993, p. 155), but if a different style of editing works for you, stick with it. Remember, connect the personal with the professional. Edit in a manner that is personally appropriate for you. Systematic people develop systematic systems. Intuitive people develop intuitive approaches" (Rankin, 2001, p. 90).

DON'T WORRY ABOUT MEMORIZING FORMAL RULES

Now, before you start worrying about having to memorize formal rules of written language to be able to write "correctly," we want to reassure you that we (Janet and Sharon) don't know all the grammatical rules and terms that authors list in stylebooks. For example, we just read in one of our favorite stylebooks that compound modifiers, also known as unit modifiers or compound adjectives generally must be hyphenated" (Walsh, 2000, p. 8). It doesn't matter whether we know what a compound modifier is or not; in fact, knowing this rule will not make one bit of difference in our writing abilities, and as Patricia O'Conner (1996) says, "most people don't know a gerund from a gerbil and don't care" (p. XI). Regardless of our skills in identifying rules of grammar, we are experienced users of language. We've been using language quite well for nearly all of our lives, and our experience with usage assists us in our writing, despite not knowing the formal rules.

Most published authors probably don't know all of the formal rules of written language either. In fact, a study published in *College Communication and Composition* (Sloan, 1990) found that professional writers make as many grammatical errors as freshman English students. We think many professional writers probably don't know how to diagram sentences either, and they recognize that it isn't a prerequisite for effective writing. If they get stuck on an editing concern, such as where to insert a comma, or when to use the words *which* or *that,* like all good writers, they ask an expert to help them, rely on their finely tuned ear for language, or look it up in a writing stylebook. There are many fine writing stylebooks to guide writers and we refer to them throughout this chapter, and list some of our favorites in the "Relevant Readings" section at the end of this chapter.

So, please be assured—our intentions in this chapter are not to provide an extensive list of rules for you to follow as you edit your work for faulty grammar, misspellings, and flawed punctuation. You will find all of the rules you might possibly want and need, and their examples listed in stylebooks, such as Bill Walsh's *Lapsing Into a Comma* (2000), Lynn Truss's best seller, *Eats, Shoots & Leaves* (2003), and Patricia O'Connor's *Woe Is I* (1996). Rather than repeat what Walsh, O'Connor, and other stylebook authors tell you, our purpose in this chapter is to raise your awareness of the importance of editing, and develop your ability to take charge of the editing process (Barzun, 2001).

WE EDIT FOR OUR READERS

Regardless of your preferred individual writing style or your knowledge of conventions, there comes a time when you must step back from your writing and concentrate carefully on editing your finished manuscript to make it smooth and reader friendly—polished like just-shined silver, and as error free as possible (Fletcher, 2000). Donald Murray (2001) tells us we have to edit because we are our readers' representatives. Patricia O'Connor (1996) says if language were flawless, rules were few, and English were easy, we wouldn't need to worry about editing our writing. However, rules of language constantly evolve, and as O'Connor says, English is weird, with "the largest lexicon (that is, the most words) of any modern language" (p. x).

Jacques Barzun, history teacher, writer of more than 30 books, critic, and author of *Simple and Direct: A Rhetoric for Writers* (2001), explains that we have to edit our manuscripts critically because written language differs considerably from speech. He says that when we speak with someone, we can listen to his or her inflections, and use the speaker's facial expressions and hand signals to help acquire meaning. If we are confused and need clarification, we can even ask questions, or request the speaker to repeat or rephrase what he or she has said.

Barzun (2001) continues, "with a written text [however,] there are no opportunities to ask questions" (p. 5). Readers must rely on the conventions of written language, such as standard spelling, punctuation, capitalization, and syntax (i.e., the order of words in a sentence) to get meaning. Consider your readers, Barzun tells us, and take responsibility for detecting and removing errors. Written expression is as important as the facts and findings of one's research.

Ralph Fletcher (2000) uses a dramatic arts metaphor to help us understand why we need to edit our work. He explains:

> Imagine that you are acting in a play. You spend weeks learning your lines, practicing while standing on the stage of an empty theater. During these rehearsals would you wear makeup and costumes? Use props? Probably not. It wouldn't make much sense to do all that until the seats were filled with real people watching the play. The same thing is true in writing. Proofreading [i.e., editing] becomes important when you move from private to public with what you have written. When the time comes for someone other than yourself to read your sentences, you will want them to be correct. (p. 85)

AUDIENCE AS AN IMPORTANT FACTOR

We believe that, when editing, audience is the most important factor. Heather Brown's thoughts illustrate this importance.

> *I used to not be able to edit my own work. I couldn't even look at it when I completed a writing assignment. I realize now, that without a real audience (my teacher didn't count), I had no real motive to care about correctness. As I started writing for larger audiences (whether it's my writing group or a professional journal), I started caring more about editing. As an English teacher, constantly reading reams of papers, I have fine-tuned my eye and my ear for editing.*

In the broader context of her dual role as a teacher of young writers and a teacher who chooses to write for and about her profession, she makes a distinction between her differing purposes for editing.

> *I have become an editing junkie. When people ask me to edit their writing, I actually enjoy it. My problem is I go too far. They get their piece back, covered in purple ink. Of course, I don't do this to my students, because I realize this would overwhelm them. With them, I am more concerned with content. I see conventions as something they will master gradually. With adults, however, I assume they are equally concerned with correctness, that their audience expects them to have mastered conventions. I am aware of the sad reality that our writing is often judged on correctness alone.*

She draws the distinction between how we approach editing in the process of teaching writing to students who have not yet mastered the craft, let alone the conventions of writing, and how we approach editing when we are working with colleagues for whom publication in professional journals, or a top grade from their university professor is the goal. There are very different expectations in each situation. The role of audience is critical, and she notes that when we only write for the teacher we are writing for no audience at all—or at least for an audience for whom we have a very narrow purpose—that is, to get a grade.

PERSONAL REFLECTIONS

Stop for a moment and reflect on your attitude and beliefs about the editing process. Is it difficult for you? If so, what makes it particularly difficult? Is it a lack of confidence in your knowledge of the rules of written language, or is it the anticipation of finally putting your writing out for review? If it isn't difficult, what skills do you bring to this part of the writing process? What do you actually do when you edit? Do you edit as you write, defer editing tasks until you have completed a draft, or engage in a combination of both? Do you use stylebooks or other print or online resources to support your editing? Do you ask colleagues, friends, or family to help you edit? Write your reflections.

DISTINGUISHING EDITING FROM REVISING

We briefly discussed the differences between editing and revision in chapter 5, and we think it's important to further clarify this distinction now. Some writers have never thought about the differences between editing and revising. Janet confesses that until she did research to write this book, she used the terms *revising* and *editing* interchangeably, although Sharon always corrected her. You may remember that Kim Shea, in chapter 5, said, "I've always thought of revising and editing as being the same thing." This is likely because, in general, when we are rereading to check organization or meaning, we simply can't skip over the surface errors we encounter. We revise and edit simultaneously, so we again blur the boundaries between aspects of the writing process. Nonetheless, we believe it is important to distinguish between these two aspects of the writing process, because when you are making decisions about changes in your draft, you should have a clear understanding of why these changes are necessary. Are they meant to more clearly communicate content (revision) or are they to polish the language, word choice, and conventions so that language issues either (a) enhance the delivery of the content, or (b) do not interfere with it?

Lindal Buchanan offers a metaphor to help us distinguish between revision and editing. She explains:

Editing is the polishing that occurs after the revision process is over (in other words, organization feels solid, arguments are in place and well developed, all major lines of thought have been laid out). To use a jewelry making metaphor, I see the revision stage as akin to crafting a metal framework for a jewel and setting the jewel in place. The editing phase is akin to tightening the prongs around the jewel, making sure the jewel is set/placed properly in its setting and will stay in place, and then polishing the whole thing so that it is shiny, beautiful, and desirable.

During one of our Round Table writing sessions at the University of South Florida, Janet and the group members tried to figure out how they might distinguish between revision and editing tasks. After a lengthy discussion, Karen Kelley, doctoral student, and Codirector of the Tampa Bay Writing Project, came up with an easy-to-understand and perceptive explanation. "Somebody else can't revise your work, but they can edit it," she stated.

We think Karen's explanation precisely defines the difference. Revision entails discovery of new insights, and adding or changing ideas that are distinctly yours. Only authors can rethink, enhance, enrich, and reshape views presented in their manuscripts. Mary Embree, professional editor, educator, and author of *The Author's Toolkit* (2003), agrees with Karen. She says revising or rewriting an author's work changes the author's voice. Nancie Atwell (1987) urges teachers of young writers not to write on students' pieces during in-process, content conferences, where the goal is to help students rethink, focus, and develop their drafts. She reminds us to "[r]emember the centrality of ownership in students' growth as writers. The piece of writing belongs to the writer" (p. 95).

The same principle applies to our efforts to support our colleagues' writing. We must not appropriate the writer's voice in terms of content, and when helping colleagues with editing issues, our goal is not to teach our colleagues conventions of language but, rather, to help them polish their manuscript. Because the editing process relies on universally accepted rules to structure punctuation, capitalization, spelling, and the like, editing-savvy friends, spouses, and even strangers can point out errors of this type to authors who wish to improve their writing. That's why you hear our contributors talk about taking a big, red pencil (or the equivalent) to someone else's work or doing the same thing for others when they describe their editing experiences.

FEELING OVERWHELMED WITH THE EDITING PROCESS

Although Drew Lamm thinks editing is easy (cited in Fletcher, 2000, p. 84) some writers feel overwhelmed with the editing process. In fact, Kathy Perez, Professor at St. Mary's College in California, says, "I get so bogged down with editing tasks that I hire someone to do it for me. I simply do not edit well. It is not my forte."

Victoria Ridgeway, Associate Professor at Clemson University, is another writer who dislikes editing. She explains:

> *I enjoy the revising process—but almost loathe the editing process! I try to wait until I've finished—or nearly finished the revision process before I tackle editing, but sometimes errors are glaring, and I can't complete the revision until I've fixed the grammar or spelling. I learned to edit painfully in graduate school.*

Kathy and Victoria are not alone in their dislike of editing. Jacques Barzun (2001) notes that he has worked with many bright and highly motivated graduate students who were so concerned about their underdeveloped editing abilities they preferred to concentrate on the facts and findings of their research rather than give attention to written expression.

THINKING THE EDITING PROCESS IS EASY

Contrary to Kathy and Victoria's editing concerns, some writers think the editing process is easy. For example, Jody Fernandez, a recent PhD graduate from the University of South Florida, credits her journalism background and her teaching experiences for honing her editing abilities. Jody explains:

> *I have a background in journalism and in teaching college preparatory/developmental writing. I am very aware of the importance of editing. I edit consciously at least twice with anything that I write. Grammar is easy for me because of my background. When my manuscript is finished, I rarely have to go back and put in commas, etc. When my ideas stop flowing freely, however, I go back and do my first conscious edit usually for spelling, mostly typos, but also for word choice. Word choice is very important—the suitability of words for my audience. If I'm writing and can't think of the exact word that I want, I hit my computer bold button and type in several close-but "not-it" words. When I see the bold type later, I know I have to recheck for word choice. Once I've finished a section, I reread and edit for clarity. When it comes to the end product, I have to print it out and get out my red (or green or purple) pen and do the English teacher thing and REALLY edit. I have to do it on paper; the computer screen doesn't work for me.*

Karen Kelly, who so succinctly explained the differences between revision and editing, finds editing tasks uncomplicated, but she does not remember being taught to edit. Karen tells us:

I view editing as very important. When I reflect about how I write on a computer, I realize that every time I sit down with a piece of writing in progress, I always begin by re-reading what I already have written. I find myself making all kinds of changes each time I do this—some editing/some revision. Sometimes I think I need to not edit and just get on with the writing.

I don't recall ever being taught to edit. That's something I have become more aware of as a part of the Tampa Bay Writing Project. I do remember diagramming sentences in middle school. I think that is where I gained much of my conception of sentence structure and punctuation. I think that the most common problem I see—something we don't really talk or read about—is sentence structure and how that impacts the tone of a piece.

FOLLOWING A SYSTEMATIC EDITING PLAN

Lindal Buchanan, who devised the jewelry-making metaphor to distinguish between revision and editing, is one of those writers who follows a specific plan when she edits her work. She explains:

In concrete terms, when I edit, I place myself in the role of critical reader. After I've finished substantial revision—in other words, when I feel like the main structure of my thoughts are pretty well in place—then I move into the editing stage. Here I'm dealing with style and punctuation, and fine points of writing rather than arrangement. I look at four areas: 1) I attempt to eliminate word repetition as much as possible, especially in closely connected sentences, 2) I make sure elements that should be parallel are parallel in structure, 3) I strive for a variety of sentence structures within paragraphs, 4) I check for my own personal grammatical demons like subject/verb agreement. Although items 1–3 sound a bit mundane when taken separately, in unison they work together to build my own particular "style" of academic writing, which I always hope is clear and well crafted.

Regarding more rhetorical issues, by this point in the writing process, I've already thought through issues of context and audience in terms of my larger argument and the genre I'm working in, but I continue to ask myself these kinds of audience-related questions: Will my readers understand my point? Will they think this point is interesting and well expressed? Will they be stumped by jargon? I comb sentences and paragraphs looking for places to improve readability and flow.

Not surprisingly, considering her systematic approach to outlining and organizing, Debbie Dimmett also has a systematic plan, along with a cautionary note, for editing. She says:

I'm very secretive about my work, and I don't like to have other people read it until it has gone through at least a couple of revisions. Normally, when I edit, I return to the outline or conceptual map that framed my writing. I look to see that all of the sections I wanted to include are there, if they add or detract from the initial question or proposition I put forward, and if the sections of the paper flow together in a logical way. Are there gaps in the paper that need to be filled?

After I have a fairly readable document, then I might ask others to read it. Usually, I will only have someone read it if the development of my argument might need tweaking or if there could be dreaded consequences if there are mistakes or misunderstandings (such as not getting a grant). Otherwise, I often find the input of others to be more confusing—particularly if it's a husband who is critiquing it. Advice—Don't let your husband critique your work or help you edit/revise. Editing is painful enough without adding marital discord.

Generally speaking, I am my own editor. However, I do enjoy the feedback that I get from my writing group because the feedback tends to have less to do with editing and more to do with new directions or thoughts that might influence how I finish the paper. I see the feedback of the group as being "food for thought" and focusing less on surface issues. I don't use any stylebooks other than EndNote.[1]

While Debbie avoids having her husband read and edit her work, Sandra Engoron-March relied on her husband extensively when working on her dissertation:

My husband, Richard, an English major, provided me with abundant assistance in the editing of my dissertation. I recall that he would insist that I simplify my language. He would drive home that ideas should be expressed simply. For example, he advised me to avoid superfluous adverbs. Another of his suggestions was not to use pronouns when their use rendered the meaning of the text vague.

He observed that my thirty years of experience with writing in academic Spanish impinged on my syntax when writing in English. I would frequently employ Spanish syntax with English lexicon. I still fall into this linguistic pattern, although I am now more conscious of this tendency and, therefore, do it less frequently.

---

[1] EndNote™ (2004) is a computer application that automatically records your citations and develops the source list based on which style (e.g., APA) you have chosen. More information can be found at http://www.EndNote.com

HAVING AN EDITING MENTOR

Sandra's husband was, in many ways, a mentor, but not all of us are lucky enough to live with an expert. Sometimes we must depend on our professional or academic relationships for support. Nancy Williams, Associate Professor at the University of South Florida, had a helpful editing mentor who taught her how to edit. Nancy says:

> Initially, I was not a good editor of my work when I was in graduate school. Fortunately, I had the best editing mentor in the world! Bonnie Konopak was my advisor at Louisiana State University and the director of my doctoral dissertation. She and I became co-researchers and co-authors that began with my doctoral work and continues today. She served on editorial boards, and was an editor for several publications and taught me well.
>
> Bonnie preached APA style and "corrected" my writing by using a big first grade sized red pencil. I would carefully read her comments and interject them into the writing. By writing WITH her, I was able to learn from her style of writing as well. I learned from Bonnie that editing also involves looking for the suitability of words and sentence length.

ENHANCING EDITING SKILLS THROUGH EXPERIENCE: JOHN BARNITZ

John Barnitz, Professor of Language and Literacy at the University of New Orleans, who is a scholarly writer on applied linguistics and topics in literacy education, sharpened his editing skills when he served on his high school newspaper editorial board and worked as a writer-producer of high school television documentaries. John explains:

> I learned much about the editing process while working on the weekly school newspaper, especially as layout-production editor. I saw how student prose had to be "cut" to fit into a finite space of column inches. I also served as a writer-producer of documentary television programs at my high school, so I edited across multiple sign systems. I coordinated the written prose of the script, the musical score sequences, and various visual sequences. I had to coordinate and adjust all of this with an audience in mind. Also, I copy-edited school TV news stories and scripts written by fellow students, and this activity helped me develop an awareness of the difference between spoken and written language.

John goes on to describe exactly how he edits his writing by keeping his audience and purpose for writing in mind.

I edit at the end of the writing process and throughout various stages of the draft formations. If I leave a draft overnight to review the next day or so, I may start with reading it and editing it. There are different purposes for editing depending on the manuscript and audience, and stage of development. For example, when I wrote this narrative and sent it to Janet via e-mail, I did not edit it because Janet was my audience. I wrote informally, and I knew as one of the authors of this book, she would edit my writing for this chapter. However, I am in the process of completing a biographical newsletter article for a historical society in Chicago. So I am editing for language, which will sound more like journalese in the popular press. Also, I am editing to cut down the wording of longer sentences because of the nature of the general public audience.

DEVELOPING A TALENT
AND A FINELY TUNED EAR FOR EDITING

Some people have an innate talent for editing. They seem to have a finely tuned ear, or a subconscious sense that makes them relish editing, and helps them make appropriate editing decisions. Christine Miranda, Graduate Program Coordinator at the University of South Florida, is an editorial whiz kid. Many faculty and students hire Christine to edit their academic writing, including dissertations, department letters, scholarly articles, and student papers. Christine explains:

I'm a good editor. I only took one secretarial course in grammar, but for some reason, I have a natural editing talent. I have a good ear for language, and I'm careful and thorough so that helps me with my editing work. I love to edit. I even want to edit the daily newspaper as I read it. (By the way, there are many articles in the daily newspaper that need editing help.) When I was quite young, no one wanted to write a letter to me because I'd pick it apart. I'd actually tell people who wrote letters to me what was incorrect with their writing. I wouldn't do that now, but when I receive a letter I still edit it in my head. I guess I just like to correct writing.

When I edit someone's academic manuscript, it's like my brain is split into sections. Part of me is looking for mechanics and the other part is looking for order. I like to shorten things. "Use fewer words," I tell writers. Wordiness complicates manuscripts and I think manuscripts should be easy to read. Always consider the reader.

I have a structure I use when I edit. I just don't rely on my innate abilities or my finely tuned ear. I follow the rules advocated by the American Psychological Association. That's the style used in the discipline of education. Other disci-

plines, such as history, follow other guidelines, using The Chicago Manual of Style, for example.

I put sticky notes on sections that tell me to go back to parts of a manuscript and recheck things. I use a lot of pencils. I can't edit without a sharp pencil. I occasionally look up a word in a thesaurus. I look up words in the dictionary.

When I edit, I always consider the reader. Writing has to be clear and logical, or readers will get lost. My advice to new authors and those who want to enhance their academic writing is this: Everything has to follow an order. If you give a statement, provide examples. In the introduction, state facts, and then, provide examples. At the end of your manuscript—summarize—sum it up.

I keep track of everything when I edit. I have those sticky notes all over the manuscript—I read something and I say to myself, "They said that two pages ago." I put myself in a place where I pretend I don't know anything about the topic in a manuscript, and I read the piece, and then I actually go to my computer and summarize what I've learned. If it doesn't make sense, or if there is a missing part, my summarizing technique vividly points it out.

Sharon, too, was always a good editor, with a finely tuned ear for the sound of language. One source of her skills, she believes, came from being a voracious reader.

Even as a youngster, I was a student of language. When I read, I always took note of what I later called the "finely wrought sentence." (I'm sure I didn't coin that phrase, but I have no idea where I first heard it.) I would marvel at the skill of such writers as George Orwell and Mark Twain, for example. As a student, unlike so many of my peers, I liked diagramming sentences. (As an English teacher, though, I never inflicted it on my students.) I still consciously examine sentence structure and language when I read popular novels—Steven King and Barbara Kingsolver are masters of language.

I always liked grammar, finding it easy to learn and to apply. As a result, I was a pretty good editor, even in high school. Later, as an English teacher, I was often pressed into service as an editor for other teachers who had graduate papers to do. I remember editing a dissertation on glaciers for a science teacher. I knew very little about glaciers, but I was able to edit by examining sentence structures and questioning the writer on his intent and identifying sentences that failed to advance his thesis clearly for his reader, along with fixing up punctuation and regular conventions of language.

EDITING FOR MORE THAN CONVENTIONS
OF WRITTEN LANGUAGE

Did you notice that in several of the preceding narratives, the writers extended their editing concerns beyond the familiar conventions of written language, such as, spelling, syntax, and punctuation? "Consider your reader," they suggested. They emphasized the need to refine word choice, sentence structure, flow, and variety of sentences, as well as being alert for unnecessary repetition and jargon.

In addition to her previous advice, Christine provided us with a list of editing problems that go well beyond surface conventions. She emphasizes the following common issues that can be serious problems for writers who do not attend to them:

- Use of the word *which* for the word *that*.
- Incorrect references.
- References left out of the reference section.
- References in the reference section but not in the body of the paper.
- Writing in a dry, academic tone.
- Excessive use of passive voice or unintentional switching between active and passive voices.
- Wordiness and redundancies.
- Writing that is boring and dull because it does not move readers forward.

We see the problems in Christine's list as very important and urge you to consult a stylebook for guidance in these and other areas.

The last four problems in Christine's list are closely connected to issues we would like to explore more thoroughly. The dry, academic tone we often criticize may be the result of excessive use of the passive voice and wordiness, which can produce unclear, boring text that does not "move the reader forward." We believe that the objections Christine raises here can be remedied through attention to clarity and pace. In the next section, we focus on the issues of clarity (i.e., clearly saying what you want to say in simple, straightforward prose) and pace (i.e., rhythm and movement forward).

Finally, we discuss editing for correctness; that is, for the surface errors that may interfere with readers' understanding or that, in publication, might reflect poorly on us as writers.

Editing for Clarity

Writers edit for clarity so that their readers can follow what they are trying to say. Donald Murray (2001) explains, "What we write is often correct, but the reader doesn't get it because it is not clear. We need to develop our drafts so the meaning is not only clear to us but to our skeptical reader" (p. 159). Strunk and White (2000) support Murray's ideas. Above all, "Be clear," they advise. "When you say something, make sure you have said it" (p. 79).

Toby Fulwiler (2002) notes that unlike editing for correctness, where we follow specified rules, editing for clarity "is more a matter of making choices than following rules" (p. 178). That means as authors, it is our responsibility to look for clutter in our work, and when we find it, we must "prune it away ruthlessly" (Zinsser, 2001, p. 17).

One way to edit for clarity is to remove confusion and untidiness at the word and phrase level of our manuscripts. Carefully scrutinize each word and phrase to make sure they are accurate and suit your audience. Vary vocabulary, cut unnecessary phrases and clauses, omit needless words, use active verbs, and weed out jargon (i.e., professional and work-specific words and terms that readers might not understand).

Too often, what Christine refers to as the "dry, academic tone" is the culprit in problems of clarity. This tone is frequently characterized by large words, convoluted sentence constructions, and use of jargon. It is, in fact, a genre of its own, and one that we work very hard at learning to be successful in the academy. Remember how Andrea Fishman and Debbie Dimmett adopted the voice of the academy as a matter of expediency, but they never believed it represented them well. Again, consider the audience for your writing; if it is your graduate professor who fervently abides by the old rules of academic writing, then, by all means, the formal, academic tone will be successful. However, if you aspire to write for real audiences, people who will actually read your work and be somehow moved by it, your tone should be more natural and the language accessible.

William H. Teale (1992), onetime editor of *Language Arts,* offers advice to aspiring writers about writing for professional journals. He says you are "writing for people who will read what you have to say.... [it's] not an academic exercise.... Don't pontificate, obfuscate, or otherwise 'jargonize.' You are writing for real people, not trying to reproduce the language of some poorly written textbook you used in a graduate course last year" (p. 114).

In editing for clarity, you will need to know your audience well and avoid lapsing into academic jargon if it is inappropriate. Look for excessive use of the passive voice. We don't mean to suggest that the passive voice is always inappropriate; it is, in fact, appropriate in some instances. The problem is that it has earned a bad reputation because of its role in producing objective, academic prose as we discussed in chapter 2. If you recall, many of us were cautioned to use third-person and "it" constructions to avoid introducing the personal in our research reports, as in "It was concluded that …" instead of "I concluded …"

Passive constructions change the dynamic of the sentence. The doer of the action is hidden behind the words and emphasis is shifted away from him or her. Remember Gary Natriello's plea in chapter 2 for writers to come out from behind the "curtain" and reveal themselves to their readers. There are times, though, even in informal discourse, when passive constructions are appropriate and effective. Intentional use of the passive shifts the focus of the sentence from the doer of the action to the receiver of the action. For example, in chapter 1, in Sharon's reflection about Freshman Comp 101, she originally used the sentence, "It was whispered that 101 had done them in." Janet edited it into the active voice: "We whispered that 101 had done them in." Sharon believed the active voice didn't work there. The emphasis was not on who whispered, but rather what was whispered. For that reason, the passive voice was more effective. Additionally, the passive voice suggests the conspiratorial nature of the whispering and echoes a commonly used phrase, "It was whispered that …" In other words, if you have used the passive voice in your writing, was it intentional and purposeful? If not, change it to the active voice.

We also suggest that you edit to ensure you have used parallel constructions that "repeat an identical grammatical pattern within the same sentence which creates symmetry and balance" (Fulwiler, 2002, p. 180). For example, Abraham Lincoln made effective use of parallelism in his Gettysburg Address: "Government *of the people, by the people, for the people* shall not perish from the earth" (Buscemi, Nicolai, & Strugala, 2000, p. 296). The repetition of prepositional phrases supports fluency and readability. Other forms of parallelism include presenting contrasting ideas in similarly constructed sentences, as in Shakespeare's "The evil that men do lives after them; the good is oft interred with their bones" (Buscemi et al., 2000, p. 297). A good stylebook will provide you with many additional examples.

Further, we urge you to delete worn-out clichés (e.g., "the tip of the proverbial iceberg"), and tired metaphors, such as "My principal threw down the gauntlet." Clichés and tired metaphors not only demonstrate a lack of originality, they make your writing uninteresting and boring. Try to think of fresh, original ways to express your ideas.

Gender-biased, or sexist language, can, in fact, be an issue of clarity for readers and writers. Its use is often the result of an earlier practice of using the neutral, or generic, *he* when the gender is not specified in a sentence. For example, some years ago, it was common to say, "A writer should carefully proofread his work." The assumption implicit in this construction is that writers are predominantly men. Too often the careful writer will correct this by writing, "A writer should carefully proofread his or her work." This creates a clumsy structure and can be overdone when the construction arises several times in a document. Then there is the increasing use of *s/he* as a way around the problem, but exactly how do you pronounce it? Increasingly, we are seeing constructions that result in an error of agreement: "Everyone should carefully proofread their work" (everyone = singular; their = plural). One effective revision to avoid gender bias as well as grammar problems would be to recast the sentence in the plural: "Writers should carefully proofread their work." Another solution is to alternate the use of male and female pronouns in successive paragraphs where you are using a series of examples, illustrations, and anecdotes. Be alert for these problems in your writing and be prepared to edit them effectively.

Being cautious about gender bias is important. According to the online *American Heritage Book of English Usage* (1996):

> There is little to be gained by offending people in your audience. It makes sense to educate yourself about the issues involved and to try to accommodate at least some of these concerns. Even if you are not convinced of the need for reforms to reduce gender bias, you ought to recognize that the use of language that has been called out as sexist can sometimes lead to ambiguity. Using a term like *policemen,* for instance, may leave your readers wondering whether you are excluding women police officers from the discussion or whether you are tacitly allowing *policemen* to stand for the entire police force. You owe it to your readers to be clear. (Para. 4–5)

Additionally, we need to be concerned about language that reflects cultural bias. Again, we don't want to offend any of our readers, so we must be aware of appropriate terms for the various cultural groups who are part of our readership.

Edit for concrete nouns (e.g., use *Persian* instead of *cat*). Concrete nouns, as opposed to abstract ones, enable the reader to "see" what you are saying. They "create a vivid and more lively reading experience" (Fulwiler, 2002, p. 179). Be cautious using adjectives and adverbs that don't contribute much to the text. In fact, Strunk and White (2000) suggest that you be stingy with adjectives and adverbs. "Write with nouns and verbs" (p. 71), they advise. (See Strunk & White, 2000, and Fulwiler, 2002, for in-depth discussions of these editing concerns.)

In addition to considering word choice, read each sentence in your manuscript, line by line, and determine if each one conveys exactly the ideas you intend. As you edit for clarity, keep asking yourself these two questions: "Am I saying what I want to say? And, am I saying it as clearly and as consistently as possible?"

Editing for Pace

Pace is an important editing consideration that is often ignored by authors of stylebooks and writing manuals (Murray, 2001). "Pace is the speed at which the writer causes the reader to move through the text" (Murray, 2001, p. 171). The pace "should be slow enough so the reader can absorb the information and its meaning, [and] fast enough to keep the reader interested" (Murray, 2001, p. 193). Pace, or movement, is the distinction between writing that reads at an agreeable speed and writing that is slow and tedious (Barzun, 2001). When the pace of a manuscript is sluggish, readers want to abandon it because they think, "Boy, this is boring."

Conversely, when a manuscript flows smoothly, readers want to continue reading what the author has to say. We've all read good novels that have moved us along in a smooth, rapid manner. We don't want to put these fast-paced novels down, and we read as fast as possible to discover what happened at the end of the story. There is no reason that academic writing cannot and should not flow as smoothly as fiction. But what steps might you take to ensure that your writing moves readers forward?

Robert Weir has a few suggestions for enhancing the tempo or pace of academic writing. He says, "Every time you make a general point, provide a clear example to illuminate it. In addition, write shorter sentences and paragraphs. Long passages where a reader isn't sure of a point, or has gotten it already are a sure path to tedium" (Personal communication, March 9, 2004).

Donald Murray (2001) also asserts that one way to speed up the pace of academic writing is to use shorter sentences and paragraphs. "Pace can be slowed down by longer words and longer sentences with clotting clauses," he tells us (p. 171). He also wants us to ask ourselves two questions as we consider the pace of our manuscripts: "How fast is fast enough? How much is enough?" (p. 172). Murray's questions are good examples of the editing choices all exemplary authors make. To determine how fast is fast enough (i.e., the pace of a manuscript and what information to delete) and how much is enough (i.e., how much information, explanation, and description to incorporate), we have to rhetorically consider our audience and the purpose of our writing. Lindal Buchanan defines rhetoric as a negotiation between the writer and the reader. She explains:

> *A rhetorical approach to writing considers the text as a negotiation of sorts. A writer attempts to accomplish a purpose (say to inform or persuade) with a particular audience (e.g., readers of a particular journal). All of this occurs in concert with the writer's audience and topic which in turn, dictates what style of writing is appropriate and ultimately determines what pace is needed in the manuscript.*

Christine Miranda, who we described as an "editorial whiz kid," points out that understanding your audience is critical to your decisions about pace. Christine tells us:

> I like to explain pace this way. I know a lot about indigenous plants and trees of Florida. If my writing audience already knows a lot about this topic I can speed up the pace of my manuscript. I don't have to supply so many definitions and "For examples." But if my audience knows little about Florida's indigenous plants and trees, I have to slow down my pace. I have to start at the beginning, and go slower and include lots of description and definitions.

According to Toby Fulwiler (2002), using headings throughout your manuscript can enhance its pace: Fulwiler believes that "subtitles do two things at once: they serve as categorizers for concepts and they operate as transitions from one concept to the next" (p. 22).

Fulwiler's comments about transitions are important. Jacques Barzun (2001) thinks making transitions from one paragraph to another often is difficult, especially for beginning writers. Therefore, some writers resort to inserting trite, unoriginal phrases to bridge sentence and paragraph gaps, such as "In addition to," "Nonetheless," and "On the other hand." We (Janet and Sharon) are guilty of using these types of transitional phrases, and we plan to monitor our writing more carefully so we can reduce our need for these kinds of transitions. "Each sentence should lead to the next and grow out of the last sentence of the previous paragraph" (Zinsser, 2001, p. 267).

Besides using shorter sentences and paragraphs and attending to transitions, another way to increase a manuscript's pace is to combine groups of words in ways that lead readers forward. For example, write in first person (I or we) and then use a strong verb. Write in the active voice whenever possible (Murray, 2001), and use standard syntax (the conventional order of words in a sentence) to give readers the feeling of forward motion (Barzun, 2001)

Here are a few other tips: Break up a series of long sentences by inserting some shorter ones, and convert short, choppy, awkward sentences into sentences that are rhythmic and pleasing. To provide a change, vary sentence patterns so that you don't begin each sentence with the same word phrase, or clause. Make sure your sentences contain a complete thought and never be afraid to break a long sentence into two short ones, or even three.

Editing for Correctness

Editing for correctness refers, of course, to the conventional notion of editing for style—fixing errors of punctuation, capitalization, spelling, and syntax (i.e., the order of the words at the sentence level). Such errors can divert readers' attention away from the information presented. Therefore, as authors, we need to check to make sure that we follow the accepted conventions or principles of written language because we want our readers to concentrate on what we have to say. For example, we use appropriate singular and plural possessives, (e.g., the teacher's lesson; two teachers' lessons). We end a question with a question mark. We insert commas where they are needed, and we spell words in standard English. These conventions of English serve as road maps for our readers as they travel through a manuscript.

As Georgia Heard (1995) notes, "It's good not to worry too much about punctuation in the beginning. But after a while. the punctuation [and other written language conventions] becomes part of what we're trying to say" (p. 125). Of course, if you've recently glanced through *Elements of Style* (Strunk & White, 2000), or Ross-Larsen's (1996) *Edit Yourself: A Manual for Everyone Who Works With Words*, you know there are more editing rules than you could possibly learn and we could conceivably cover here. We urge you to purchase one or two good stylebooks and refer to them often. However, Bill Walsh (2000), in his humorous stylebook, *Lapsing Into a Comma*, cautions, "It's relatively easy to pick a stylebook, any stylebook, and learn the rules it imposes. It's harder to apply those rules correctly and consistently, and harder still to truly understand the reasons behind the rules—and therefore know when they should be ignored" (p. 1). Walsh continues: "A finely-tuned ear is at least as important as formal grammar, and that's not something you can acquire by memorizing a stylebook" (p. 3).

We agree with Walsh. Since Robert Lowth wrote the first one in 1762, stylebooks have proven their worth. They can help us determine how to deal with the minute and rule-driven grammatical complexities of English. In addition to a good stylebook, we also recommend a good, current handbook of usage.

English usage continues to change with changing times, and we must be informed regarding what is currently acceptable. Informal usage creeps into formal usage, and new words come into the language while other words become obsolete. Think of all of the new terms brought into the language as a result of the Internet and the computer revolution. A common source of new words is the result of a relatively new practice called *verbing*, which, according to Slangsite.com (2001), is "the act of transforming a regular noun into a non-existent verb form." Specific examples include words commonly accepted in education, such as *conferencing*, and *mentoring*, and in economics, such as *offshoring*. Interestingly, when we typed the previous sentence, the Spell Check feature of Microsoft Word accepted the first two words (conferencing and mentoring) and rejected the last (offshoring). It also rejected verbing, which is not surprising. We imagine that newer versions of Word might accept offshoring. In any case, you will want to be certain that you use a lexicon that represents current accepted usage. Be careful with slang and colloquialisms that might suggest you lack an understanding of what is correct and acceptable.

KNOWING YOU ARE FINISHED EDITING

You've looked for your common errors, checked your word choice, and considered clarity and the pace of the text. You might still worry about whether or not there is more to do. Sandra Engoron-March explains how she knows she is finished and ready to get the final response from her writing group.

> I feel I've finished editing once the text sounds natural to me; that is, the language flows (no stops and starts), and there is a clear, logical progression of thought. When no more editing is required, I don't have to stop and re-read a sentence or paragraph to discover the intended meaning of the passage. Further editing is not required when the language of the text sounds natural to the ear and its meaning is evident.

Note her emphasis on achieving a natural quality in the language. It is this natural flow of our language, our voice, that makes us as the writer visible in the text, and makes the personal connection we strive for in our writing.

PERSONAL REFLECTIONS

By now, you are aware of the importance of editing. When you edit your writing, what do you look for? Do you edit like Janet and Sharon used to edit—on automatic pilot—or do you follow a plan like Lindal Buchanan, Christine Miranda, and Debbie Dimmett? Do you have a colleague or close friend on whom you depend? Do you have a "finely tuned ear" for language? How did you develop it? How might you develop it? Write your reflections.

IDENTIFYING EDITING ERROR PATTERNS

Sandra Engoron-March examined her own editing process and made a list of her common editing problems, making significant discoveries about her writing. She returned to a document she had written, revised, and published, and carefully examined the changes she had made in the first draft. From this examination, she was able to determine what editing issues were common in her writing.

In the area of clarity, Sandra discovered the following problems:

Omission of essential information.

Poor sentence construction.

Use of impersonal references, e.g., "the students" instead of "my students."

Failure to specify locations of foreign towns, cities, or states, i.e., Sonora (a northern, border state of Mexico).

Failure to present, at the beginning of an article, the initials to be used in its body, e.g., English Language Learners (ELL).

Wordiness, e.g., making unnecessarily explicit that which is already implicit in the text.

Improper order of adjectives, e.g., "English spoken language" as opposed to "spoken English language" or simply, "spoken English."

In the area of pace, Sandra discovered:

Overuse of pet phrases, e.g., "on the other hand," and "in terms of."

Attempting to cover too much content in one sentence.

Overuse of specific words, e.g., "assessment" instead of varying it with synonyms.

Undesirable formality, e.g., "I experienced great distress when I observed ..." instead of "I observed ..."

In the area of correctness, she discovered:

Omission or improper use of articles, e.g., "a," and "the."

Improper punctuation.

After completing this activity, Sandra reflected on the experience of examining her editing process:

Making this list of my most common mistakes on a first draft has directed my attention to weaknesses in my style. I had never created such a list before this one. I have learned the types of errors I need to look for, especially in the area of clarity. I expect that I will be able to write more effectively as a result of this activity. I recommend it.

PRACTICAL APPLICATIONS:
EXAMINING YOUR OWN EDITING PROCESS

As you have made your way through this book, we have asked you to engage in prewriting, drafting, and revising something personally and professionally important to you. Now we'd like to invite you to edit that piece, focusing on clarity, pace, and correctness. In addition to editing, though, we'd like you to look carefully at the kinds of editing you do and develop a list of writing problems that define your typical patterns of error. Record these problems and patterns in your Think-Writing Log.

Return to your first draft as well as your subsequent drafts, and examine the changes you made. How many of the changes had to do with clarity, pace, or correctness? Use your Think-Writing Log to date and record the editing decisions you made so you have a permanent record of your work. Activate your metacognitive abilities and monitor your editing decisions. Think about why you made specific editing decisions and write your reasons in your Think-Writing Log. What do these error patterns teach you about your writing practices? How will this knowledge help you in future writing endeavors?

SUMMARY

In this chapter, we intentionally chose not to provide an extensive list of editing rules for you to follow. There are many good stylebooks and usage handbooks on the market to which you can turn for writing rules. Our intentions were to raise your awareness of the importance of editing and develop your ability to take charge of the editing process.

As we wrote this chapter, we gained a new respect for the editing phase of writing. We also raised our levels of consciousness about editing. We no longer believe that editing is boring and dull. We no longer edit on automatic pilot either. We discovered that editing can be just as exciting as the other stages of the writing process.

Editing differs considerably from revision. Revision entails discovery of new information, and adding or changing ideas that are distinctly the domain of writers. Only authors can revise their work.

Exemplary writers edit for three purposes: to achieve clarity, to enhance the pace, and to correct surface errors. Clarity refers to how clearly the ideas are presented at the word and sentence level. To make writing as clear as possible, authors remove clutter and untidiness. They vary vocabulary, cut unnecessary phrases, omit needless words, and weed out jargon and sexist and biased language. They also delete worn-out clichés, get rid of tired metaphors and are judicious with the use of adjectives and adverbs.

The pace of a manuscript keeps readers moving forward. Not many stylebooks or writing texts discuss the importance of pace. Yet, the pace of a manuscript determines if readers will want to continue reading what authors have to say. Some suggestions for speeding up the pace of a manuscript are writing shorter sentences and paragraphs, alternating between long and short sentences, inserting subheadings, making smooth transitions, and using strong verbs. Write in the active voice, if possible, and craft the order of the words at the sentence level (i.e., the syntax) to move readers forward.

Editing for correctness involves attention to universally accepted rules to detect and mend errors of punctuation, capitalization, spelling, and syntax. Professional editors and editing-savvy colleagues and friends can point out these sorts of written language convention problems.

In summary, just as in other stages of the writing process, we need to make choices as we edit. The main consideration is to become consciously aware of the importance of editing and to rhetorically consider our readers. That means we have to step back once more from our writing self and become a reader of our own writing.

RELEVANT READINGS

Bartleby.com: Great Books Online. (2004). Retrieved March 31, 2004, from http://www.bartleby.com/reference/

This Web site is a virtual library of reference materials: encyclopedias, thesauri, dictionaries, handbooks of English usage (including the 1918 version of Strunk & White), books of quotations, gazetteers, fact books, literature and history, and much, much more. The American Heritage Book of English Usage (1996), available through this site, is an extremely valuable resource. The URL also links to an extensive online library of classic books.

Harnack, A., & Kleppinger, E. (2001). *Online! A reference guide to using Internet sources.* Boston: Bedford/St. Martin's

This little handbook provides detailed explanations and models for citing online documents, Web sites, newsgroups, listservs, e-mail messages, and many other aspects of the World Wide Web. MLA, APA, Chicago, and CBE are fully represented. It is an essential resource for anyone who uses the Internet for research and support for academic writing.

Ross-Larson, B. (1996). *Edit yourself: A manual for everyone who works with words*. New York: Norton.

Ross-Larson believes that by learning to write clearly, we learn to think clearly. In the first part of the book he offers suggestions for improving common problems of writing, such as what he calls "hop scotching" between the words which *and* that. *The second section of the book provides an alphabetized list of more than 1,500 recommendations for common cuts, changes, and comparisons that editors make to produce writing that is clear, concise, and effective.*

Strunk, W., & White, E. B. (2000). *The elements of style* (4th ed.). Boston: Allyn & Bacon.

This timeless, tiny reference book offers rules and principles of writing in simple, succinct language. The authors are direct and waste few words. They believe writers should not overwrite or overstate. Writers should use orthodox spelling and simplify.

Truss, L. (2003). *Eats, shoots, and leaves: The zero tolerance approach to punctuation*. New York: Gotham Books.

Those of us who cringe upon seeing signs in grocery stores, in front of apartment buildings, or on passing city buses that prove large numbers of people cannot distinguish between plural and possessive forms will be delighted with this little book. Truss not only takes sign makers to task for egregiously misusing the apostrophe ("egg's, $1.29 a dozen"); she also berates those who misuse and abuse commas, dashes, semicolons, and even the little-used hyphen. She presents the rules of punctuation with grace and humor, offering examples of errors throughout the history of the English language, while calling for greater attention to correct usage today. If you, like Truss, are a "stickler," barely able to restrain yourself from carrying a marker and single-handedly correcting those public errors, you will love this surprise bestseller.

Chapter 7

Integrating the Personal
and the Professional

*If you find yourself consciously avoiding any mention of the personal in your profes-
sional writing, ask yourself why you are doing it.... If it's only because you think you
shouldn't, it might be worth reexamining your assumptions. (Rankin, 2001, p. 69)*

*As a writer your goal is to find voices within yourself. These voices will, of course, be
colored by many outside influences including the books you've read, the people you
know ... but all of these influences should pass through filters of your own psyche and
come out imbued with your own touch. (Gardner, 2001, p. 1)*

In chapter 1, we explored who we are as writers, looking back on those experiences that have defined our identities and shaped the kind of writers we
are now. We examined the traditional conflict between personal and professional writing in chapter 2. In the next four chapters, we offered an overview of the writing process. Although we presented these stages in a linear,
chapter-by-chapter rendering, one of our goals was to blur the boundaries
between the stages, emphasizing the recursive nature of writing. Also, we
hoped you would be able to find yourself at various points along the way.
Throughout the text, we invited our friends and colleagues, and called on
noted experts in the field of writing, to tell their stories. As you read and
considered these stories, we suspect you discovered that you have much in
common with these writers. By the same token, we'd like for you to see just
how different they are from you and from each other. We believe that both
the commonalities and the differences bring us together as writers who

179

share a common destination, but who sometimes follow quite different routes to get there.

In this chapter, we'd like to explore the challenge of connecting the personal and the professional and to guide your thinking as you seek final direction for the journey you have begun. Again, writers' stories provide the guideposts.

WRITING IN YOUR OWN VOICE

As we dealt with the various stages of the writing process, we emphasized the importance of situating yourself in your writing. We wanted you to think about the use of the personal "I" in your academic writing and to think about how to be *in* the writing even when the personal "I" is not permitted. We wanted you to be aware of when, where, and under what circumstances personal narrative and an experiential approach to writing is acceptable and even invited. When we do not put ourselves into our writing, not only might it lack voice and passion, it might not communicate effectively.

Tilly Warnock (2003), writing professor at the University of Arizona, tells the story of an undergraduate who came to the Writing Center with a draft of a book review that was largely unintelligible. In the conference, she listened as the young woman spoke clearly and convincingly about her ideas and wondered why her writing bore such little resemblance to what she had said. After the young woman made unsuccessful efforts to revise for clarity, Warnock realized that the clarity of her spoken ideas was characterized by the personal "I," but that pronoun was nowhere in the draft. When she asked her why, the young woman explained, sincerely, that "she was not supposed to, … that was what she was taught" (p. 530). The poorly written draft came about as a result of her "ingenuity in expressing her views without using the first person pronoun" (p. 530). Once she was given permission to use "I," her writing became clear.

This incident illustrates the effect of writing "outside" of ourselves. This young woman had not mastered the academic voice she believed was required. As a result, her writing was unintelligible. All of us, however, can benefit from identifying and confronting the theories and rules that inhibit us when we write. Are you afraid to reveal yourself in your professional writing? Have you been taught that the personal pronoun has no place in your writing? Does it work for you as a writer? If not, think about what Rankin (2001) means when she tells us we should reexamine our assumptions about writing. In chapter 1, we urged you to consider your writing history and to define yourself as a writer. Your memories and your writer's identity may help you uncover the origins of these assumptions and understand better how they affect your writing today. If you believe the personal "I," or a narrative stance, has no place in your writing, where did this idea come from? Are you committed to changing your thinking?

It is not surprising that the young woman in Warnock's tale needed permission to use the personal pronoun in her academic writing. Often, the injunction against it begins in high school, with well-meaning teachers carefully schooling their college-bound students to avoid it at all costs. They perpetuate the myth that "I" has no place in college and university writing. In fact, many incoming freshmen bring with them a practiced "pseudo-academic" voice they used successfully in their advanced high school classes. The more talented among them will gain credibility with their college professors as they develop skill in actually communicating the intended information through this disembodied voice. When that happens, it becomes all the more difficult to reclaim our real voices in either the undergraduate or graduate setting.

Andrea Fishman describes the events that led to the liberation of her voice.

I was a good writer. A successful English major. A graduate student who could churn out twenty pages of academic writing without breaking a sweat or a rule. As far back as tenth grade in a New York City public high school, I had developed strategies for leaving myself out of my writing. I could efface myself from beginning to end, disappearing behind pithy quotes from respected sources. I was a rhetorical magician: now you see me, now you don't. I hid behind the words of my betters and they/we/I got A's. Until my doctoral program began, that is.

At the age of 35, with 13 years of high school teaching experience and a master's (degree) + 15 (credits) in hand, I got my first ever "See me" paper. No grade. Just "See me" where the grade should have been.

"You wanted to see me?" I winced, standing in the doorway of his office. Professor Botel looked up, flashed his leading-man smile, and invited me to sit down. I was clutching the offending document in my lap.

Botel looked at the paper in my hand then looked at me. He began by saying that he knew, by many measures, I was a good writer. (I exhaled.) In fact, I had written a substantial, well-researched piece. (I actually breathed.) But he had to ask: "Where are you in that paper?"

Where was I? What kind of question was that? I was where I was supposed to be: nowhere. Missing, and without a trace, I hoped. "What do you mean?" was all I could muster.

"I want to hear your voice," Botel explained. "I want to know what you think."

In that moment my life changed forever. I could not believe what I had heard, but 30 minutes of professor–student conference persuaded me that Profes-

sor Morton Botel—he who was always named in the pantheon of stars at Penn—actually meant what he said. Neither my classmates nor I had been admitted to this doctoral program in Writing because the faculty saw us as traditional students or potential professional clones. Rather, we had been admitted because the faculty wanted to learn from and with us as much as we expected to learn from them.

"You bring knowledge and experience we all need to share," Botel told me. "We don't expect you to silence yourself. Quite the contrary, we expect you to develop and hone your own voice. That's why you're here. To be part of the program."

Were those Mort Botel's exact words to me in July of 1982? Probably not. With the exception of his initial concerted stare and opening question, I'm fairly sure the preceding scene is what we'd now call memoir or even creative nonfiction. Yet it is as true as Truth can be, for it conveys the message he sent—and the lesson I learned—26 years ago. Writers should be in their writing, and readers should hear writers' voices, English majors and doctoral candidates notwithstanding. Unless, of course, you believe that knowledge is separate from the knower; lives are separate from those who live them; and you can always distinguish the dancer from the dance. In 1982, I began to question those beliefs. For two years I struggled to overcome them for—like many bad habits—they had seemed to serve me well.

Sharon and Janet remember, like Andrea, learning how to maintain invisibility in our academic writing. The younger generation of educators, perhaps, have benefited from the more liberalized approach to writing that is becoming more common in colleges and universities today (see chapter 2). Keep in mind, though, that it is extremely difficult to get doctoral committees to accept the use of a first-person, personal voice in a dissertation, unless, of course, it is an ethnographic study. It is encouraging, however, that a number of scholarly journals are inviting teachers' stories, personal narratives of teacher research studies.

LETTING YOUR VOICE BE HEARD

One way to find yourself in your writing is to examine it to determine whether or not your voice is heard in the text. So much has been said about voice in writing, but it remains a mysterious element for many writers. Exactly what does it mean? How do we convey voice in our writing and why is it important?

Murray (1989) describes voice as "the key element in effective writing. It is what attracts the reader and communicates to the reader. It is that element that gives the illusion of speech.... It is the music in writing that makes the meaning clear" (p. 150). When we write, he says, we adapt our own personal voices to the written language and convey our subject to the audience we have in mind. He urges us to "hear what we're writing as we write it" (p. 151), to "write with our ear" (p. 223).

Sheridan Baker (1976) emphasizes the importance of voice when he insists on writing "in the language of intelligent conversation.... [Your writing] should be alive with a human personality—yours—which is probably the most persuasive rhetorical force on earth. Good writing should have a voice, and the voice should be unmistakably your own" (p. 8).

According to the Northwest Regional Educational Laboratory (NWREL) rubric[1] for assessing voice in student writing, teachers should look for specific characteristics in the writing to rate the writer's use of voice. The rubric describes the successful use of voice as follows: "The writer speaks directly to the reader in a way that is individual, compelling, and engaging. The writer crafts the writing with an awareness and respect for the audience and the purpose for writing."

In an effort to provide teachers more guidance in assessing voice, the rubric includes descriptions of what this might look and feel like to a reader:

- The tone of the writing adds interest to the message and is appropriate for the purpose and audience.
- The reader feels a strong interaction with the writer, sensing the person behind the words.
- The writer takes a risk by revealing who he or she is consistently throughout the piece.
- Expository or persuasive writing reflects a strong commitment to the topic by showing why the reader needs to know this and why he or she should care.
- Narrative writing is honest, personal, and engaging and makes you think about, and react to, the author's ideas and point of view.

In many parts of the country, state writing assessments use the 6 + 1 rubric to assess student writing, and elementary, middle, and high school students are expected to demonstrate effective use of voice, among other things, in writing. Such state assessments are not without controversy in various parts of the country, but beyond that, given that youngsters are now focusing on voice in their writing assignments, should we, also, be examining voice and what it means to us as professional and academic writers?

---

[1]The NWREL 6+1 Traits™ rubric is based on research into what effective writers do. It assesses the following writing traits: Ideas and Content, Organization, Voice, Sentence Fluency, Word Choice, and Conventions. The +1 trait, Presentation, is optional. The rubric and related materials are available at nwrel.org, or http://www.nwrel.org/assessment/department.asp?d=1.

If, in fact, voice is important in writing, doesn't it follow that we should find ourselves inextricably bound up in that which we are writing? Should we not be "honest, personal and engaging," and invite our reader to "feel a strong interaction with" us, "sensing the person behind [our] words"? In chapter 2, we cited Toby Fulwiler (2002), who pointed out the importance of belief and persuasion in college writing. Remember, he says that writers must believe in what they write, and then, through language, must persuade readers that what they say is true. Although he also honors objectivity, his emphasis of "truth" as a guiding factor in our writing seems to be supported by the descriptions of voice in the NWREL rubric, specifically that the reader recognizes the writer's commitment to the topic and that the writer takes a risk by revealing himself or herself in the writing.

How do we do that? How do we help the reader sense our presence in the text? How do we, as writers, speak to our readers? How do we convey our belief and commitment to our topic? How do we convey the "meanings that are not within the world"? as Murray (1989, p. 223) says. Do we really want to take the risk of revealing ourselves in the writing, to reveal our character along with the text (Murray, 1989)?

We wish we could answer these questions simply. We wish it could be as simple as just telling you to use the personal "I" in your writing. Unfortunately, voice is not exclusive to first-person writing. It should be, of course, explicit in that mode, but it should be implicit even when we are not writing in the first person. Perhaps, though, it is through our first-person narratives that we can discover our voice and then focus on how to use voice more effectively in other writing modes.

Murray (1989) describes his own process of dictating his writing, which allows him to monitor his voice, pace, and rhythm. He suggests that you go back and read aloud as you write, and if you use a word processor, turn off the screen and write, listening to yourself as you do it. When you go back to read it later, you should be able to make changes that lead to the voice you want your reader to hear. He urges us to listen for our voices as we rehearse lines in our heads, as we draft.

Revealing ourselves in our writing can be risky. How much of us should we put into our texts? Michael Robinson (2003), a Teaching Advisor in the writing program at the University of Arizona, describes his ambivalence about his writing and its potential to reveal too much of himself.

> As much as writing has always been my lens, into myself and onto the world, I have never completely trusted it.... Do we ever completely trust the things that compel us, the things to which we must either submit if we want to stay whole, or deny by surrendering a piece of ourselves? I have a nagging suspicion that my writing will never be satisfied until I have exposed every scrap of error, sorrow, fear that I have ever endured. And so in every text I compose,

even the writing in my journal, I negotiate between the need for expression and the desire for safety, the impulse to protect myself and the drive to tell my own small version of the truth. (pp. 188–189)

For Robinson, the risk is great, but yet he writes. For most of us, however, it's a matter of believing in ourselves, and in our own voices, which can bring our individual truths to the page.

Throughout this book, you have heard the voices of teachers, professors, and our colleagues in their stories and reflections. Go back and re-read some of these and listen to the voices you hear. All of them are, of course, first-person, "I" stories, and as such they express deeply personal experiences and firmly held beliefs of the storytellers. We hear their voices explicitly in these reflections. However, these writings are not typical of the writing we, as professional educators, must do. In fact, unless we keep a personal, or teaching journal, we don't often have the opportunity to indulge ourselves through this kind of writing. However, we can learn something about the character of our personal voices through such informal, reflective writing. We can locate ourselves in these informal texts and then use that to move forward in the search for voice in our academic and professional writing.

PERSONAL REFLECTIONS

Go back to the previous reflections you wrote as you read through this book. Try to "hear" your own voice in them. Read them aloud. Find the natural rhythm in your writing. What "rules" do you commonly break? An occasional fragment, perhaps? What do you hear in your text? Who is the you that is revealed in these informal writings? Now, look at some of your professional or academic writings. Find one you really like, one that was satisfying to write. Are there commonalities between this one and your informal ones? Find one you really hated. What are the differences? Which one represents your voice? Reflect on your experience of comparing these different writings. Write your reflections.

MERGING VOICE AND ACADEMIC WRITING

To what extent is your voice welcome in your professional and academic writing expectations? To what extent are you free to use first person in your writing? The controversy over the use of the personal "I" in academic writing is, in many respects, a controversy over voice. What is the voice of the academy? Is there a collective voice or are multiple voices welcome? What are the characteristics of those voices that are welcome in the academy? In chapter 2, we explored the formal voice—objective, sometimes obscure, and sometimes inaccessible—that is commonly associated with academic writing.

Debbie Dimmett, on beginning her doctoral program, describes the conflict of voices in the writing expectations.

> *I don't always find myself in my writing [for the program]. The more structured the writing assignment, the more contrived and unnatural my writing seems to be. For example, I am writing a case study for one of my classes. Even though the research is qualitative, the structure of the reporting almost has the feel of a quantitative study. I want to write a narrative, almost like a story. The professor on the other hand, wants me to have sections that refer to the rationale, theoretical framework, literature review, data collection, data analysis, findings, discussion, and implications. Okay, I know this is all well and good, but it leads to uninspiring and uninteresting writing. I want to write like the authors of the books that professors hail as being so interesting you could read it in one sitting. This style of writing just doesn't do that.*

It's interesting that Debbie's professors seem to promote reading texts that are engaging and interesting, but they do not expect their students to write such texts. They encourage and accept qualitative research, but they expect a traditional, formal writing structure based on a quantitative model. Perhaps they are on the cusp of change, but simply not there yet.

No doubt, because she lives a block from the campus, Debbie's choice of universities might have been influenced by geography. But what if geographical convenience isn't a factor? What do we need to know before we enroll in a university program? Is it possible to find one that welcomes the more personal voice in academic writing? How does one investigate the program's philosophy? Andrea Fishman offers thoughts based on her experience.

> *I understand, now, that there is no monolithic Academy (if there ever was one). Instead, there are different academies with different expectations, each existing in and writing for its own reality.*
>
> *Not that I knew or even wondered about these aspects of doctoral life when I chose my doctoral program. I made my selection topically (which I suspect is the #1 criterion, followed closely by geographic and financial accessibility). I'd never heard of a doctoral program in Writing before I heard about Penn's. I'd never even heard of Rhetoric and Composition as a field of study,*

traditional English (read: Literature) major that I was. So when friends in my small central Pennsylvania hometown introduced me to people from Penn, I was too naïve to wonder about their rhetorical perspective and expectations. It was not until my first summer in Philadelphia that I learned another local university had a writing program—one in which doctoral research was quantitative instead of qualitative and one requiring courses in statistics as well as decontextualized, "laboratory experiments" with human subjects. But I'd found my congenial home by accident because I knew no other way. (I do not recommend that strategy for such a major investment.)

For Andrea, then, investigating a program prior to enrollment had not occurred to her. It was serendipity that led her to a university with a program that invited her to engage in qualitative research and to express herself both personally and professionally in her academic writing. She has important advice for others, though.

Now I tell people considering doctoral pursuits to ask my unrecognized questions before they enroll, even before they apply. Ask what kinds of research professors in a prospective program do. Ask what kinds of research they expect graduate students to do. Ask to see dissertation proposals they approved. Do stories count as data? Are case studies encouraged? Do they worry about regression analyses? Controlling for variables? How big must N be, anyway? If the answers are no, no, yes, yes, and "big," you know what kind of academic writing their world values: the kind I was once so good at. The kind in which Mort Botel couldn't find me. Personally, I'm just glad he kept looking.

Many of our contributing writers have described negative experiences in their efforts to come to terms with this academic voice. As Andrea said of her academic writing, "I was where I was supposed to be: nowhere. Missing, and without a trace I hoped." Others, like Debbie Dimmett, learned how to write in that voice to satisfy professors, even though they felt marginalized and unconnected to it. Although Debbie and Andrea have a good deal in common, we sense that Andrea was a bit more comfortable with her practiced academic voice than Debbie was. Debbie resented her capitulation to her professors and wrote to fulfill the requirements. There is a certain pride in Andrea's voice when she says she "could churn out twenty pages of academic writing without breaking a sweat or a rule." She recognized her talent and enjoyed her success. It did not occur to her that she belonged in the text until Morton Botel challenged her absence.

Debbie recently began to assert herself and insist on having her voice heard. She decided that she can combine her personal connection with Caribbean culture and the Haitian community of educators with whom she works with the academic demands of the program. She says:

> *Just recently I made the decision to expand on my future dissertation topic in a way that was previously discouraged by one of my professors. Initially, I wanted to focus my research on finding alternative teaching methods for Haitian teachers who have no books or teaching materials in their classrooms and where public and school libraries just don't exist. One of my professors strongly nudged me into another area. She really wanted me to pursue an oral history project I have been working on for three, going on four, years. Another professor agreed that this would be the quickest and easiest way to finish. I could always pursue those other interests later. A couple days ago, I attended a workshop on place-based education. As I chatted it up over lunch with another doctoral student in my department, I realized that there was nothing stopping me (short of an unfriendly dissertation committee) from combining both areas. As soon as I arrived home, I began typing up all of my ideas.*
>
> *I would complete a two-part dissertation. The first part would be looking at a specific Tucson model of an oral history project and a place-based education initiative. Since I'm teaching these techniques to Haitian teachers, I would focus the second part of my research on the application of these in a developing country where the resources are so scarce. My husband referred to this as my life's work.*

Debbie is determined, to the extent it is possible, to keep herself in her academic writing and to write about that which is both personally and professionally important to her, and hopefully she will succeed. Earlier in this book, you met other doctoral candidates who demanded and found their voices through their academic writing. Remember Ramona Moore Chauvin's experience writing her dissertation (chapter 2), which she said, "helped me to reclaim pieces from my past that are continually helping me to construct who I am as an individual and as a teacher." Kim Shea (chapter 2) declared that her "voice deserves to be heard, and it will be heard even though my voice may not be the traditional voice of the academy.... What is the point of being in the academy if I cannot express myself in writing from the perspective of my African American heritage? I feel a need to control my own texts."

THE UNIVERSITY AS A COMMUNITY OF VOICES

In some ways, universities are honoring and accepting a variety of voices among their professional staff, even as they demand more traditional writing of their graduate students. The University of Arizona is an example. By way of introducing first-year composition students to the writing community in the university, it publishes an anthology, entitled *The University Book: An Anthology of Writings from the University of Arizona* (Nowotny-Young, Miller, Baliani, & Price, 2003). This book is a collection of essays, research papers, articles, poems, and stories that provides students "with a general sense of the university as a diverse community of writers" (p. 1). The writers represent different fields of study throughout the university from poet and writer Luci Tapahanso to Dr. Andrew Weil, whose work with alternative medicine is internationally recognized. Virtually all instructional programs are represented: the composition and English programs, of course, but also astronomy, engineering, medicine, and so on. The book presents a variety of voices and approaches to writing and clearly illustrates that any definition of academic writing must be broad-based and inclusive.

The anthology presents many models for writing in the university that enable undergraduates to "think critically about the university as an institution" (p. 14), and how they, as initiates in this community, can, in fact, influence it. By focusing on the variety of rhetorical situations they will encounter when writing for the academy, they come to understand their own relationship to the institution more clearly while they hone their own writing skills. The range of voices in this anthology is remarkable. Even so, Debbie Dimmett's experience makes us wonder about the extent of any universitywide commitment to the same goals for graduate students.

It is important to remember that using your own voice in your academic writing is not dependent on using the first person and telling your own stories. When we believe in the topic, it is much easier to express ourselves and to tell the "truth" as we know it. One of the descriptors of voice in writing, from the NWREL rubric, points out that the "writing reflects a strong commitment to the topic" and makes clear the reader's need for the information and its value. If we believe in what we are saying, we should feel free to allow our voices to emerge in the text. In that way, we will be more convincing and the reader will be engaged more deeply.

WRITING FROM CLASSROOM TEACHERS

Rod Winters (1992), a teacher at Orchard Hill Elementary School in Cedar Falls, Iowa, finds irony in the fact that many classroom teachers who have helped their students find their voices and write freely cannot find their own voices. He asks, "How do we redefine professional writing to include ourselves?" (p. 81). He suggests that, as readers of professional writing, we have this notion that it's all about someone writing what is true for them for an audience of readers who do not share that truth. He believes that we are often stymied by the fear that we cannot well serve this audience, so we should write first for ourselves, finding our own insights, meanings, and truths.

Further, he suggests that we must get beyond the idea that we can't put ourselves into the writing, that we must remain objective. Classroom teachers' voices derive from "personally meaningful questions" (Winters, 1992, p. 83), so why should we value only "third person, detached writing" (p. 83)? He cites the publication of Lucy Calkins's (1983) *Lessons from a Child* as proof that "research needs to be understood in terms of the researcher and the context at least as much as in terms of the content" (p. 83). He believes we have confused the scientific and the professional, that we have "distanced ourselves right out of the picture" (p. 83). He urges classroom teachers to take advantage of their "unique position to write from their own perspective about the day-in, day-out experience of the classroom" (p. 83).

"Perhaps the reason many teachers don't write about teaching is that we have forgotten that we can have a voice; forgotten that we have a right to bring to the page the voice of who we are, what we are, and where we are" (Winters, 1992, p. 84). There are avenues for educators, both in the academy and in public and private school settings, to follow that will support their efforts to find and raise their voices.

When Heather Brown was struggling with her ideas for the article she would eventually write about her teacher research, she initially thought she might just work from her research report and revise it for the journal audience who would, she hoped, eventually read it. However, you may remember that she feared doing so would position her as an expert, a role in which she was not comfortable. She wrote about her classroom, telling the story of how she ultimately shared power in the classroom with her students and created a classroom in which students were more motivated to learn and in which they all learned from each other. Originally, however, she wondered if the article should be more about herself as an Anglo woman in a Native American school, but in the end, it related more to her identity as a teacher.

> *Re-reading my reflection of a year ago, when I first conceived of the focus of my article, it occurred to me that my ideas of what my article would be and what actually occurred was not that different. What is different is that the article is not so much about the cultural differences between me and my students, and any conflicts that might arise from this, but more of the assumptions that I made as a teacher.*

In writing about her classroom and her teaching experience, Heather enacted the thinking of Rod Winters (1992), who asserted the right of classroom teachers to bring their voices and themselves to the page. In the long run, doing the writing may be the easy part; putting it out there for an anonymous audience is exceedingly difficult for some. Heather completed the article and submitted it to the *English Journal*. Once the article was written and submitted, Heather realized just how scary it is to put yourself so deeply into your writing and then to submit it to public scrutiny.

> *The thought of publishing my article really makes me nervous. In fact, I would feel very relieved if it was rejected, because, by publishing, I expose myself. My ideas, my words, are laid out for nationwide criticism. I have built up enough tough skin to not take criticisms from my writing group personally, and in the small group, I can incorporate their suggestions into my writing. But after publishing, the audience is huge, anonymous, and there is no space to incorporate their suggestions or to defend my thinking. There is no more revision. It's done. There is nothing more I can do. I change my thinking, sure, but the document remains there, permanent, a constant reminder.*

In spite of her fears, Heather was delighted when her article was accepted for publication. "Walking Into the Unknown: Challenging Assumptions and Overcoming Resistance to Research in the English Classroom" was scheduled to appear in the November 2004, issue of the *English Journal*.

BENEFITING FROM A WRITING GROUP

A number of the contributors you have met while reading this book have been or are members of ongoing writing groups. Sharon's Southern Arizona Writing Program group began, in part, as a result of our book proposal and the members' desire to publish the outcomes of their teacher research projects. Janet's Round Table began in response to the needs of her graduate students and colleagues to find a supportive community for their writing requirements. Each summer, across the nation, at the invitational institutes of the NWP, teachers come together to write and to learn about teaching writing. It is a common practice for writing groups that formed in a summer institute to continue meeting, sometimes for years, after their summer work has concluded. A supportive community, once found, is difficult for some of us to abandon.

Writing groups serve a number of functions, not the least of which is providing feedback on ideas for writing, on drafts, and on their subsequent revisions and editing. Perhaps one of the most overlooked functions, however, is serving as a forum for raising our voices in a supportive community. When writing groups meet, there is a great deal of talk, which is not always focused on someone's drafts and resolving writing dilemmas. Sometimes the talk involves venting frustrations, arguing issues, and just plain gossip. Sharon's experience with the Southern Arizona Writing Project group may be typical of some writing groups.

We almost always met at Deborah's house on a Sunday morning. It was very rare for us to begin a session by jumping right into someone's draft. We always started with coffee and conversation before getting down to business. Then we'd get busy, and after some serious writing support, we'd break and over lunch have more conversation. Afterwards, it was usually back to the business at hand. Sometimes I wondered if we were wasting time with our chatting and gossiping and laughing, and if I should insist that we get back to work. However, I began to see that these informal conversations served a number of purposes.

First, it allowed us to relax and reestablish community and a sense of group comfort. We had, of course, met many times before, either as a writing group or in our collaborations for teacher research, so there was a strong sense of community. I came to believe that this conversation time was an important group "ritual," and I was more tolerant of the time it seemed to take from our work.

Second, the conversation raised issues and helped us clarify our thinking on issues that we cared about. At times, we discovered new insights into topics for consideration and came up with ideas for future writing endeavors.

Third, and perhaps most important, it validated our voices. It was a forum in which ideas were encouraged and respected. We believed in what we had to say and we gathered strength from our mutual respect and support.

Janet describes the dynamics of the Round Table writing group at the University of South Florida similarly to Sharon—lots of talk and support, and also laughter.

One particular meeting sticks in my mind. It was near the end of the semester, and we continued for the third week in a row to devote a portion of our time discussing the processes of revision and editing. We had become fascinated with the power of revision, but we still had some confusions about the differences between revision and editing. We became so animated in our discussion that a few colleagues down the hall stopped in to ask what we were doing. They thought we were having a party. "Revision and editing?" they asked incredulously, when we explained our topic of discussion. They couldn't believe we could be so animated about writing. Well, for some reason, we thought that was REALLY funny, and we laughed for quite a while, which sent our colleagues out of our room. Then, Karen Kelly remarked, "Imagine us laughing our heads off, disturbing others, and having so much fun about revising and editing."

Writing groups, then, can be critical for us not only to find our voices but to raise them as well. Perhaps this kind of informal discourse can lead us to expressing our voices more emphatically and more confidently when we set out to write our ideas for a reading audience.

What did being in the writing group mean to those who participated in our Southern Arizona Writing Program group? Deborah, who completed an article for an NWP publication, had this to say:

> *To begin with I was intrigued by the idea of a writing group because I felt I lacked the discipline to improve my writing on my own. I thought that being responsible to the group and getting their feedback would help me stay on course and do the writing I knew I would have to do if my writing was to improve. I got a great deal out of seeing how each person went about the process of writing and how the subjects changed over time. We all started out with these lofty goals to write articles or books, and gradually the writing evolved into personal pieces. I thought I was going to write this very "objective" article about becoming a teacher researcher. I thought I was really connected to the subject, but when it came down to it I didn't have that much to say, or rather I didn't know how to put what I had learned into words.*

Deborah continued to struggle with her conflict between the objective, scientific voice and the personal voice of the teacher researcher.

> *I enjoyed the sort of theoretical discussions that we had about education and writing even when it didn't have much to do with what I was writing. The discussion made me think more deeply about a lot of issues and I'm sure that was in some way reflected in my writing. I have always wanted to write as well as I read. I haven't aspired to be a professional writer; I just wanted to be a good writer.*

Heather Brown pointed out how being a member of the group kept her writing.

> *The group made me accountable; I had to write. This alone made me write more, and by writing more, the process for me has become one that is more fluid, less frightening, less daunting. The feedback from the writing group, both the critical and the positive, has been extremely beneficial to me as well. Critical comments are always useful, but the encouragement I received from the group was very motivating. I can't imagine ever having the courage to submit an article to a scholarly journal, but I did. Regardless of whether or not I am published, I feel accomplished. I wrote an article. I submitted it. I made the first step.*

> *I think in general, I feel more confident about my writing abilities. I feel capable. I don't feel as overwhelmed when faced with writing projects. I know myself better as a writer. I understand my methods, so I just go with it. I just write.*

For both Deborah and Heather, participating in a writing group helped them understand themselves and define themselves better as writers.

DETERMINING WHAT CONSTITUTES PROFESSIONAL WRITING

Sometimes we forget that when teachers write, it isn't always for their academic pursuits or for professional journals. Sometimes, educators just have to find what is important to them and follow their hearts.

Sandra Engoron-March made a serious change in course from where she began with our writing group. At the beginning of our project, she was working on a potential article about the challenges of teaching special education students and why, in the face of incredible pressures, she chooses to persevere and continue teaching these very needy students. Sandra struggled with her article, recognizing with each draft that her descriptions of her noisy boiler room office, with cracked, peeling paint, and its crowded, inhospitable environment were just depressing. Try as she might, she couldn't find the words or the voice to explain why, in spite of all of this, she chose to stay.

Eventually, she put the article aside to work on a grant proposal, which the group helped her with. She felt positive and encouraged, and she was awarded the grant. She couldn't make herself go back to her original article and so she cast about for something that would be personally meaningful for her. She decided to write and illustrate a children's book. Our writing group supported her efforts, but, most significantly, she involved her students as test readers. Her book was about a personal experience, an unusual encounter with a family of Gambel quails, a well-loved common ground bird of the Southwest that travels in family groups from the time their eggs are hatched. As the group supported Sandra through her early drafts and plans, an appealing story emerged.

About her abandonment of the original piece, she says:

> I decided to put the "Dungeon Tale" aside, giving preference to the "Quail Tale," because I couldn't see any rewards forthcoming in terms of publishing the first. It is a tale of woe that I would rather put aside. I am obsessed with the quail story. I awake in the mornings, for example, with thoughts of the quails on my mind. What happened that morning on my walk along the desert street when I encountered the quails was remarkable. I believe I truly had a mystic experience that somehow has transformed my outlook on life, however "kooky" that might sound. Also, importantly, I look forward to developing the watercolors to accompany the text. But I wonder how defensible this project is in a professional sense.

Given Sandra's own reservations, does writing a children's book constitute professional writing? Maybe. Maybe not. But we do know that it was both personally and professionally meaningful for her and it was important for her students. As a result of this project, she foresees an article about collaborating with her students to write a children's book, an ambition that should erase any doubt that there is a professional connection.

Moreover, through writing this book, Sandra is discovering a deeper awareness of her own voice and how to use language effectively for a specific audience. She couldn't envision the audience for her first article—it felt more like she was venting frustrations for no one but herself. However, an audience of children requires careful consideration, and much of what she learns will probably transfer to better skills in considering adult audiences in the future. Because of her personal experience with the quail family, she felt a deep passion and a commitment to tell the story.

We urge you to seek out and find writing groups or writing buddies with whom you can share your ideas, your voices, and your writing. Whether you are writing for your academic requirements or for your own professional purposes, such a group can help you understand how to make certain you do not marginalize yourself through your writing efforts.

PERSONAL REFLECTIONS

What has been your experience with writing groups? Do you have a writing buddy or some colleagues on whom you can count to give you feedback and support your writing efforts? Have you found advantages to having this kind of community for your writing or do you prefer to write alone?

In what ways is your writing limited to your career, your educational pursuits, and your professional life? Have you found ways to satisfy an urge to write for purposes that are personally important to you, like Sandra did? How can you make a connection between your personally important writing and your professional expectations? Reflect on the kinds of writing you generally do, both required and "elective." Can you identify intersections of the personal and the professional in either type of writing? Write your reflections.

CONSIDERING YOUR AUDIENCE

In previous chapters we have emphasized the importance of taking your audience, your readers, into consideration whenever you write. Michael Robinson (2003) asserts that "no matter what work a text may perform for the writer, a public text must also do work for its audience" (pp. 189–190).

You should, by now, know that in any text you write, there are two "players": you, the writer, and your audience. How you develop your relationship with your reader is important. You must know where to situate yourself in terms of your reader. When you begin to write, casting about for some ideas, perhaps free writing, discovering your thoughts, there may be no specific audience in mind. As your ideas form and you recognize a need to communicate your emerging ideas to someone else, that somewhat undefined audience intrudes on your writing and your thinking and begins to influence your writing decisions.

Rus VanWestervelt describes this phenomenon in the form of a "continuum." He illustrates this idea graphically (see Fig. 7.1), demonstrating the effect of audience on our writing efforts.

Note that once the author begins to write, he or she never leaves the piece, but the audience doesn't enter until a piece of writing has been officially established as a "draft." For this reason, he asserts, as long as the writer always has the intended audience in mind during the drafting, revising, and editing stages of the manuscript, success is almost certain.

As a creative, nonfiction writer, VanWestervelt describes the initial stage in his writing process as an exercise in free writing. Many of us engage in prewriting at this stage, and we may very well know who our audience is and what they expect of our text. In either case, during this earliest stage, when ideas are unformed and unfocused, we concentrate on getting the writing started or locating the information we need; that leaves the field of ideas wide open. When we envision an audience, and we begin to define that audience more specifically, our field narrows in service of that audience's needs. The role of the audience in our writing widens, gaining more and more importance as we work toward and through revision and finally to editing. At the end of the process, when the text is ready for publication, the audience and the text have achieved a balance, so to speak. The balance must be there, VanWestervelt contends, otherwise the writing will not speak to its audience in the way we intend (personal communication, November 29, 2003).

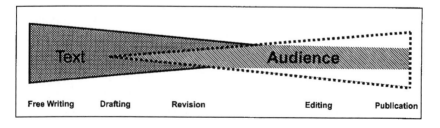

FIG. 7.1. The influence of audience on authors' writing processes.

What we like about VanWestervelt's idea is the concept of equality between the writer and the reader. The writer is not marginalized by the process, but instead remains *in* the writing. That is important, and it is through this sense of equality and balance that a writer's voice is heard.

CONNECTING THE PERSONAL AND THE PROFESSIONAL

Too often, writing for the academy is an exercise in demonstrating what we have learned from or about others, and the voices of those "others" frequently obscure our own voices. The challenge of learning from ourselves through our writing is more difficult. If we put ourselves in our writing, if we balance our needs with our audience needs, and if we allow our own voices to emerge, we may find ourselves the authors of new insights and understandings about our topics. Patrick Baliani (2003), a Teaching Advisor in the Composition Program at the University of Arizona, provides his students with a mathematical formula that ensures they, as writers, learn from and move forward through their writing.

> I ... tell my students to think of their own essays as equations: $A + B = C$. If A is a thesis, B the body, and C the conclusion, then C must be greater than A because of a relation among parts. Merely restating your thesis in the conclusion ($A + B = A$) means the body has not moved you forward.... Devise your own equations, I say, but don't solve them too formulaically. Every essay you write—assigned or not—has to be written for you. (p. 149)

This idea—writing for ourselves—even when doing the required work of the academy, is critical for making certain that we are, indeed, *in* the text; that we are, in fact, personally connected to what we write. Using Baliani's (2003) strategy applies whether we use the personal "I" or not, whether we are writing for university requirements or professional journals in which we want to report our research or simply tell our stories. Our passion and commitment to the topic will be clear and our readers will engage with our ideas more easily.

PRACTICAL APPLICATIONS: PUTTING IT ALL TOGETHER

When you began this book, we invited you to write along with us. In each chapter, when we presented an aspect of the writing process, we asked you to use the writing process to work with a text that is personally and professionally important to you. By now, you will have engaged in invention, drafting, revision, and editing. You might, at this point, feel like you have "finished." However, we urge you to review your writing and try to determine whether or not your voice is well-represented in the text. Do you convey a sense of yourself and your commitment to the topic? Will your readers know you from your words? Try reading your text aloud, to hear your words as they are spoken. Try having someone read it to you; do you hear your voice in the expression and timbre of the reader's voice? You might recognize a need to go back to the revision stage to focus on voice and audience needs to assure that your text is a true reflection of you.

SUMMARY

In the foreword to this book, Donald Murray used the terms *male text* and *female text* to describe the voices of the academy and our own natural voices. He did not mean to disparage either of the sexes, but rather to make a point about the opposing natures of these voices. In the desert Southwest, there are two rainy seasons: the summer rains, or monsoons, and the winter rains. Native Americans describe the summer rains (loud, boisterous, torrential downpours with great crashes of thunder and lightning) as male rains, and the winter rains (gentle, quiet rains that linger over the desert) as female. In summer, the precious rainwater rushes across the parched sand and into gullies and washes, offering little sustenance to the land. In winter, the rainwater soaks into the ground, replenishing the groundwater and nourishing the soil.

Applying the metaphor to our writing voices seems particularly apt. Our academic voice, our male voice, struts around wearing big words, inflated vocabulary, and convoluted sentences, what Rus VanWestervelt called "pushed purple prose," but we might not think it represents us well. Our personal voice, our female voice, carries our message more gently and brings us satisfaction. It's an interesting thought.

Consider the voices you bring to your texts. Recognize that different voices are appropriate for different audiences. More important, though, recognize your voice. What is the voice that most clearly represents you and carries your message to your intended audience?

As closure to this book, we want to wish you well as you connect the personal with the professional in your academic writing. Some of you, dear readers, have just started your writing journey. Others are moving full speed ahead. Wherever you find yourself, write with passion. Write with confidence. Write in your own voice. Above all—write.

References

Accelerated Reader™ (n.d.). Wisconsin Rapids, WI: Renaissance Learning.

Alfke, J. (1994). Stickies™ by Antler Software. Cupertino, CA: Apple Computers.

The American heritage book of English usage: A practical and authoritarian guide to contemporary English. (1996). Retrieved March 31, 2004, from http://www.bartleby.com.com/64/5html

Atwell. N. (1987). *In the middle: Reading and learning with adolescents.* Portsmouth, NH: Boynton/Cook.

Baker, S. (1976) *The practical stylist.* New York: Harper & Row.

Baliani, P. (2003). Composing the self. In C. Nowotny-Young & T. Miller (Eds.), *The university book: An anthology of writings from the University of Arizona* (pp. 145–149). Boston: Pearson Custom.

Bartholomae, D. (1990). A reply to Stephen North *PRE/TEXT 11*(1–2), 121–130.

Bartholomae, D. (1995). Writing with teachers: A conversation with Peter Elbow. *College Composition and Communication, 46,* 62–71.

Bartleby.com. (2004). *Great books online.* Retrieved March 31, 2004, from http://www.bartleby.com/ reference

Barzun, J. (2001). *Simple and direct: A rhetoric for writers* (4th ed.). New York: HarperCollins.

Berkenkotter, C. (1983). Decisions and revisions: The planning strategies of a publishing writer. *College Composition and Communication, 34,* 156–172.

Bishop, W. (1999). Places to stand: The reflective writer-teacher-writer in composition. *College Composition and Communication, 51,* 9–31.

Bissex, G. (1998). Foreword. In A. Fishman, *Amish literacy: What and how it means* (pp. ix–xi). Portsmouth, NH: Heinemann.

Bizzell, P. (1982). College composition: Initiation in the academic discourse community. *Curriculum Inquiry, 12,* 191–207.

Bizzell, P. (2002). The intellectual work of "mixed" forms of academic discourse. In C. Schroeder, H. Fox, & P. Bizzell (Eds.), *Alt-Dis: Alternative discourses in the academy* (pp.1–10). Portsmouth, NH: Heinemann.

Bloodgood, J. (2002). Quintilian: A classic educator speaks to the writing process. *Reading Research and Instruction, 42*(1), 30–43.

Bloom, H. (Ed.). (1987). *Michael De Montaigne's essays: Modern critical interpretations.* Broomall, PA: Chelsea House.

Bloom, L. (1981). Why graduate students can't write: Implications of research on writing anxiety for graduate education. *JAC: A Journal of Composition and Theory, 2*, 1-1. Retrieved July 1, 2003, from http://jac.gsu.edu/jac/2/Articles/11.html

Brace, T. (1996). *Rethinking the dissertation in the digital world.* Austin: University of Texas, Office of Graduate Studies. Retrieved July 7, 2003, from http://www.utexas.edu/ogs/etd/project/history.html

Bratcher, S., & Ryan, L. (2004). *Evaluating children's writing: A handbook of grading choices for classroom teachers.* Mahwah, NJ: Lawrence Erlbaum Associates.

Brodkey, L. (1994). Writing on the bias. *College English, 56,* 527–547.

Brooke, R. (1988). Modeling a writer's identity: Reading and imitation in the writing classroom. *College Composition and Communication, 39,* 23–41.

Brown, H. (2004).Walking into the unknown: Inquiry-based learning transforms the English classroom. *English Journal, 94*(2), 43–48.

Buscemi, S., Nicolai, A., & Strugala, S. (2000).*The basics: A rhetoric and handbook.* Boston: McGraw Hill.

Calkins, L. (1983). *Lessons from a child.* Portsmouth, NH: Heinemann.

Calkins, L. (1994). *The art of writing.* Portsmouth, NH: Heinemann.

Cameron, J. (1992). *The artist's way: A spiritual path to higher creativity.* New York: Putnam.

Catalanello, R. (2004 February 1). Kicking 'FCAT essay' habit. *The St. Petersburg Times* (Tampa Edition), pp. 1, 14A.

Chauvin Moore, R. (1995). *Constructing a narrative of teacher development: Piecing together teacher stories, teacher lives, and teacher education.* Unpublished doctoral dissertation, University of New Orleans, New Orleans, LA.

Check, J. (2001). Three myths that keep teachers from writing. In T. Fox, K. O'Shaughnessy, J. Check, & C. Tateishi (Eds.), *Professional writing retreat handbook* (pp. 23–26). Berkeley, CA: National Writing Project.

Coles, N., & Wall, S. (1987). Conflict and power in the reader-responses of adult basic writers. *College English, 49,* 298–314.

Cooke, E. (2001). Interview with a published writer. In D. Murray, *The craft of revision* (pp. 26–31). New York: Harcourt College.

Crème, P., & Lea, M. (2000). *Writing at university: A guide for students.* Philadelphia: Open University Press.

Dahl, K. (Ed.). (1992). *Teacher as writer: Entering the professional conversation.* Urbana, IL: NCTE.

Dewey, J. (1933). *How we think.* Lexington, MA: D. C. Heath. (Original work published 1901)

Ede, L. (1989). *Work in progress: A guide to writing and revising.* New York: St. Martin's Press.

Eisner, E. (1990, April). *Objectivity in educational research.* Paper presented at the Annual Meeting of the American Educational Research Association, Boston.

Elbow, P. (1973). *Writing without teachers*. New York: Oxford University Press.

Elbow, P. (1985). The shifting relationships between speech and writing. *College Composition and Communication, 36,* 283–303.

Elbow, P. (1987). *Embracing contraries: Explorations in learning and teaching*. New York: Oxford University Press.

Elbow, P. (1991). Reflections on academic discourse: How it relates to freshman and colleagues. *College English, 53,* 135–155.

Elbow, P. (1993). Being a writer vs. being an academic: A conflict of goals. *College Composition and Communication, 46,* 72–83.

Elbow, P. (1997). Options for getting feedback. In J. Bolker (Ed.), *The writer's home companion: An anthology of the world's best writing advice* (pp. 117–128). New York: Owl Books.

Elbow, P. (1998). *Writing without teachers* (25th anniversary ed.). New York: Oxford University Press.

Elbow, P. (2000). *Everyone can write: Essays toward a hopeful theory of writing and teaching writing*. New York: Oxford University Press.

Ellis, C., & Botchner, A. (2000). Autoethnography, personal narrative, and reflexivity. In N. Denzin & Y. Lincoln (Eds.), *Handbook of qualitative research* (2nd ed., pp. 733–768). Thousand Oaks, CA: Sage.

Ellis, J. (1996). *American sphinx: The character of Thomas Jefferson*. New York: Alfred Knopf.

Embree, M. (2003). *Authors' toolkit*. New York: Allworth Press.

Emery, D., Kierzek, J., & Lindblom, P. (1990). *English fundamentals* (9th ed.). New York: Macmillan.

EndNote™. (2004). Carlsbad, CA: ISI ResearchSoft. Retrieved March 12, 2004, from http://www.ENDNOTE.com

Ernst da Silva, K. (2001). Drawing on experience: Connecting art and language. *Primary Voices K-6, 10*(2), 2–8.

Fishman, A. (1988). *Amish Literacy: What and how it means*. Portsmouth, NH: Heinemann.

Fishman, S., & McCarthy, L. (1992). Is expressivism dead? *College English, 54,* 647–661.

Fletcher, R. (1999). *Live writing: Breathing life into your words*. New York: Avon.

Fletcher, R. (2000). *How writers work: Finding a process that works for you*. New York: Avon.

Flower, L., & Hayes, J. (1981). Images, plans, and prose: The representation of meaning in writing. *Written Communication, 32,* 365–387.

Fontaine, S. (1988). The unfinished story of the interpretive community. *Rhetoric Review, 7,* 86–96.

Fulwiler, T. (2002). *College writing: A personal approach to academic writing* (3rd ed.). Portsmouth, NH: Heinemann Boynton/Cook.

Gardner, J. (2001). *A seminar on writing prose*. Retrieved March 8, 2004, from http://www.thinkage.ca/~jim/prose.htm

Gleason, B. (2001). Teaching at the crossroads: Choices and challenges in college composition. *The Writing Instructor, A Network Journal and Digital Community for Writers and Teachers of Writing*. Retrieved January 30, 2004, from http://www.writnginstructor.com/essays/gleason2.html

Goldberg, N. (1986). *Writing down the bones: Freeing the writer within*. Boston: Shambhala.

Goldberg, N. (1990). *Wild mind: Living the writer's life*. New York: Bantam

Goldberg, N. (2001). *The essential writer's notebook: A step-by-step guide to better writing*. White Plains, NY: Peter Pauper Press.

Golden. J. (1969). Cicero and Quintilian on the formation of the orator. *Speech Journal, 6*, 29–34.

Goldenveizer, A. (1969). *Talks with Tolstoy* (S. Koteliansky & V. Woolk, Trans.). New York: Horizon.

Graves, D. (1983). *Writing: Teachers and children at work*. Portsmouth, NH: Heinemann.

Graves, D. (1994). *A fresh look at writing*. Portsmouth, NH: Heinemann.

Hardawanes, J. (2003, August 17). What is success? For some it's more than a well-lined wallet. *Tampa Tribune*, Career Seekers Section, p. 2.

Harnack, A., & Kleppinger, E. (2001). *Online! A reference guide to using Internet sources*. Boston: Bedford St. Martin's.

Harris, M. (1983). Modeling: A process method of teaching. *College English, 45*, 74–84.

Heard, G. (1995). *Writing toward home*. Portsmouth, NH: Heinemann.

Hillocks, G. (1995). *Teaching writing as reflective practice*. New York: Teachers College Press.

Hillocks, G. (2002). *The testing trap: How statewide assessments control learning*. New York: Teachers College Press.

Hubbard, R., & da Silva, K. (1996). *New entries: Learning by writing and drawing*. Portsmouth, NH: Heinemann.

Hubbard, R., & Power, B. (1993). *The art of classroom inquiry: A handbook for teacher-researchers*. Portsmouth, NH: Heinemann.

Hult, C. (1994). Over the edge: When reviewers collide. *Writing on the Edge, 5*(2), 24–28.

Inspiration™ (n.d.). (Version 7.5) [Computer Software]. Portland, OR: Inspiration Software. Available at http://www.writingcenters.org

Invention Strategies. (2004). Albany, OR: LBCC Media Services, Linn-Benton Community College. Retrieved February 1, 2004, from http://cf.linnbenton.edu. depts/lrc/web.cfm?pgID=350

Jalongo, M. (2002). *Writing for publication: A practical guide for educators*. Norwood, MA: Christopher Gordon.

Jarmon, L. (1996). Leslie Jarmon's dissertation. Retrieved May 23 from http://www.edb.utexas.edu/projects/mmdesign/fall96project/How/Dissertation/leslie.html

Jennings, D. (2001). Interview with a published author. In D. Murray, *The craft of revision* (pp. 247–255). New York: Harcourt College.

Judson, P. (2001). *How will instruction in prewriting strategies affect the quality of written products and student attitude toward their writing?* Retrieved January 23, 2003, from http://mwp.cla.umn.edu/anthology/2001/judson-ar.html

Kozinski, J. (1968). *Steps*. New York: Random House.

Kozinski, J. (1977). *Blind date*. New York: Grove Press.

Kuckla, J. (2003, April 12). Purchase power: Writer found voice in spy novel. *Times Picayune*, pp. E-1, E-3.

La March, J. (2000). *The raft.* New York: HarperCollins.

Lamb, B. (1997). *Booknotes: America's finest authors on reading, writing, and the power of ideas.* New York: Times Books/Random House.

Lamm, D. (1999). *The prog frince: A mixed up tale.* New York: Orchard Books.

Lamott, A. (1995). *Bird by bird.* New York: Anchor.

Lieberman, A., & Wood, D. (2002a). *Inside the National Writing Project: Connecting network learning and classroom teaching.* New York: Teachers College Press.

Lieberman, A., & Wood, D. (2002b, March). The National Writing Project. *Educational Leadership,* 40–43.

Lowth, R. (1762). *A short introduction to English grammar: With critical notes.* London: J. Hughes.

Luce-Kapler, R. (1999). As if women writing. *Journal of Literacy Research, 31,* 267–291.

Lunsford, A. (1990). Composing ourselves: Politics, commitment, and the teaching of writing. *College Composition and Communication, 41,* 71–82.

Lunsford, A. (1991). The nature of composition to composition studies. In E. Lindemann & G. Tate (Eds.), *An introduction to composition studies* (pp. 1–14). New York: Oxford University Press.

MacLean, M., & Mohr, M. (1999). *Teacher-researchers at work.* Berkeley, CA: National Writing Project.

Macrorie, K. (1985). *Telling writing.* Portsmouth, NH: Boynton/Cook.

Marek, R. (1993). How books are chosen: What goes into making an editorial decision. In G. Gross (Ed.), *Editors on editing: What writers need to know about what editors do* (pp. 83–90). New York: Grove Press.

Mason, J. (2000). *From Gutenberg's galaxy to cyberspace: The transforming power of electronic hypertext.* Doctoral dissertation, McGill University, Montréal, Canada. Retrieved April 10, 2004, from http://www.masondissertation.elephanthost.com

Matkin, R. (1991). *Persist and publish: Helpful hints for academic writing and publishing.* Boulder: University Press of Colorado.

Miles, T. (1990). *Critical thinking and writing for science and technology.* Philadelphia: Harcourt Brace.

Murphy, D. (1990). Quintilian's influence on the teaching of speaking and writing in the Middle Ages and Renaissance. In R. Enos (Ed.), *Oral and written communication: Historical approaches* (pp. 158–183). Newbury Park, CA: Sage.

Murray, D. (1982). Teach writing as a process not a product. In D. Murray (Ed.), *Learning by teaching: Selected articles on writing and teaching* (pp. 14–17). Portsmouth, NH: Boynton/Cook Heinemann.

Murray, D. (1989). *Expecting the unexpected: Teaching myself and others to read and write.* Portsmouth, NH: Boynton/Cook Heinemann.

Murray, D. (1990). *Shoptalk: Learning to write with writers.* Portsmouth, NH: Heinemann Boynton/Cook.

Murray, D. (1993). *Read to write* (3rd ed.). New York: Harcourt College.

Murray, D. (1994). All writing is autobiography. In S. Per (Ed.), *Landmark essays on writing process* (pp. 207–216). Davis, CA: Hermagoras Press.

Murray, D. (1996a). *Crafting a life in essay, story, poem.* Portsmouth, NH: Boynton/Cook Heinemann

Murray, D. (1996b). *Writer in the newsroom.* St. Petersburg, FL: Poynter Institute for Media Studies.

Murray, D. (1999). *Write to learn* (6th ed.). New York: Harcourt College.

Murray, D. (2000). *Writing to deadline—The journalist at work.* Portsmouth, NH: Heinemann.

Murray, D. (2001). *The craft of revision* (4th ed.). New York: Harcourt College.

National Commission on Writing in America's Schools and Colleges. (2003). *The neglected "R": The need for a writing revolution.* Princeton, NJ: The College Board.

Natriello, G. (1998). The author's voice: Revealing the person behind the curtain. *Teachers College Record, 99,* 617–621.

Nowotny-Young, C., Miller, T., Baliani, P., & Price, E. (Eds.). (2003). *The university book: An Anthology of writings from the University of Arizona* (3rd ed.). Boston: Pearson Custom.

O'Connor, P. (1996). *Woe is I.* New York: Riverhead Books.

Oyler, C. (1996). *Making room for students: Sharing teacher authority in room 104.* New York: Teachers College Press.

Polkinghorne, D. (1988). *Narrative knowing and the human sciences.* Albany: State University of New York Press.

Randall, S. (2002, September, 7). My brother doesn't have sight, but he has insight. *The Sun Herald,* Section B, p. 2.

Rankin, E. (1998, April). Changing the hollow conventions of academic writing. *The Chronicle of Higher Education,* pp. A64–65.

Rankin, E. (2001). *The work of writing: Insights and strategies for academics and professionals.* San Francisco: Jossey-Bass.

Richardson, L. (2000). Writing: A method of inquiry. In N. Denzin & Y. Lincoln (Eds.), *Handbook of qualitative research* (2nd ed., pp. 923–948). Thousand Oaks, CA: Sage.

Rider, J., & Broughton, E. (1994). Moving out, moving UP: Beyond the basement and the ivory tower. *Journal of Composition Theory, 14*(1) [Electronic version]. Retrieved May 29, 2003, from http://www.cas.usf.edu/JAC/141/rider.html

Robinson, M. (2003). Recomposing myself in an academic text: Making amends. In C. Nowotny-Young, T. Miller, P. Baliani, & E. Price (Eds.), *The university book: An anthology of writings from the University of Arizona* (pp. 188–192). Boston: Pearson Custom.

Rodriguez, R. (1983). *Hunger of memory.* New York: Bantam.

Romano, T. (1995). *Writing with passion: Life stories, multiple genres.* Portsmouth, NH: Heinemann Boynton/Cook.

Romano, T. (2000). *Blending genre, altering style: Writing multi-genre papers.* Portsmouth, NH: Heinemann.

Ross-Larsen, B. (1996). *Edit yourself: A manual for everyone who works with words.* New York: Norton.

Sadowski, M., & Paivio, A. (2001). *Imagery and text: A dual coding theory of reading and writing.* Mahwah, NJ: Lawrence Erlbaum Associates.

Safire, W., & Safire, L. (1992). *Good advice on writing.* New York: Fireside/Simon & Schuster.

Schon, D. (1983). *The reflective practitioner: How professionals think in action.* New York: Basic Books.

Schroeder, C., Fox, H., & Bizzell, P. (Eds.). (2002). *Alt-dis: Alternative discourses in the academy.* Portsmouth, NH: Heinemann.

Schuster, E. (2003). *Breaking the rules: Liberating writers through innovative grammar instruction*. Portsmouth NH: Heinemann.

Shafer, G. (1999). Negotiating audience and voice in the writing center. *Teaching English in the Two Year College*, 220–227.

Slangsite.com. (2001). Retrieved April 10, 2004, from http://www.slanfsite.com/slang/V.html

Sloan, G. (1990). Frequency of errors by college freshman and by professional writers. *College Communication and Composition, 41*, 299–303.

Sommers, N. (1992). Between the drafts. *College Composition and Communication, 43*, 23–31.

Spellmeyer, K. (1989). A common ground: The essay in the academy. *College English, 51*, 262–276.

Spigelman, C. (2001). Argument and evidence in the case of the personal. *College English, 64*, 63–87.

Strunk, W., & White, E. B. (2000). *The elements of style* (4th ed.). New York: Allyn & Bacon.

Taylor, K. (1997, September). *Word for the wise* [Script]. Albany, NY. WAMC Radio. Retrieved May 30, 2002, from http://www.m-w.com/mw/textonly/wfw/97Sept91797.html

Teale, W. (1992). Inside language arts: An editor's story of one journal. In K. Dahl (Ed.), *Teacher as writer: Entering the professional conversation* (pp. 107–117). Urbana, IL: National Council of Teachers of English.

Tips on making your own concept maps. (2003). Retrieved March 22, 2003, from http://www.classes.aces.unic.edu?ACES100/mind/-c-m3.html

Trimble, J. (2000). *Writing with style*. Upper Saddle River, NJ: Prentice Hall.

Trupe, A. (n.d.). The Bridgewater College (VA) materials posted by Alice L. Trupe. Retrieved April 10, 2004, from http://www.bridgewater.edu/~atrupe/ENG315/prewriting.htm and http://www.bridgewater.edu/~atrupe/ENG315/planning.htm

Truss, L. (2003). *Eats, shoots & leaves: The zero tolerance approach to punctuation*. New York: Gotham.

Unilearning: Academic writing. (2002). University of Wallongong, New South Wales, Australia. Retrieved January 3, 2003, from http://www.unilearning.uow.edu.au/academic/2div.html

University of Texas, Office of Graduate Studies. (1996). *Report of the ad hoc committee on digital dissertations*. Retrieved May 26, 2003, from http://www.utexas.edu/ogs/organizations/ga/cd/dissertations/html

Updike, J. (2004, March 6). A television interview with John Updike. *Making History with Roger Mudd*, The History Channel.

Urion, M. (2002). Writing selves, establishing academic identity. In N. Welsh, C. Latterell, C. Moore, & S. Carter-Tod (Eds.), *The dissertation and the discipline: Reinventing composition studies* (pp. 1–12). Portsmouth, NH: Boynton/Cook.

Villanueva, V. (1993). *Bootstraps: From an American academic of color*. Urbana, IL: National Council of Teachers of English.

Walsh, B. (2000). *Lapsing into a comma*. Lincolnwood, IL: Contemporary Books.

Warnock, T. (2003). How I write. In C. Nowotny-Young, T. Miller, P. Baliani, & E. Price (Eds.), *The university book: An anthology of writings from the University of Arizona* (pp. 523–532). Boston: Pearson Custom.

Weinstein, L. (2001). *Writing at the threshold*. Urbana, IL: National Council of Teachers of English.

White, E. B. (1995). Sootfall and fallout. In C. Anderson & I.. Runciman (Eds.), *A forest of voices* (pp. 492–500). Mountain View, CA: Mayfield.

Wilcox, B. (2002). *Thinking and writing for publication: A guide for teachers*. Newark, DE: International Reading Association.

Willis, M. (1993). *Deep revision: A guide for teachers, students, and other writers*. New York: Teachers and Writers Collaborative.

Winters, R. (1992). Professional writing: Redefining teaching as learning. In K. Dahl (Ed.), *Teacher as writer: Entering the professional conversation* (pp. 81–85). Urbana, IL: National Council of Teachers of English.

Wollman-Bonilla, J. (2001). Can first grade writers demonstrate audience awareness? *Reading Research Quarterly, 36,* 184–201.

The Writing Center of the University of North Carolina. (2002). *Should I use "I" in my writing? Using first person and personal experience in academic writing*. Retrieved May 23, 2004, from http://www.unc.edu.depts/wcweb/handouts_pdf/Should_I_Use_Ipdf

Zeichner, K., & Liston, D. (1985). Varieties of discourse in supervisory conferences. *Teaching and Teacher Education, 1,* 155–175.

Zinsser, W. (1988). *Writing to learn*. New York: Harper & Row.

Zinsser, W. (2001). *On writing well: The classic guide to writing nonfiction* (25th anniversary ed.). New York: Quill.

Author Index

Subject Index

A

Academic writing, xx–xxi, 1–2, 15, 23–26, 61, 185–188
  early experiences, 29–31
  traditional expectations, 39–40, 46–48, 55
  writing approaches, 66–67
Anxiety, 104–105, 160–161
Article proposal, 84–85
Audience, 140–141, 158–159, 195–197

B

Brainstorming, 78–81

C

Categorizing revisions, 137–138
Children's writing, 3–8
  teacher control, 5–8
Clarity, 168–170
Class papers, 43–44

Collaborative dissertations, 58–59
Composing styles, 15–20
Concept maps, 74–77
Confidence, 5–8, 20
Creative writing, 15, 119–121

D

Discovery drafters, 19–20, 113
Dissertations
  challenges, 50–55
  collaborative, 58–59
  electronic initiatives, 57–58
Drafting, 100–104, 113–119, 121–124
  anxiety, 104–105

E

Early writing experiences, 3–8, 29–31
Editing, 128–129, 154–174
  common issues, 167, 174–175
Electronic dissertation initiatives, 57–58

211

teacher control, 5–8
Technology, 93
Thinking aloud, 87–88
Think-writing logs, 110–113, 125, 137,
144, 147

U

University, 188–189
Using this book, xxii–xxiv

V

Voice, 48–49, 182–185

and academic writing, 185–188

W

Webs, *see* Concept maps
Writer's block, 105–106
Writing approaches, 66–67
Writing decisions, 44–45
Writing groups, 10–11, 24, 43,
138–140, 149, 191–194
Writing journey, xxi, 2–3, 25–26
Writing process, 65–66
Writing schedule, 12–15